CAPITAL
PUNISHMENT
CRUEL AND UNUSUAL?

ISSN 1538-6678

CAPITAL PUNISHMENT
CRUEL AND UNSUAL?

Mei Ling Rein

INFORMATION PLUS® REFERENCE SERIES
Formerly published by Information Plus, Wylie, Texas

GALE GROUP
™
THOMSON LEARNING

Detroit • New York • San Diego • San Francisco
Boston • New Haven, Conn. • Waterville, Maine
London • Munich

CAPITAL PUNISHMENT: CRUEL AND UNUSUAL?

Mei Ling Rein, *Author*

The Gale Group Staff:

Coordinating Editors: Ellice Engdahl, *Series Editor*; Charles B. Montney, *Series Graphics Editor*

Managing Editor: Debra M. Kirby

Contributing Editors: Elizabeth Manar, Kathleen Meek

Contributing Associate Editors: Paula Cutcher-Jackson, Prindle LaBarge, Heather Price, Michael T. Reade

Imaging and Multimedia Content: Barbara J. Yarrow, *Manager, Imaging and Multimedia Content*; Dean Dauphinais, *Imaging and Multimedia Content Editor*; Kelly A. Quin, *Imaging and Multimedia Content Editor*; Robyn Young, *Imaging and Multimedia Content Editor*; Leitha Etheridge-Sims, *Image Cataloger*; Mary K. Grimes, *Image Cataloger*; David G. Oblender, *Image Cataloger*; Lezlie Light, *Imaging Coordinator*; Randy Bassett, *Imaging Supervisor*; Robert Duncan, *Imaging Specialist*; Dan Newell, *Imaging Specialist*; Luke Rademacher, *Imaging Specialist*; Christine O'Bryan, *Graphic Specialist*

Indexing: Susan Kelsch, *Indexing Supervisor*

Permissions: Kim Davis, *Permissions Associate*; Maria Franklin, *Permissions Manager*

Product Design: Michelle DiMercurio, *Senior Art Director and Product Design Manager*; Michael Logusz, *Graphic Artist*

Production: Evi Seoud, *Assistant Manager, Composition Purchasing and Electronic Prepress*; Keith Helmling, *Buyer*; Dorothy Maki, *Manufacturing Manager*

Cover photo © PhotoDisc.

ISBN 0-7876-5103-6 (set)
ISBN 0-7876-6054-X (this volume)
ISSN 1538-6678 (this volume)
Printed in the United States of America
10 9 8 7 6 5 4 3 2 1

TABLE OF CONTENTS

PREFACE

Capital Punishment: Cruel and Unusual? is one of the latest volumes in the Information Plus Reference Series. Previously published by the Information Plus company of Wylie, Texas, the Information Plus Reference Series (and its companion set, the Information Plus Compact Series) became a Gale Group product when Gale and Information Plus merged in early 2000. Those of you familiar with the series as published by Information Plus will notice a few changes from the 2000 edition. Gale has adopted a new layout and style that we hope you will find easy to use. Other improvements include greatly expanded indexes in each book, and more descriptive tables of contents.

While some changes have been made to the design, the purpose of the Information Plus Reference Series remains the same. Each volume of the series presents the latest facts on a topic of pressing concern in modern American life. These topics include today's most controversial and most studied social issues: abortion, capital punishment, care for the elderly, crime, health care, the environment, immigration, minorities, social welfare, women, youth, and many more. Although written especially for the high school and undergraduate student, this series is an excellent resource for anyone in need of factual information on current affairs.

By presenting the facts, it is Gale's intention to provide its readers with everything they need to reach an informed opinion on current issues. To that end, there is a particular emphasis in this series on the presentation of scientific studies, surveys, and statistics. These data are generally presented in the form of tables, charts, and other graphics placed within the text of each book. Every graphic is directly referred to and carefully explained in the text. The source of each graphic is presented within the graphic itself. The data used in these graphics are drawn from the most reputable and reliable sources, in particular the various branches of the U.S. government and major independent polling organizations. Every effort has been made to secure the most recent information available. The reader should bear in mind that many major studies take years to conduct, and that additional years often pass before the data from these studies is made available to the public. Therefore, in many cases the most recent information available in 2002 dated from 1999 or 2000. Older statistics are sometimes presented as well, if they are of particular interest and no more recent information exists.

Although statistics are a major focus of the Information Plus Reference Series, they are by no means its only content. Each book also presents the widely held positions and important ideas that shape how the book's subject is discussed in the United States. These positions are explained in detail and, where possible, in the words of their proponents. Some of the other material to be found in these books includes: historical background; descriptions of major events related to the subject; relevant laws and court cases; and examples of how these issues play out in American life. Some books also feature primary documents, or have pro and con debate sections giving the words and opinions of prominent Americans on both sides of a controversial topic. All material is presented in an even-handed and unbiased manner; the reader will never be encouraged to accept one view of an issue over another.

HOW TO USE THIS BOOK

Few topics are as controversial as capital punishment. Capital punishment has been debated since the colonial period in America and is currently a worldwide issue. This book includes the history of capital punishment, plus discussions of numerous court cases, legal decisions, and historical statistics. Also included is information about execution methods, minors and the death penalty, public attitudes, and capital punishment around the world.

Capital Punishment: Cruel and Unusual? consists of eleven chapters and three appendices. Each of the chapters is devoted to a particular aspect of capital punishment. For a summary of the information covered in each chapter, please see the synopses provided in the Table of Contents at the front of the book. Chapters generally begin with an overview of the basic facts and background information on the chapter's topic, then proceed to examine sub-topics of particular interest. For example, Chapter Seven: Under Sentence of Death begins with a discussion of the increasing number of prisoners on death row. It then details the race, gender, and characteristics of prisoners awaiting execution, and the criminal history of death row inmates. Also covered are methods of getting off death row, including the appeals process, legal resources, exoneration, moratoriums, and DNA testing. Federal and state studies of the death penalty and costs of administering the death penalty are also included. Readers can find their way through a chapter by looking for the section and sub-section headings, which are clearly set off from the text. Or, they can refer to the book's extensive index if they already know what they are looking for.

Statistical Information

The tables and figures featured throughout *Capital Punishment: Cruel and Unusual?* will be of particular use to the reader in learning about this issue. These tables and figures represent an extensive collection of the most recent and important statistics on capital punishment, as well as related issues—for example, graphics in the book cover capital offenses, by state; federal laws providing for the death penalty; minimum age authorized for capital punishment; methods of execution; number of prisoners executed, by state; number of persons under sentence of death; death row exoneration; support for capital punishment; countries retaining the death penalty; and countries which have abolished the death penalty. Gale believes that making this information available to the reader is the most important way in which we fulfill the goal of this book: to help readers understand the issues and controversies surrounding capital punishment in the United States and reach their own conclusions.

Each table or figure has a unique identifier appearing above it, for ease of identification and reference. Titles for the tables and figures explain their purpose. At the end of each table or figure, the original source of the data is provided.

In order to help readers understand these often complicated statistics, all tables and figures are explained in the text. References in the text direct the reader to the relevant statistics. Furthermore, the contents of all tables and figures are fully indexed. Please see the opening section of the index at the back of this volume for a description of how to find tables and figures within it.

In addition to the main body text and images, *Capital Punishment: Cruel and Unusual?* has three appendices. The first is the Important Names and Addresses directory. Here the reader will find contact information for a number of government and private organizations that can provide information on capital punishment. The second appendix is the Resources section, which can also assist the reader in conducting his or her own research. In this section, the author and editors of *Capital Punishment: Cruel and Unusual?* describe some of the sources that were most useful during the compilation of this book. The final appendix is the index. It has been greatly expanded from previous editions, and should make it even easier to find specific topics in this book.

COMMENTS AND SUGGESTIONS

The editors of the Information Plus Reference Series welcome your feedback on *Capital Punishment: Cruel and Unusual?* Please direct all correspondence to:

Editors
Information Plus Reference Series
27500 Drake Rd.
Farmington Hills, MI 48331-3535

ACKNOWLEDGEMENTS

The editors wish to thank the copyright holders of material included in this volume and the permissions managers of many book and magazine publishing companies for assisting us in securing reproduction rights. We are also grateful to the staffs of the Detroit Public Library, the Library of Congress, the University of Detroit Mercy Library, Wayne State University Purdy/Kresge Library Complex, and the University of Michigan Libraries for making their resources available to us.

Following is a list of the copyright holders who have granted us permission to reproduce material in Information Plus: Capital Punishment. Every effort has been made to trace copyright, but if omissions have been made, please let us know.

Acknowledgements are listed in the order the tables and figures appear in the text of Capital Punishment. For more detailed citations, please see the sources listed under each table and figure.

Table 5.1. Snell, Tracy L. "Table 1. Capital offenses, by State, 1999," from *Capital Punishment 1999*. Bureau of Justice Statistics, Washington, DC, December 2000.

Table 5.2. Snell, Tracy L. "Table 2. Federal laws providing for the death penalty, 1999," from *Capital Punishment 1999*. Bureau of Justice Statistics, Washington, DC, December 2000.

Table 5.3. Snell, Tracy L. "Table 4. Minimum age authorized for capital punishment, 1999," from *Capital Punishment 1999*. Bureau of Justice Statistics, Washington, DC, December 2000.

Table 5.4. Snell, Tracy L. "Table 3. Method of execution, by State, 1999," from *Capital Punishment 1999*. Bureau of Justice Statistics, Washington, DC, December 2000.

Figure 6.1. Snell, Tracy L. "Executions, 1930-2000," from *Capital Punishment 1999*.

Retrieved from [Online] http://www.ojp.usdoj.gov/bjs/glance/exe.htm [accessed October 9, 2001]. Bureau of Justice Statistics, Washington, DC.

Figure 6.2. "Executions from 1976-2000," retrieved from [Online] http://www.deathpenaltyinfo.org/dpicexec.html [accessed October 12, 2001]. Death Penalty Information Center, Washington, DC. Reproduced by permission.

Table 6.1. "Number of Executions by State since 1976," retrieved from [Online] http://www.deathpenaltyinfo.org/dpicreg.html#region [accessed November 1, 2001]. Death Penalty Information Center, Washington, DC. Reproduced by permission.

Table 6.2. "Execution Update (1976 to July 1, 2001)," from *Death Row USA, Summer 2001*. NAACP Legal Defense & Educational Fund, Inc., New York, NY, 2001. Reproduced by permission.

Table 6.3. Streib, Victor L. "Table 1: Executions of Female Offenders by Decade, 1900-2000," from *Death Penalty for Female Offenders: January 1, 1973, to December 31, 2000*, retrieved from [Online] http://www.law.onu.edu/faculty/streib/femdeath.htm [accessed October 11, 2001]. Reproduced by permission.

Table 6.4. "Table 6.95: Prisoners executed under civil authority," from *Sourcebook of Criminal Justice Statistics 1999*. Edited by Kathleen Maguire and Ann L. Pastore. Bureau of Justice Statistics, Washington, DC. 2000.

Table 6.5. Snell, Tracy L. "Executions, by State and method, 1977-99," from *Capital Punishment 1999*. Bureau of Justice Statistics, Washington, DC, December 2000.

Table 6.6. Snell, Tracy L. "Advance count of executions: January 1, 2000-December 31, 2000," from *Capital Punishment 1999*.

Bureau of Justice Statistics, Washington, DC, December 2000.

Figure 7.1. Snell, Tracy L. "Persons under sentence of death, 1953-99," from *Capital Punishment 1999*. Bureau of Justice Statistics, Washington, DC, December 2000.

Table 7.1. Snell, Tracy L. "Number sentenced to death and number of removals, by jurisdiction and reason for removal, 1973-99," from *Capital Punishment 1999*. Bureau of Justice Statistics, Washington, DC, December 2000.

Table 7.2. "Summary of State Lists of Prisoners on Death Row (As of July 1, 2001)," from *Death Row USA, Summer 2001*. NAACP Legal Defense & Educational Fund, Inc., New York, NY, 2001. Reproduced by permission.

Table 7.3. Streib, Victor L. "Table 3: State-by-State Breakdown of Death Sentences for Female Offenders, January 1, 1973, to December 31, 2000," from *Death Penalty for Female Offenders: January 1, 1973, to December 31, 2000*, retrieved from [Online] http://www.law.onu.edu/faculty/streib/femdeath.htm [accessed October 11, 2001]. Reproduced by permission.

Table 7.4. Snell, Tracy L. "Table 8. Age at time of arrest for capital offense and age of prisoners under sentence of death at yearend 1999," from *Capital Punishment 1999*. Bureau of Justice Statistics, Washington, DC, December 2000.

Table 7.5. Snell, Tracy L. "Table 7. Demographic characteristics of prisoners under sentence of death, 1999," from *Capital Punishment 1999*. Bureau of Justice Statistics, Washington, DC, December 2000.

Table 7.6. Snell, Tracy L. "Table 9. Criminal history profile of prisoners under sentence of death, by race and Hispanic origin, 1999," from *Capital Punishment 1999*. Bureau of

Justice Statistics, Washington, DC, December 2000.

Table 7.7. Snell, Tracy L. "Table 12. Time under sentence of death and execution, by race, 1977-99," from *Capital Punishment 1999*. Bureau of Justice Statistics, Washington, DC, December 2000.

Table 7.8. Snell, Tracy L. "Appendix table 2. Prisoners under sentence of death on December 31, 1999, by State and year of sentencing," from *Capital Punishment 1999*. Bureau of Justice Statistics, Washington, DC, December 2000.

Table 7.9. Snell, Tracy L. "Appendix table 1. Prisoners sentenced to death and the outcome sentence, by year of sentencing, 1973-99," from *Capital Punishment 1999*. Bureau of Justice Statistics, Washington, DC, December 2000.

Figure 7.2. "Death Row Exonerations by Year," retrieved from [Online] http://www.deathpenaltyinfo.org/innoc.html#year [accessed October 12, 2001]. Death Penalty Information Center, Washington, DC. Reproduced by permission.

Figure 7.3. "Death Row Exonerations by State," (chart), retrieved from [Online] http://www.deathpenaltyinfo.org/innoc.html#state [accessed October 12, 2001]. Death Penalty Information Center, Washington, DC. Reproduced by permission.

Table 7.10. "Table 1A: Distribution of Defendants Within Each Stage of the Federal Death Penalty Process (1995-2000)," from *The Federal Death Penalty System: A Statistical Survey (1988-2000)*. U.S. Department of Justice, Washington, DC, September 12, 2000.

Figure 7.4. "Federal Death Penalty Cases by Year of Indictment," from *Federal Death Penalty Cases: Recommendations Concerning the Cost and Quality of Defense Representation*. Judicial Conference of the United States, Committee on Defender Services, Subcommittee on Federal Death Penalty Cases, Washington, DC, 1998.

Table 7.11. "Average Number of Attorney Hours Billed in Capital and Non-Capital Homicide Cases," from *Federal Death Penalty Cases: Recommendations Concerning the Cost and Quality of Defense Representation*. Judicial Conference of the United States, Committee on Defender Services, Subcommittee on Federal Death Penalty Cases, Washington, DC, 1998.

Table 8.1. Taylor, Humphrey. "Table 1: Believe in Capital Punishment," from *The Harris Poll #41*, retrieved from [Online] http://www.harrisinteractive.com/harris_poll/index.asp [accessed October 19, 2001]. Harris Interactive, Rochester, NY, August 17, 2001. Reproduced by permission.

Table 8.2. "Table 2.60: Attitudes toward the death penalty," from *Sourcebook of Criminal Justice Statistics*. Edited by Kathleen Maguire and Ann L. Pastore. Bureau of Justice Statistics, Washington, DC, 2000. Reproduced by permission.

Table 8.3. Taylor, Humphrey. "Table 5: What Percent of People Convicted of Murder are Innocent?" from *The Harris Poll #41*, retrieved from [Online] http://www.harrisinteractive.com/harris_poll/index.asp [accessed October 19, 2001]. Harris Interactive, Rochester, NY, August 17, 2001. Reproduced by permission.

Table 8.4. Taylor, Humphrey. "Table 2: Is Capital Punishment a Deterrent?" from *The Harris Poll #41*, retrieved from [Online] http://www.harrisinteractive.com/harris_poll/index.asp [accessed October 19, 2001]. Harris Interactive, Rochester, NY, August 17, 2001. Reproduced by permission.

Table 9.1. *The Death Penalty: List of Abolitionist and Retentionist Countries,* June 1, 2001, © Amnesty International Publications. Reproduced by permission.

Table 9.2. *The Death Penalty: List of Abolitionist and Retentionist Countries*, June 1, 2001, © Amnesty International Publications. Reproduced by permission.

Table 9.3. *The Death Penalty: List of Abolitionist and Retentionist Countries*, June 1, 2001, © Amnesty International Publications. Reproduced by permission.

Table 9.4. *The Death Penalty: List of Abolitionist and Retentionist Countries*, June 1, 2001, © Amnesty International Publications. Reproduced by permission.

Table 9.5. *The Death Penalty: List of Abolitionist and Retentionist Countries*, June 1, 2001, © Amnesty International Publications. Reproduced by permission.

Text statement, Chapter 10: Stewart, Steven D. Quote retrieved from http://www.clarkprosecutor.org/html/death/death.htm. Reproduced by permission.

CHAPTER 1

A CONTINUING CONFLICT—
A HISTORY OF CAPITAL PUNISHMENT IN AMERICA

THE COLONIAL PERIOD

Since the first European settlers arrived in America, the death penalty has been accepted as just punishment for a variety of offenses. The English Penal Code, which applied to the British colonies, listed 14 capital offenses, but actual practice varied from colony to colony. In the Massachusetts Bay Colony 12 crimes warranted the death penalty—idolatry, witchcraft, blasphemy, rape, statutory rape, kidnapping, perjury in a trial involving a possible death sentence, rebellion, murder, assault in sudden anger, adultery, and buggery (sodomy). In the statute each crime was accompanied by Old Testament quotations justifying capital punishment. Later arson, treason, and grand larceny were added.

In 1608 the first recorded execution in the new colonies occurred in the Jamestown colony of Virginia. Captain George Kendall, accused of spying for Spain, received the death penalty. In 1632 Jane Champion, a slave, became the first woman to be put to death in the new colonies. She was hanged in James City, Virginia, for the murders of her master's children.

In contrast to the Massachusetts Bay Colony, the Quakers adopted much milder laws. The Royal Charter for South Jersey (1646) did not permit capital punishment for any crime, and there was no execution until 1691. In Pennsylvania William Penn's Great Act of 1682 limited the death penalty to treason and murder. Most states, however, followed the much harsher British codes. For example, in New York hitting one's parent was punishable by death.

THE FIRST ABOLITIONISTS OF THE DEATH PENALTY

Although the Founding Fathers commonly accepted the death penalty, many early Americans opposed capital punishment. In the late eighteenth century Dr. Benjamin Rush (1745–1813), a physician considered the founder of the American abolition movement, decried capital punishment. He attracted the support of Benjamin Franklin (1706–1790), and it was at Franklin's home in Philadelphia that Rush became one of the first Americans to propose a "House of Reform," a prison where criminals could be detained until they changed their antisocial behavior. Consequently, in 1790 the Walnut Street Jail, the primitive seed from which the American penal system grew, was built in Philadelphia.

Dr. Rush published numerous pamphlets, the most notable of which was *Inquiry into the Justice and Policy of Punishing Murder by Death* (1792). Rush argued that the biblical support given to capital punishment was questionable and that the threat of hanging did not deter crime. Influenced by the philosophy of the Enlightenment (the Age of Reason in the mid- to-late 1700s), Rush believed the state exceeded its granted powers when it executed a citizen. In addition to Franklin, Rush attracted many other Pennsylvanians to his cause, including Pennsylvania's attorney general, William Bradford. Bradford suggested the idea of different degrees of murder, some of which did not warrant the death penalty. As a result, in 1794 Pennsylvania repealed the death penalty for all crimes except first-degree murder, defined as "willful, deliberate, and premeditated killing or murder committed during arson, rape, robbery, or burglary."

THE ABOLITIONIST MOVEMENT

Dr. Rush's proposals attracted many followers, and numerous petitions aiming to abolish all capital punishment were presented in Ohio, New Jersey, New York, and Massachusetts. No state, however, reversed its laws.

The second quarter of the nineteenth century was a time of reform in America. Capital punishment opponents rode the tide of righteousness and indignation created by antisaloon and antislavery advocates. Abolitionist societies sprang up, especially along the Atlantic Coast. In 1845 the American Society for the Abolition of Capital Punishment was founded.

In the late 1840s Horace Greeley (1811–1872), the editor and founder of the *New York Tribune* and a leading advocate of most abolitionist causes, led the crusade against the death penalty. In 1846 Michigan, then a U.S. territory, was the first to abolish the death penalty for all crimes except treason. The law took effect in 1847 after Michigan became a U.S. state, making Michigan, for all practical purposes, the first English-speaking jurisdiction in the world to abolish the death penalty for common crimes. (Common crimes, also called ordinary crimes, are crimes committed during peacetime. Ordinary crimes that could lead to the death penalty include murder, rape, and, in some countries, robbery or embezzlement of very large sums of money. In comparison, exceptional crimes are military crimes committed during exceptional times, mainly wartime. Examples are treason, spying, or leaving the armed services without permission.) In 1852 and 1853, Rhode Island and Wisconsin, respectively, became the first two states to outlaw the death penalty for all crimes. Most states began limiting the number of capital crimes. Outside the South, murder and treason became the only acts punishable by death.

Opponents of the death penalty initially benefited from abolitionist sentiment, but as the Civil War (1861–1865) neared, concern about the death penalty was lost amid the growing antislavery movement. It was not until after the Civil War that Maine and Iowa abolished the death penalty. Almost immediately, however, their legislatures reversed themselves and reinstated the death penalty. In 1887 Maine again reversed itself and abolished capital punishment. It has remained an abolitionist state ever since. Colorado abolished capital punishment in 1897, a decision apparently against the will of many of its citizens. At least twice, these citizens lynched convicted murderers. In response, the state restored the death penalty in 1901.

Meanwhile, the federal government, following considerable debate in the U.S. Congress, reduced the number of federal crimes punishable by death to treason, murder, and rape. In no instance was capital punishment to be mandatory.

A DECLINE IN ABOLITIONIST FORTUNES

At the start of the twentieth century, death penalty abolitionists again took advantage of American reformism as the Progressives (liberal reformers) tried to correct the deficiencies of the American system. Between 1907 and 1917 six states and Puerto Rico, a U.S. territory, abolished capital punishment, but the momentum did not last. By 1921 five states had reinstated it. The Prohibition Era (1920–1933), characterized by frequent disdain for law

and order, almost destroyed the abolitionist movement as many Americans began to believe that the death penalty was the only proper punishment for gangsters who committed murder.

Only the determined efforts of the famed Clarence Darrow, the "attorney for the damned"; Lewis E. Lawes, the abolitionist warden of Sing Sing Prison in New York; and the American League to Abolish Capital Punishment (founded in 1927) prevented the movement's complete collapse. Nonetheless, of the 16 states and jurisdictions that outlawed capital punishment after 1845, only seven—Maine, Michigan, Minnesota, North Dakota, Rhode Island, Wisconsin, and Puerto Rico—had no major death penalty statute at the beginning of the 1950s. Between 1917 and 1957, no state abolished the death penalty.

The abolitionist movement made a mild comeback in the mid-1950s, and the issue was discussed in several state legislatures. In 1957 the U.S. territories of Alaska and Hawaii abolished the death penalty. In the states, however, the movement's singular success in Delaware (1958) was reversed three years later (1961), a major disappointment for death penalty opponents.

The abolitionists were able to recover during the civil rights movement of the 1960s. In 1963 Michigan, which in 1847 had abolished capital punishment for all crimes except treason, finally outlawed the death penalty for that crime. Oregon (1964), Iowa (1965), and West Virginia (1965) all abolished capital punishment, while many other states sharply reduced the number of crimes punishable by the death penalty. Oregon reinstated capital punishment in 1978. In 1995 New York became the thirty-eighth state to reinstate the death penalty, ending its 18-year ban of capital punishment. At year-end 2000, 38 states, the federal government, and the U.S. military had the death penalty.

FEDERAL DEATH PENALTY

The federal government no longer lists rape as one of the crimes punishable by death, but it continues to impose the death penalty for murder, treason, and espionage. Over the years, the federal government has added to the number of federal offenses punishable by death. In 1790 Thomas Bird became the first inmate executed under the federal death penalty. He was hanged in Maine for murder. Between 1790 and 1963 the federal government put to death 336 men and 4 women. On February 15, 1963, Victor Feguer was hanged in Iowa for kidnapping and murder. This was the last execution by the federal government until nearly 40 years later. On June 11, 2001, federal execution resumed when the U.S. government carried out Timothy McVeigh's death sentence. McVeigh was sentenced to death in 1997 for bombing the Alfred P. Murrah Federal Building in Oklahoma City, Oklahoma, on April 19, 1995, killing 168 people.

Anti-Drug, Violent Crime, and Antiterrorism Laws

In 1988 Congress reinstated the death penalty by enacting the Anti-Drug Abuse Act (Public Law 100-690), which included a drug-kingpin provision allowing the death penalty for murder resulting from large-scale illegal drug dealing. The act did not provide for the method of federal execution. In 1993 then President George H. W. Bush authorized the use of lethal injection under this law. Since its enactment six people have been sentenced to death under this provision.

In 1994 the Violent Crime Control and Law Enforcement Act (Public Law 103-322; also known as the Federal Death Penalty Act of 1994) added more than 50 crimes punishable by death. Among these federal crimes are murder of certain government officials, kidnapping resulting in death, murder for hire, fatal drive-by shootings, sexual abuse crimes resulting in death, carjacking resulting in death, and other crimes not resulting in death, such as running a large-scale drug enterprise. The method of execution will be the same as that used in the state where the sentencing occurs. If the state does not allow the death penalty, the judge would choose a state with the death penalty. Under the act, 15 persons have been sentenced to death, including McVeigh.

Antiterrorism legislation came about in the wake of the Oklahoma City bombing in 1995. In 1996 Congress passed the Antiterrorism and Effective Death Penalty Act (AEDPA; Public Law 104-132). The act, signed into law on April 24, 1996, just after the first anniversary of the Oklahoma City bombing by Timothy McVeigh, was intended "to deter terrorism, provide justice for victims, [and] provide for an effective death penalty." The law also restricts death row inmates' use of *habeas corpus* petitions, federal appeals by which state and federal inmates request a federal court to determine whether they are being held in violation of their constitutional rights. The law requires that *habeas corpus* petitions be filed within six months after the inmate's final state court sentencing.

Federal prisoners used to be imprisoned in the state where the trial was held, but between 1993 and 1996 the U.S. Bureau of Prisons built a 50-cell federal death house in Terre Haute, Indiana, to accommodate the condemned. It started housing death row inmates in 1999.

Federal Government Resumes Executions

After being sentenced to death for conspiracy and murder in 1997, Timothy McVeigh received an execution date of May 16, 2001. U.S. Attorney General John Ashcroft, however, delayed the execution following the discovery that the Federal Bureau of Investigation (FBI) failed to turn over more than three thousand documents to the defense and prosecution during the trial. McVeigh appealed for a second stay of execution, but the 10th U.S. Circuit Court of Appeals denied his request, affirming a U.S. District Court's ruling that there was no evidence that the U.S. government intentionally hid the FBI files from the defense. On June 11, 2001, the execution was carried out.

Eight days later, on June 19, 2001, Texas drug boss Juan Raul Garza became the second federal prisoner to be executed in 2001. He was the first person to be executed under the Anti-Drug Abuse Act of 1988 for murders resulting from a drug enterprise. Garza received the death sentence in 1993 for the 1990 murders of three associates.

Garza was initially scheduled to be executed in August 2000. In July 2000 the Clinton administration granted a four-month reprieve (a stay of execution for a short time to resolve an issue) to allow the Justice Department to establish clemency guidelines by which a death row inmate could plead for his life after exhausting all appeals. Some critics noted that the administration, which had been running the government for seven years, should have taken the time to put in place a clemency protocol for capital cases. Others claimed the government could have applied to capital cases the clemency guidelines that it uses for noncapital cases. It should be noted that, even with no formal guidelines in place, Garza could have pleaded for clemency.

On September 13, 2000, Garza asked President Clinton to commute his death sentence to life imprisonment without parole. Garza's lawyer argued that the Justice Department study of the federal death penalty system, released the day before, showed that the federal capital punishment is "plagued by systemic bias, disparity and arbitrariness." Defense counsel claimed that it would be unfair to put Garza to death because the federal death penalty discriminates against members of minorities and is administered unevenly geographically. (Of the 18 men on federal death row at that time, 16 were minorities, and 6 had been convicted in Texas.) Again, the president delayed the execution, this time to December 12, 2000. It took another six months for the U.S. government to carry out Garza's death penalty. President George W. Bush refused to stay the execution.

THE U.S. MILITARY

The U.S. military has its own death penalty law, with lethal injection as the method of execution. As of July 1, 2001, seven men were on the military death row. No execution has occurred since 1961.

NATIVE AMERICANS

The U.S. government has let Native American reservations use their own discretion regarding the death penalty. Most of the tribes have decided against using the death penalty, though according to the NAACP Legal

Defense Fund & Educational Fund, as of July 1, 2000, there were 46 Native Americans on state death rows.

RESOLVING THE CONSTITUTIONAL ISSUES

Until the 1960s there was legally no question that the death penalty was acceptable under the U.S. Constitution. Then, in 1963 U.S. Supreme Court Justice Arthur J. Goldberg (joined by Justices William O. Douglas and William J. Brennan), dissenting from a rape case in which the defendant had been sentenced to death (*Rudolph v. Alabama*, 375 U.S. 889), raised the question of the legality of the death penalty. The filing of a large number of lawsuits in the late 1960s led to an implied moratorium (a temporary suspension) on carrying out the death penalty, which lasted until 1977, when the state of Utah executed Gary Gilmore.

Since 1972, with *Furman v. Georgia* (408 U.S. 238) and the accompanying cases, the Supreme Court has been defining and refining what is and is not acceptable under the U.S. Constitution. With the replacement of Chief Justice Earl Warren by Chief Justice Warren Burger, and his later replacement by Chief Justice William Rehnquist, the Court majority has generally interpreted the death penalty as worthy of extra attention because of the seriousness of the consequences, though it is most assuredly considered an acceptable punishment for murder. There can be little question that the high court's position reflects that of the majority of the American public.

CHANGES IN CAPITAL PUNISHMENT IN THE UNITED STATES

New Restrictions to Federal Review

Under the AEDPA, inmates are required to file their petitions "not later than 180 days after final state court affirmance of the conviction and sentence on direct review or the expiration of the time for seeking such review." Opponents of capital punishment have noted that a growing number of death row inmates have no lawyers to help them meet this new deadline. In addition, they believe that the unclear language of the AEDPA has allowed for varying interpretations in federal appeals courts. For the first time, in 2000, the U.S. Supreme Court, addressed the lower courts' interpretation of the AEDPA.

The number of executions rose dramatically from 1994 to 1999. In 1994 there were 31 executions, which nearly doubled to 56 in 1995. The number of prisoners put to death (98) in 1999 was the largest yearly number since 1951, when 105 prisoners were executed. Some claim that the AEDPA restrictions on federal review were responsible for these high numbers, while others observed that the high numbers were more a product of inmates' appeals eventually being exhausted. In 2000 the number of executions decreased 13 percent to 85. As of November 15, 2001, 60 persons had been executed since January 1,

2001. Experts noted that the slowdown of executions was due partly to the growing concern that innocent people might be put to death and partly to the increasing number of states that were suspending executions to conduct investigations about the application of the death penalty.

Some States Take Careful Steps

In January 2000 Illinois became the first state to declare a moratorium. In March 2001 the Massachusetts House of Representatives voted 94 to 60 against bringing back the death penalty. In 1997 a similar bill was defeated by just one vote.

In March 2001 Maryland's lower legislature passed a bill providing for a moratorium on executions. The bill called for the suspension of executions pending completion of a study to determine if racial bias plays a role in the imposition of the death penalty. No further action, however, was taken after the session adjourned in April 2001. In July 2001 a *de facto* (in practice, as different from *de jure*, in law) moratorium occurred pending the resolution by the state's high court of an appeal by death row inmate Steven Oken challenging the constitutionality of Maryland's capital punishment.

Some leading death penalty states, such as Texas and Virginia, seemed to be practicing more caution. In June 2000 Texas governor George W. Bush ordered a stay of execution for Ricky McGinn to allow for new DNA testing. This was the first time Governor Bush granted a reprieve. In the first half of 2001 the Texas Court of Criminal Appeals stayed the execution of two inmates— Michael Moore and Mack Oran Hill—each just a day before the scheduled date. In August 2001 the court granted a fifth stay of execution to Napoleon Beazley, who was convicted of murder when he was 17.

Some States Retain the Death Penalty

Other states, however, executed more prisoners in 2001, compared to 2000. They included Delaware, Missouri, North Carolina, and Oklahoma. As of October 3, 2001, Oklahoma executed 15 inmates versus 11 in 2000. During the same time period, North Carolina's executions rose from 1 to 3, and those of Delaware increased from 1 to 2. Missouri put five inmates to death in 2000, compared to 6 in 2001. On November 6, 2001, New Mexico executed its first inmate since 1960. Terry Clark was executed for the 1986 murder of a nine-year-old girl, whom he had raped.

In March 2000 the New Hampshire House of Representatives and in May 2000 the New Hampshire Senate passed a bill to abolish the death penalty. Governor Jeanne Shaheen, however, vetoed the bill. A similar bill introduced in its House in January 2001 was defeated three months later. Although the death penalty is in the statute books, New Hampshire has not sentenced anyone to death since reinstating capital punishment in 1991 and had not had an execution since 1939.

New York State Expands Its Death Penalty Law

On September 17, 2001, in the aftermath of the September 11, 2001, attacks on the World Trade Center and the Pentagon, the New York legislature enacted the Antiterrorism Act of 2001. The act stated, "Our death penalty statute must be strengthened so that the cold-blooded execution of an individual for terrorist purposes is a capital offense."

CLEMENCY

All states provide for clemency, which may take the form of a reprieve, a commutation of sentence (replacing the death sentence with a lesser sentence, such as life without parole), or a pardon. The power of clemency may rest solely with the governor, with the clemency board, or with the governor and a board of advisers. In federal cases the president alone has clemency power.

Between the reinstatement of the death penalty in 1976 to November 2001, 46 death row inmates had received a commutation of their death sentences. In 1999 five death row inmates received reprieve, the most notable being that of Darrell Mease, who was scheduled for execution on February 10, 1999. On January 28, 1999, as a tribute to Pope John Paul II, who requested clemency for Mease during the pope's visit to St. Louis, Missouri, Governor Mel Carnahan commuted Mease's sentence to life imprisonment without parole.

In 2000 Maryland and North Carolina each commuted the death sentence of a death row inmate to life without parole. Before leaving office in January 2001, President Bill Clinton commuted the death sentence of federal inmate David Ronald Chandler to life imprisonment without parole. Two other prisoners, one from Oklahoma and one from North Carolina, received commutations of their death sentences to life without parole in 2001.

SUPREME COURT JUSTICES AND THE DEATH PENALTY

On July 2, 2001, Supreme Court Justice Sandra Day O'Connor, a long-time supporter of the death penalty and the swing justice in the Court, expressed concern about capital punishment. She said in a speech before the Minnesota Women Lawyers (Minneapolis, MN), that "If statistics are any indication, the system may well be allowing some innocent defendants to be executed." On October 18, 2001, Justice O'Connor told the Nebraska Bar Association (Lincoln, NE) that, unless qualified lawyers are willing to work for indigent defendants who cannot afford counsel, innocent people may be sentenced to death. Justice O'Connor said, "More often than we want to recognize, some innocent defendants have been convicted and sentenced to death."

On April 9, 2001, Justice Ruth Bader Ginsburg had expressed similar concerns at a lecture at the University of the District of Columbia. Justice Ginsburg stated:

> I have yet to see a death case among the dozens coming to the Supreme Court on eve-of-execution stay petitions, in which the defendant was well represented at trial... Public funding for the legal representation of poor people in the United States is hardly generous. In capital cases, state systems for affording representation to indigent defendants vary from adequate to meager.

WORLDWIDE TREND

The *de facto* moratorium on the death penalty in the United States from 1967 to 1976 paralleled a general worldwide movement, especially among Western nations, toward the abolition of capital punishment. While the United States resumed executions in 1977, most of the Western world either formally or informally abolished capital punishment.

Today among the Western democratic nations (with which the United States traditionally compares itself), only the United States imposes the death penalty. There are technical exceptions: Israel, for example, maintains the death penalty in its statute books for "crimes against mankind" but has executed only Adolf Eichmann (1962). Eichmann was responsible for the murder of millions of Jews in occupied Europe during World War II (1939–1945). Some countries still maintain the death penalty for treason—although no Western democracy has actually imposed it. One of the first acts of the parliaments of many of the Eastern European countries after the fall of communism was to abolish capital punishment.

In 1999 then President Boris Yeltsin of Russia commuted 716 death sentences to life imprisonment. In July 2001, at a meeting with the World Bank in the Kremlin, President Vladimir Putin stated that he opposed the reinstatement of the death penalty. As of November 2001, however, Russia continued to retain the death penalty in national law, and public opinion continued to lean toward reintroducing the death penalty. Although Russia had joined the Council of Europe in 1996, it had not ratified (became a party to) Protocol No. 6 to the European Convention on Human Rights, requiring member nations to abolish the death penalty during peacetime. The council had made ratification of Protocol 6 a requisite for membership. In 1999 Ukraine ratified Protocol 6 in order to join the council.

Extradition and Capital Punishment

An increasing number of countries refuse to extradite (surrender for trial) U.S. criminals who might face the death penalty. In March 2000 French authorities arrested fugitive James Charles Kopp who was accused of murdering Buffalo, New York, abortion provider Dr. Barnett Slepian. It took months of negotiations before the French government sent Kopp back to New York for trial. The U.S. Justice Department had to agree in writing that the United States would not charge Kopp with capital murder. In spring 2001 the supreme courts of Canada and South Africa ruled that both nations would not extradite any criminal to the United States or any country that advocates capital punishment. In November 2001 Spain made a similar announcement, saying it will not extradite terrorist suspects to the United States unless the U.S. government agrees not to seek the death penalty.

A very controversial case also involving France concerned a fugitive convicted and sentenced to life imprisonment in absentia. Ira Einhorn was accused of murdering his girlfriend, Helen Maddux, in 1977. Her body was found in 1979, 18 months after she disappeared, in a closet in his apartment. Before his trial in 1981, Einhorn fled to Ireland, and eventually to France. The state of Pennsylvania held a trial without him, and he was convicted of Maddux's murder in 1993. In 1997, after French authorities arrested Einhorn, the United States requested his extradition. France, following rules of the European Convention on Human Rights, does not recognize verdicts handed down in trials in absentia or verdicts that result in the death penalty and refused to extradite the fugitive. Four years later, on July 20, 2001, France finally turned Einhorn over to U.S. officials after receiving assurance that he would be retried and not face the death penalty, forcing the Pennsylvania General Assembly to create a new law allowing for a condemned man to have another trial.

CHAPTER 2

SUPREME COURT RULINGS—CRUEL AND UNUSUAL?

In 1967 a coalition of antideath penalty groups sued Florida and California, the states with the most inmates on death row at that time, challenging the constitutionality of state capital laws. An unofficial moratorium (temporary suspension) of executions resulted, pending Supreme Court decisions on several cases on appeal. The defendants in these cases claimed that the death penalty is "cruel and unusual punishment" in violation of the Eighth Amendment to the U.S. Constitution. Moreover, they alleged that the death penalty also violated the Fourteenth Amendment, which prevents states from denying anyone "equal protection of the laws." This moratorium lasted until January 17, 1977, when Gary Gilmore, virtually at his own request, was executed by the state of Utah.

"AS THE STATUTES ARE ADMINISTERED"

On June 29, 1972, a split 5–4 Supreme Court reached the landmark decision *Furman v. Georgia* (408 U.S. 238, that included *Jackson v. Georgia* and *Branch v. Texas*), which held that "as the statutes are administered ... the imposition and carrying out of the death penalty [constitute] cruel and unusual punishment in violation of the Eighth and Fourteenth Amendments." In other words, the justices did not address whether capital punishment as a whole is unconstitutional. Rather, they chose to consider capital punishment in the context of its application in state statutes. The justices, whether they were of the majority opinion or of the dissenting opinion, could not agree on the arguments explaining why they opposed or supported the death penalty. As a result, the decision consisted of nine separate opinions, the lengthiest ruling in court history to date.

Justice William O. Douglas, in his concurring majority opinion quoted former Attorney General Ramsey Clark's statement: "It is the poor, the sick, the ignorant, the powerless, and the hated who are executed." Douglas added:

We deal with a system of law and of justice that leaves to the uncontrolled discretion of judges or juries the deter-

mination whether defendants committing these crimes should die or be imprisoned. Under these laws no standards govern the selection of the penalty. People live or die, dependent on the whim of one man or of 12.... Thus, these discretionary statutes are unconstitutional in their operation. They are pregnant with discrimination, and discrimination is an ingredient not compatible with the idea of equal protection of the laws that is implicit in the ban on "cruel and unusual" punishments.

Justice William J. Brennan stated,

At bottom, ... the Cruel and Unusual Punishments Clause prohibits the infliction of uncivilized and inhumane punishments. The State, even as it punishes, must treat its members with respect for their intrinsic worth as human beings. A punishment is "cruel and unusual," therefore, if it does not comport with human dignity.

Justice Potter Stewart stressed another point, saying,

These death sentences are cruel and unusual in the same way that being struck by lightning is cruel and unusual. For, of all the people convicted of rapes and murders in 1967 and 1968, many just as reprehensible as these, the petitioners are among a capriciously (unpredictably) selected random handful upon whom the sentence of death has in fact been imposed.

This did not mean that Justice Stewart would rule out the death penalty. He believed that the death penalty was justified but would like to see a more equitable (fair) system of determining who should be executed. He explained,

I cannot agree that retribution (punishment or vengeance for a wrong or injury) is a constitutionally impermissible ingredient in the imposition of punishment. The instinct for retribution is part of the nature of man, and channeling that instinct in the administration of criminal justice serves an important purpose in promoting the stability of a society governed by law. When people begin to believe that organized society is unwilling or unable to impose upon criminal offenders the punishment they "deserve," then there are sown the seeds of anarchy—of self help, vigilante justice, and lynch law.

Justice Byron White, believing that the death penalty was so seldom imposed that executions were ineffective deterrents to crime, chose instead to address the role of juries and judges ruling imposing the death penalty. He concluded that the cases before the courts violated the Eighth Amendment because the state legislatures, having authorized the application of the death penalty, left it to the discretion of juries and judges whether or not to impose the punishment.

Justice Thurgood Marshall thought that "the death penalty is an excessive and unnecessary punishment which violates the Eighth Amendment." He added that "even if capital punishment is not excessive, it nonetheless violates the Eighth Amendment because it is morally unacceptable to the people of the United States at this time in their history." Justice Marshall also noted that the death penalty was applied with discrimination against certain classes of people (the poor, the uneducated, and members of minority) and that innocent people had been executed before they could prove their innocence. He also believed that it hindered the reform of the treatment of criminals, and that it promoted sensationalism during trials.

Differing Opinions

Chief Justice Warren Burger, dissenting, observed that "the constitutional prohibition against 'cruel and unusual punishments' cannot be construed to bar the imposition of the punishment of death." Justice Harry A. Blackmun was disturbed by Justices Stewart's and White's remarks that as long as capital punishment was mandated for specific crimes, it could not be considered unconstitutional. Justice Blackmun feared "that statutes stricken down today will be re-enacted by state legislatures to prescribe the death penalty for specified crimes without any alternative for the imposition of a lesser punishment in the discretion of the judge or jury."

Justice Lewis Powell declared,

I find no support—in the language of the Constitution, in its history, or in the cases arising under it—for the view that this Court may invalidate a category of penalties because we deem less severe penalties adequate to serve the ends of penology....

This Court has long held that legislative decisions in this area, which lie within the special competency of that branch, are entitled to a presumption of validity. (The Court would not question the validity of a government entity properly doing its job unless its actions were way out of line.)

Justice William H. Rehnquist agreed with Justice Powell, adding the following comment:

How can government by the elected representatives of the people co- exist with the power of the federal judiciary, whose members are constitutionally insulated from responsiveness to the popular will, to declare invalid laws duly enacted by the popular branches of government?

Therefore, only Justices Brennan and Marshall concluded that the Eighth Amendment prohibited the death penalty for all crimes and under all circumstances. Justice Douglas, while ruling that the death penalty statutes reviewed by the high court were unconstitutional, did not necessarily require the final abolition of the death penalty. Justices Stewart and White also did not rule on the validity of the death penalty, noting instead that, because of the capricious imposition of the sentence, the death penalty violated the Eighth Amendment. On the other hand, Justices Rehnquist, Burger, Powell, and Blackmun concluded that the U.S. Constitution allows capital punishment.

Consequently, most state legislatures went to work to revise their capital punishment laws. They strove to make these laws more equitable in order to swing the votes of Stewart and White (and later that of John Stevens, who replaced the retired Justice Douglas).

PROPER IMPOSITION OF THE DEATH PENALTY

Four years later, on July 2, 1976, the Supreme Court ruled decisively on a series of cases. In a 7–2 decision, the justices ruled that the death penalty was, indeed, constitutional as presented in some new state laws. With Brennan and Marshall dissenting, the Court stressed (just in case *Furman* had been misunderstood) that "the death penalty is not a form of punishment that may never be imposed, regardless of the circumstances of the offense, regardless of the procedure followed in reaching the decision." Furthermore, "the infliction of death as a punishment for murder is not without justification and ... is not unconstitutionally severe."

The ruling upheld death penalty statutes in Georgia (*Gregg v. Georgia*, 428 U.S. 153, the source of the above quote), Florida (*Proffitt v. Florida*, 428 U.S. 242), and Texas (*Jurek v. Texas*, 428 U.S. 262), but struck down laws in North Carolina (*Woodson v. North Carolina*, 428 U.S. 280) and Louisiana (*Roberts v. Louisiana*, 428 U.S. 40). It ruled the latter two states' laws as too rigid in imposing mandatory death sentences for certain types of murder.

Citing the new Georgia laws in *Gregg v. Georgia*, Justice Stewart supported the bifurcated (two-part) trial system, in which the accused would first be tried to determine his or her guilt. Then, in a separate trial, the jury would consider whether the convicted person deserved the death penalty or whether mitigating factors (circumstances that may lessen responsibility for a crime) warrant a lesser sentence, usually life imprisonment. This system meets the requirements demanded by *Furman*. Noting how the Georgia statutes fulfilled these demands, Justice Stewart observed,

These procedures [established by the Georgia statutes] require the jury to consider the circumstances of the crime and the criminal before it recommends sentence. No longer can a Georgia jury do as *Furman*'s jury did: reach a finding of the defendant's guilt and then, without guidance or direction, decide whether he should live or die. Instead, the jury's attention is directed to the specific "circumstances of the crime: Was it committed in the course of another capital felony? Was it committed for money? Was it committed upon a peace officer or judicial officer? Was it committed in a particularly heinous way or in a manner that endangered the lives of many persons?" In addition, the jury's attention is focused on the characteristics of the person who committed the crime: Does he have a record of prior convictions for capital offenses? Are there any special facts about this defendant that mitigate against imposing capital punishment (e.g., his youth, the extent of his cooperation with the police, his emotional state at the time of the crime)? As a result, while some jury discretion still exists, "the discretion to be exercised is controlled by clear and objective standards so as to produce non-discriminatory application."

In addition, the Georgia law required that all death sentences be automatically appealed to the state supreme court, an "important additional safeguard against arbitrariness and caprice." The two-part trial system has since been adopted in the trials of all capital murder cases.

In *Proffitt v. Florida*, the high court upheld Florida's death penalty laws that had a bifurcated trial system similar to Georgia's. In Florida, however, the sentence was determined by the trial judge rather than by the jury, who assumed an advisory role during the sentencing phase. The Court found Florida's sentencing guidelines adequate in preventing unfair imposition of the death sentence.

PREDICTABILITY OF FUTURE CRIMINAL ACTIVITY

In *Jurek v. Texas*, the issue centered on whether a jury can satisfactorily determine the future actions of a convicted murderer. The Texas statute required that during the sentencing phase of a trial, after the defendant had been found guilty, the jury would determine whether it is probable the defendant would commit future criminal acts of violence that would threaten society. While agreeing with Jurek's attorneys that predicting future behavior is not easy, Justice Stewart noted,

> The fact that such a determination is difficult, however, does not mean that it cannot be made. Indeed, prediction of future criminal conduct is an essential element in many of the decisions rendered throughout our criminal justice system. The decision whether to admit a defendant to bail, for instance, must often turn on a judge's prediction of the defendant's future conduct. Any sentencing authority must predict a convicted person's probable future conduct when it engages in the process of determining what punishment to impose. For those sentenced to prison, these same predictions must be made by parole authorities. The task that a Texas jury

must perform in answering the statutory question is thus basically no different from the task performed countless times each day throughout the American system of criminal justice.

Is the Testimony of a Psychiatrist Valid?

In 1978 Thomas Barefoot was convicted of murdering a police officer. During the sentencing phase of the trial, the prosecution put two psychiatrists on the stand. Neither psychiatrist had actually interviewed Barefoot nor did either ask to do so. Both psychiatrists agreed that an individual with Barefoot's background and who had acted as Barefoot had in murdering the policeman represented a future threat to society. Partially based on their testimony, the jury sentenced Barefoot to death.

Barefoot's conviction and sentence were appealed numerous times, and in 1983 his case was argued before the U.S. Supreme Court. Barefoot's attorneys claimed that psychiatrists could not reliably predict that a particular offender would commit other crimes in the future and be a threat to society. They further argued that psychiatrists should also not be allowed to testify about an offender's future dangerousness in response to hypothetical situations presented by the prosecutor and without having first examined the offender.

In *Barefoot v. Estelle* (463 U.S. 880, 1983), the Supreme Court ruled 6–3 that local juries were in the best position to decide guilt and impose a sentence. The Court referred to *Jurek v. Texas*, which upheld the testimony of laypersons concerning a defendant's possible future actions. The Court, therefore, looked upon psychiatrists as just another group of people presenting testimony to the jury for consideration.

The high court dismissed a brief presented by the American Psychiatric Association (APA), indicating that psychiatric testimony was "almost entirely unreliable" in determining future actions. The Court countered that such testimony had been traditionally accepted. The high court also dismissed Barefoot's contention that the psychiatrists should have personally interviewed him. Such methods of observation and conclusion were quite normal in courtroom procedures and the psychiatric observations had been based on established facts. Barefoot's appeal was denied.

FLEXIBLE GUIDELINES FOR JUDGES AND JURORS ARE REQUIRED

In *Woodson v. North Carolina*, the Supreme Court addressed for the first time the question of whether the jury's handing down of a death sentence pursuant to North Carolina's mandatory death penalty for all first-degree murders constituted cruel and unusual punishment within the meaning of the Eighth and Fourteenth Amendments. The justices held that North Carolina's new statute provided "no standards to guide the jury in its inevitable exercise of the power to determine which first-degree murderer shall live and which shall die." Furthermore, the North Carolina law did not let the jury consider the convicted defendant's character, criminal record, or the circumstances of the crime before the imposition of the death sentence.

The Louisiana mandatory death sentence for first-degree murder suffered from similar inadequacies. It did, however, permit the jury to consider lesser offenses such as second-degree murder. In *Roberts v. Louisiana*, the Supreme Court rejected the Louisiana law because it forced the jury to find the defendant guilty of a lesser crime in order to avoid imposing the death penalty. The jury did not have the option of first determining if the accused was indeed guilty of first-degree murder for the crime he had actually committed and then recommending a lesser sentence if there were mitigating circumstances to support it.

As a result of either *Furman* or *Gregg*, or both, virtually every state's capital punishment statute had to be rewritten. These statutes would provide flexible guidelines for judges and juries so that they might fairly decide capital cases and consider, then impose, if necessary, the death penalty.

EXCLUSION FROM JURIES OF THOSE AGAINST CAPITAL PUNISHMENT

In *Witherspoon v. Illinois* (391 U.S. 510, 1968), the Supreme Court found unconstitutional the exclusion from juries of all who opposed the death penalty without determining whether their ethical beliefs would compel them to reject capital punishment. This selective process would result in a jury that would not be representative of the community.

The findings in *Witherspoon*, however, did not mean that a person against the death penalty could not be excluded. According to the justices,

[A prospective juror must] be willing to *consider* all the penalties provided by [the] state law, and ... not be irrevocably committed before the trial has begun, to vote against the penalty of death regardless of the facts and circumstances that might emerge in the course of proceedings.

[Based on] presently available knowledge, we simply cannot conclude ... that the exclusion of jurors opposed to capital punishment results in an unrepresentative jury on the issue of guilt or substantially increases the risk of conviction.

Consequently, based on *Witherspoon*, it has become the practice in most states to exclude prospective jurors who indicate that they could not possibly in good conscience return a death penalty. In *Lockett v. Ohio* (438 U.S, 586, 1978), the Supreme Court upheld *Witherspoon*

when it dismissed Lockett's contention that the exclusion of four prospective jurors who opposed the death penalty denied her an impartial jury.

Weakening Witherspoon

In *Wainwright v. Witt* (469 U.S. 412, 1985), a 7–2 Supreme Court majority eased the strict requirements of *Witherspoon*. Writing for the majority, Justice Rehnquist declared that the new capital punishment procedures left less discretion to jurors. Rehnquist indicated that potential jurors in capital cases should be excluded from jury duty in a manner similar to how they were excluded in noncapital cases.

No longer would a juror's "automatic" bias against imposing the death penalty have to be proved with "unmistakable clarity." A prosecutor could not be expected to ask all the questions necessary to determine if a juror would automatically rule against the death penalty or fail to convict a defendant if he or she were likely to face execution. Fundamentally, the question of exclusion from a jury should be determined by the interplay of the prosecutor and the defense lawyer and by the decision of the judge based on his or her initial observations of the prospective juror. Judges can see firsthand whether prospective jurors' beliefs would bias their ability to impose the death penalty.

In his dissent, Justice Brennan claimed that making it easier to eliminate those who opposed capital punishment from the jury created a jury not only more likely to impose the death sentence, but also more likely to convict. He also attacked the majority interpretation that now treated exclusion from a capital case as being similar to exclusion from any other case.

IT DOES NOT MATTER IF "DEATH-QUALIFIED" JURIES ARE MORE LIKELY TO CONVICT

In *Lockhart v. McCree* (476 U.S. 162, 1986), the Supreme Court resolved the issue of a fair trial with a "death-qualified" jury. Ardia McCree was convicted of murdering Evelyn Boughton while robbing her gift shop and service station in Camden, Arkansas. In accordance with Arkansas law, the trial judge removed eight prospective jurors because they indicated they could not, under any circumstances, vote for the imposition of the death sentence. The resulting jury then convicted McCree and, although the state sought the death penalty, sentenced the defendant to life imprisonment without parole.

McCree appealed, claiming that the removal of the so-called *Witherspoon*-excludables violated his right to a fair trial under the Sixth and Fourteenth Amendments. These amendments guaranteed that his guilt or innocence would be determined by an impartial jury selected from a representative cross-section of the community, which would include people strongly opposed to the death penalty. Both the federal district court and the federal court of appeals agreed with McCree, but in a 6–3 decision, the Supreme Court disagreed.

The high court majority did not accept the validity of the studies presented to show that those strongly opposed to the death penalty were less likely to convict and those who supported the death penalty were more likely to convict. Justice Rehnquist, speaking for the majority, argued that, even if the justices did accept the validity of these studies, "the Constitution does not prohibit the States from 'death qualifying' juries in capital cases." Justice Rehnquist further observed,

> The exclusion from jury service of large groups of individuals not on the basis of their inability to serve as jurors, but on the basis of some immutable [unchangeable] characteristic such as race, gender, or ethnic background, undeniably gave rise to an "appearance of unfairness."

> [Nevertheless], unlike blacks, women, and Mexican-Americans, "*Witherspoon*-excludables" are singled out for exclusion in capital cases on the basis of an attribute that is within the individual's control. It is important to remember that not all who oppose the death penalty are subject to removal for cause in capital cases; those who firmly believe that the death penalty is unjust may nevertheless serve as jurors in capital cases so long as they state clearly that they are willing to temporarily set aside their own beliefs in deference to the rule of law. Because the group of "*Witherspoon*-excludables" includes only those who cannot and will not conscientiously obey the law with respect to one of the issues in a capital case, "death qualification" hardly can be said to create an "appearance of unfairness."

Writing in dissent, Justice Marshall observed that if the high court thought in *Witherspoon* that excluding those who opposed the death penalty meant that a convicted murderer would not get a fair hearing during the sentencing part of the trial, it would also logically mean that he or she would not get a fair hearing during the initial trial part. The Court minority generally accepted the studies showing "that 'death qualification' in fact produces juries somewhat more 'conviction-prone' than 'nondeath-qualified' juries."

JURY MAY CONSIDER A LESSER CHARGE

Along with an accomplice, Gilbert Beck entered the home of Roy Malone. While they were tying up the victim, Beck's accomplice unexpectedly struck and killed Malone. Beck admitted to the robbery, but claimed the murder was not part of the plan. Beck was tried under an Alabama statute for "robbery or attempts thereof when the victim is intentionally killed by the defendant."

Under Alabama law, the judge was specifically prohibited from giving the jury the option of convicting the defendant of a lesser-included offense. Instead, the jury was given the choice of either convicting the defendant of the capital crime, in which case he possibly faced the death penalty, or acquitting him, thus allowing him to escape all penalties for his alleged participation in the crime. The judge could not have offered the jury the lesser alternative of felony-murder, which did not deal with the accused's intentions at the time of the crime.

Beck appealed, claiming this law created a situation in which the jury was more likely to convict. The Supreme Court, in *Beck v. Alabama* (447 U.S. 625, 1980), agreed and reversed the lower court's ruling. The high court observed that, while not a matter of due process, it was virtually universally accepted in lesser offenses that a third alternative be offered. The Court noted,

> That safeguard would seem to be especially important in a case such as this. For when the evidence unquestionably establishes that the defendant is guilty of a serious, violent offense—but leaves some doubt with respect to an element that would justify conviction of a capital offense—the failure to give the jury the "third option" of convicting on a lesser included offense would seem inevitably to enhance the risk of an unwarranted conviction.

According to the ruling, such a risk could not be tolerated in a case where the defendant's life was at stake. *Beck*, however, did not require a jury to consider a lesser charge in every case, but only where the consideration would be justified.

DOES THE BUCK STOP WITH THE JURY?

During the course of a robbery, Bobby Caldwell shot and killed the owner of a grocery store. He was tried and found guilty. During the sentencing phase of the trial, Caldwell's attorney pleaded for mercy, concluding his summation by emphasizing to the jury,

> I implore you to think deeply about this matter.... You are the judges and you will have to decide his fate. It is an awesome responsibility, I know—an awesome responsibility.

Responding to the defense attorney's plea, the prosecutor played down the responsibility of the jury, stressing that a life sentence would be reviewed by a higher court:

> [The defense] would have you believe that you're going to kill this man and they know ... that your decision is not the final decision.... Your job is reviewable.... [T]hey know, as I know, and as Judge Baker has told you, that the decision you render is automatically reviewable by the Supreme Court.

The jury sentenced Caldwell to death, and the case was automatically appealed. The Mississippi Supreme Court upheld the conviction, but split 4–4 on the validity of the death sentence, thereby upholding the death sentence by an equally divided court. Caldwell appealed to the U.S. Supreme Court.

In a 5–3 decision (Justice Powell took no part in the decision), the Supreme Court, in *Caldwell v. Mississippi* (472 U.S. 320, 1985), vacated (annulled) the death sentence. Writing for the majority, Justice Marshall noted,

> It is constitutionally impermissible to rest a death sentence on a determination made by a sentencer who has been led to believe that the responsibility for determining the appropriateness of the defendant's death rests elsewhere.... [This Court] has taken as a given that capital sentencers would view their task as the serious one of determining whether a specific human being should die at the hands of the State.

Furthermore, the high court pointed out that the appeals court was not the place to make this life-and-death decision. Most appellate courts would presume that the sentencing was correctly done, which would leave the defendant at a distinct disadvantage. The jurors, expecting to be reversed by an appeals court, might choose to "send a message" of extreme disapproval of the defendant's acts and sentence him or her to death to show they will not tolerate such actions. Should the appeals court fail to reverse the decision, the defendant might be executed when the jury only intended to "send a message."

The three dissenting judges believed "the Court has overstated the seriousness of the prosecutor's comments" and that it was "highly unlikely that the jury's sense of responsibility was diminished."

KEEPING PAROLE INFORMATION FROM THE JURY

In 1990 Jonathan Dale Simmons beat an elderly woman to death in her home in Columbia, South Carolina. The week before his capital murder trial began, he pleaded guilty to first-degree burglary and two counts of criminal sexual conduct in connection with two prior assaults on elderly women. These guilty pleas resulted in convictions for violent offenses, which made him ineligible for parole if convicted of any other violent crime.

At the capital murder trial, over the defense counsel's objection, the court did not allow the defense to ask prospective jurors if they understood the meaning of a "life" sentence as it applied to the defendant. Under South Carolina law, a defendant who was deemed a future threat to society and receiving a life sentence was ineligible for parole. The prosecution also asked the judge not to mention parole.

During deliberation, the jurors asked the judge if the imposition of a life sentence carried with it the possibility of parole. The judge told the jury,

> You are instructed not to consider parole or parole eligibility in reaching your verdict.... The terms life impris-

onment and death sentence are to be understood in the plan [sic] and ordinary meaning.

The jury convicted Simmons of murder, sentencing him to death. On appeal the South Carolina Supreme Court upheld the sentence. The case was brought before the U.S. Supreme Court. The high court, in a 6–2 decision (*Simmons v. South Carolina* [512 U.S. 154, 1994]), overruled the South Carolina Supreme Court, concluding,

> Where a defendant's future dangerousness is at issue, and state law prohibits his release on parole, due process requires that the sentencing jury be informed that the defendant is parole ineligible. An individual cannot be executed on the basis of information which he had no opportunity to deny or explain.... Petitioner's jury reasonably may have believed that he could be released on parole if he were not executed. To the extent that this misunderstanding pervaded its deliberations, it had the effect of creating a false choice between sentencing him to death and sentencing him to a limited period of incarceration. The trial court's refusal to apprise the jury of information so crucial to its determination, particularly when the State alluded to the defendant's future dangerousness in its argument, cannot be reconciled with this Court's well-established precedents interpreting the Due Process Clause.

JUDGE SENTENCING INSTEAD OF JURY

Under Florida's capital trial system, the jury decides the guilt or innocence of the accused. If the jury finds the defendant guilty, it recommends an advisory opinion of either life imprisonment or the death sentence. The trial judge considers aggravating and mitigating circumstances, weighs them against the jury recommendation, and then sentences the convicted murderer to either life or death.

A Florida jury convicted Joseph Spaziano of torturing and murdering two women. The jury recommended that Spaziano be sentenced to life imprisonment, but the trial judge, after considering the mitigating and aggravating circumstances, sentenced the defendant to death. In his appeal, Spaziano claimed the judge's overriding of the jury's recommendation of life imprisonment violated the Eighth Amendment's prohibition against cruel and unusual punishment. The Supreme Court, in a 5–3 decision, in *Spaziano v. Florida* (468 U.S. 447, 1984), did not agree.

Spaziano's lawyers claimed juries, not judges, were better equipped to make reliable capital-sentencing decisions and that a jury's decision of life imprisonment should be inviolate (not questioned). They reasoned that the death penalty was unlike any other sentence and required that the jury have the ultimate word. This belief had been upheld, Spaziano claimed, because 30 out of 37 states with capital punishment had the jury decide the prisoner's fate. Furthermore, the primary justification for the death penalty was retribution and an expression of community outrage. The jury served as the voice of the community and knew best whether a particular crime was so terrible that the community's response must be the death sentence.

The high court indicated that, although Spaziano's argument had some appeal, it contained two fundamental flaws. First, retribution played a role in all sentences, not just death sentences. Second, a jury was not the only source of community input. "The community's voice is heard at least as clearly in the legislature when the death penalty is authorized and the particular circumstances in which death is appropriate are defined." That trial judges imposed sentences was a normal part of the judicial system. The Supreme Court continued,

> In light of the facts that the Sixth Amendment does not require jury sentencing, that the demands of fairness and reliability in capital cases do not require it, and that neither the nature of, nor the purpose behind, the death penalty requires jury sentencing, we cannot conclude that placing responsibility on the trial judge to impose the sentence in a capital case is unconstitutional.

In addition, just because 30 of 37 states let the jury make the sentencing decision did not mean states that let a judge decide were wrong. The Court pointed out that there is no one right way for a state to establish its method of capital sentencing.

Writing for the dissenters, Justice John Stevens indicated:

> Because of its severity and irrevocability, the death penalty is qualitatively different from any other punishment, and hence must be accompanied by unique safeguards to ensure that it is a justified response to a given offense.... I am convinced that the danger of an excessive response can only be avoided if the decision to impose the death penalty is made by a jury rather than by a single governmental official ... [because a jury] is best able to "express the conscience of the community on the ultimate question of life or death."

Justice Stevens also gave weight to the fact that 30 out of 37 states had the jury make the decision, attesting to the "high level of consensus" (a majority view) that communities strongly believe life-or-death decisions should remain with the people—as represented by the jury—rather than relegated to a single government official.

Advisory Juries

Louise Harris asked a coworker, Lorenzo McCarter, with whom she was having an affair, to find someone to kill her husband. McCarter paid two accomplices one hundred dollars, with a vague promise of more money after they killed the husband. McCarter testified against Harris in exchange for the prosecutor's promise that he would not seek the death penalty against McCarter. McCarter testified that Harris had asked him to kill her husband so they could share in his death benefits. An Alabama jury convicted Louise Harris of capital murder. At the sentencing hearing witnesses testified to her good background and strong character. She was rearing seven children, held three jobs simultaneously, and was active in her church.

Alabama law gives capital sentencing authority to the trial judge, but requires the judge to "consider" an advisory jury verdict. The jury voted 7 to 5 to give Harris life imprisonment without parole. The trial judge then considered her sentence. He found one aggravating circumstance (the murder was committed for monetary gain), one statutory mitigating circumstance (Harris had no prior criminal record), and one nonstatutory mitigating circumstance (Harris was a hardworking, respected member of her church).

Noting that she had planned the crime, financed it, and stood to benefit from the murder, the judge felt that the aggravating circumstance outweighed the other mitigating circumstances and sentenced her to death. On appeal, the Alabama Supreme Court affirmed the conviction and sentence. It rejected Harris's arguments that the procedure was unconstitutional because Alabama state law did "not specify the weight the judge must give to the jury's recommendation and thus permits the arbitrary imposition of the death penalty."

On appeal, the U.S. Supreme Court upheld the Alabama court's decision (*Harris v. Alabama* [513 U.S. 504], 1995). Alabama's capital-sentencing process is similar to that of Florida (see *Spaziano* above). Both require jury participation during sentencing but give the trial judge the ultimate sentencing authority. Nevertheless, while the Florida statute requires that a trial judge must give "great weight" to the jury recommendation, the Alabama statute requires only that the judge "consider" the jury's recommendation.

As in *Spaziano*, the high court ruled that the Eighth Amendment does not require the state "to define the weight the sentencing judge must give to an advisory jury verdict."

> Because the Constitution permits the trial judge, acting alone, to impose a capital sentence ... it is not offended when a State further requires a judge to consider a jury recommendation and trusts the judge to give it the proper weight.

CHAPTER 3

LEGAL DECISIONS—CIRCUMSTANCES, RIGHT TO COUNSEL, EVIDENCE, AND VICTIM IMPACT STATEMENTS

RAPE AND KIDNAPPING DO NOT WARRANT DEATH

On June 20, 1977, a 5–4 divided Supreme Court ruled, in *Everheart v. Georgia* (433 U.S. 917) and in *Coker v. Georgia* (433 U.S. 584):

> Rape is without doubt deserving of serious punishment, but in terms of moral depravity and of the injury to the person and to the public, it does not involve the unjustified taking of human life.... The murderer kills; the rapist, if no more than that, does not. Life is over for the victim of the murderers; for the rape victim, life may not be nearly so happy as it was, but it is not over and normally is not beyond repair. We have the abiding conviction that the death penalty, which is unique in its severity and irrevocability ... is an excessive penalty for the rapist who, as such, does not take human life.

The Court also held that kidnapping did not warrant the death penalty. While the victims usually suffered tremendously, they had not lost their lives. (If the kidnapped victim were killed, then the kidnapper would be tried for murder.) These high court decisions left only murder and treason as justifiable grounds for the imposition of the death penalty. So far, no cases involving the death penalty for treason have been brought to the Supreme Court.

MITIGATING CIRCUMSTANCES

Sandra Lockett was convicted for helping to plan and then driving the getaway car for a pawnshop robbery. Although it was unintended, the owner of the pawnshop was murdered. Lockett also hid her accomplices in her home. Later she was tried for the capital murder of the pawnshop owner. According to the Ohio death penalty statute, capital punishment had to be imposed on Lockett unless "(1) the victim induced or facilitated the offense; (2) it is unlikely that the offense would have been committed but for the fact that the offender was under duress,

coercion, or strong provocation; or (3) the offense was primarily the product of the offender's psychosis or mental deficiency." Lockett was found guilty and sentenced to die.

Lockett appealed, claiming that the Ohio law did not give the sentencing judge the chance to consider the circumstances of the crime and the defendant's character and record as mitigating factors (factors that may lessen responsibility for a crime). In July 1978 the Supreme Court, in *Lockett v. Ohio* (438 U.S. 586), upheld Lockett's contention. Chief Justice Warren Burger observed,

> A statute that prevents the sentencer in capital cases from giving independent mitigating weights to aspects of the defendant's character and record and to the circumstances of the offense ... creates the risk that the death penalty will be imposed in spite of factors that may call for a less severe penalty, and when the choice is between life and death, such risk is unacceptable and incompatible with the commands of the Eighth and Fourteenth Amendments.

Mitigating Circumstances Must Always Be Considered

In *Hitchcock v. Dugger* (481 U.S. 393, 1987), a unanimous Supreme Court further emphasized that all mitigating circumstances had to be considered before the convicted murderer could be sentenced. A Florida judge had instructed the jury not to consider, and he himself refused to consider, evidence of mitigating factors that were not specifically indicated in the Florida death penalty law. Writing for the Court, Justice Antonin Scalia stressed that a convicted person had the right "to present any and all relevant mitigating evidence that is available."

NOT BEING AT THE SCENE OF THE MURDER

On April 1, 1975, Sampson and Jeanette Armstrong, on the pretext of requesting water for their overheated car, tried to rob Thomas Kersey at home. Earl Enmund waited in the getaway car. Kersey called for his wife, who tried to shoot Jeanette Armstrong. The Armstrongs killed the Kerseys. Enmund was tried as an aider and abettor in the robbery-murder and sentenced to death.

In *Enmund v. Florida* (468 U.S. 782, 1982), a 5–4 split Supreme Court ruled that, in this case, the death penalty violated the Eighth and Fourteenth Amendments to the U.S. Constitution. The majority noted that only 9 of the 36 states with capital punishment permitted its use on a criminal who was not actually present at the scene of the crime. The exception was the case where someone paid a hit man to murder the victim.

Furthermore, over the years juries had tended not to sentence to death criminals who had not actually been at the scene of the crime. Certainly Enmund was guilty of planning and participating in a robbery, but murder had not been part of the plan. Since someone is killed in only one out of two hundred robberies, Enmund could not have expected the Kerseys' murders during the robbery attempt. The Court concluded that, because Enmund did not kill or planned to kill, he should be tried only for his participation in the robbery. The Court observed,

> We have no doubt that robbery is a serious crime deserving serious punishment. It is not, however, a crime "so grievous an affront to humanity that the only adequate response may be the penalty of death" [from *Gregg v. Georgia*, 428 U.S. 153, 1976]. It does not compare with murder, which does involve the unjustified taking of human life.... The murderer kills; the robber, if no more than that, does not. Life is over for the victim of the murderer; for the [robbery] victim, life ... is not over and normally is not beyond repair.

Writing for the minority, Justice Sandra Day O'Connor concluded that intent is a complex issue. It should be left to the judge and jury trying the accused to decide intent, not a federal court far removed from the actual trial.

Enmund Reviewed

Just because a person had no intent to kill, however, does not mean that he or she cannot be sentenced to death. Crawford Bullock and a friend, Ricky Tucker, had been drinking at a bar. An acquaintance, Mark Dickson, offered them a ride home. During the drive an argument ensued over money Dickson supposedly owed Tucker.

Outside the car Bullock held Dickson while Tucker hit Dickson in the face with a whiskey bottle and punched him. When Dickson fell, Tucker smashed his head with a concrete block, killing him. Tucker and Bullock disposed of the body. The next day police spotted Bullock driving the victim's car. After his arrest Bullock confessed.

Under Mississippi law a person involved in a robbery that results in murder may be convicted of capital murder regardless of "the defendant's own lack of intent that any killing take place." The jury never was asked to consider

whether Bullock in fact killed, attempted to kill, or intended to kill. He was convicted and sentenced to death as an accomplice to the crime. During the appeals process, the Mississippi Supreme Court confirmed that Bullock was indeed a participant in the murder.

In January 1986 a 5–4 divided Supreme Court, in *Cabana v. Bullock* (474 U.S. 376), modified the *Enmund* decision. It indicated that while *Enmund* had to be considered at some point during the judicial process, the initial jury trying the accused did not necessarily have to consider the *Enmund* ruling. The high court ruled that, while the jury had not been made aware of the issue of intent, the Mississippi Supreme Court had considered this question. Since *Enmund* did not require that intent be presented at the initial jury trial, only that it be considered at some time during the judicial process, the state of Mississippi had met that requirement.

The four dissenting justices claimed that it was difficult for any appeals court to determine intent from reading a typed transcript of a trial. It was important to see the accused and others involved to help determine who was telling the truth and who was not. This was why *Enmund* must be raised to the jury so it could consider the question of intent in light of what it had seen and heard directly.

A "Reckless Indifference to the Value of Human Life" Is Just as Bad as Pulling the Trigger

Gary Tison was a convicted criminal who had been sentenced to life imprisonment for murdering a prison guard during an escape. Tison's three sons, his wife, his brother, and other relatives planned and carried out a prison escape involving Tison and a fellow prisoner, Randy Greenawalt, also a convicted murderer.

Tison's family provided Gary Tison and Greenawalt with guns. During the escape their car had a flat tire, so they flagged down a passing car. The motorist who stopped to help was driving with his wife, their 2-year-old son, and a 15-year-old niece.

Gary Tison then told his sons to go get some water from the motorist's car, presumably to be left with the family they planned to abandon in the desert. While the sons were gone, Gary Tison and Randy Greenawalt shot and killed the family. Several days later two of Tison's sons and Greenawalt were captured. The third son was killed, and Tison escaped into the desert, where he later died of exposure.

The Tison sons and Greenawalt were found guilty and sentenced to death. The sons, citing *Enmund*, appealed, claiming that they had neither pulled the triggers nor intended the deaths of the family who had stopped to help them. The 5–4 Supreme Court decision (*Tison v. Arizona*, 481 U.S. 137, 1987) upheld the death sentence, indicating that the Tison sons had shown a "reckless indifference to the value of human life [which] may be every bit as shocking to the moral sense as an 'intent to kill.' "

The Tison sons may not have pulled the triggers (and the Court fully accepted the premise that they did not do the shootings or directly intend them to happen), but they released and then assisted two convicted murderers. They should have realized that freeing two killers and giving them guns could very well put innocent people in great danger. They continued to help the escapees even after the family was killed.

"These facts," concluded Justice O'Connor for the majority, "not only indicate that the Tison [sons'] participation in the crime was anything but minor, they also would clearly support a finding that they both subjectively appreciated that their acts were likely to result in the taking of innocent life." Unlike the situation in the *Enmund* case, they were not sitting in a car far from the murder scene. They were direct participants in the whole event. The death sentence would stand.

Writing for the minority, Justice William J. Brennan observed that had a prison guard been murdered (Gary Tison had murdered a prison guard in a previous escape attempt), then the Court's argument would have made sense. The murder of the family, however, made no sense and was not even necessary for the escape. The Tison sons were away from the murder scene getting water for the victims and could have done nothing to save them. While they were guilty of planning and carrying out an escape, the murder of the family who stopped to help them was an unexpected outcome of the escape.

Furthermore, the father had promised his sons that he would not kill during the escape, a promise he had kept despite several opportunities to kill during the actual prison escape. It was, therefore, not unreasonable for the sons not to have expected their father to kill in a situation that did not appear to warrant it. Justice Brennan concluded that "like Enmund, the Tisons neither killed nor attempted nor intended to kill anyone. Like Enmund, the Tisons have been sentenced to death for the intentional acts of others, which the Tisons did not expect, which were not essential to the felony, and over which they had no control."

AN "OUTRAGEOUSLY AND WANTONLY VILE" MURDER

Robert Godfrey and his wife of 28 years separated after a heated dispute. Mrs. Godfrey went to live with her mother, who supported her daughter's decision to leave her husband. During a telephone conversation, Mrs. Godfrey told her husband that reconciliation was impossible.

Later Robert Godfrey took a shotgun and went to his mother-in-law's nearby trailer. He shot through a window, killing his wife instantly. He then entered the trailer,

struck his fleeing daughter on the head with the gun, and shot his mother-in-law in the head, killing her. Godfrey then called the police, told them what he had done, and waited for the police to arrive.

The Georgia Code permits the imposition of the death penalty in the case of a murder that "was outrageously or wantonly vile, horrible, or inhuman in that it involved torture, depravity of mind, or an aggravated brutality to the victim." Aware of this law, the jury sentenced Godfrey to die. He appealed, claiming that the statute was unconstitutionally vague. After the Georgia Supreme Court upheld the lower court decision, the case was appealed to the U.S. Supreme Court.

The Supreme Court, in *Godfrey v. Georgia* (446 U.S. 420, 1980), noted that the victims were killed instantly (i.e., there was no torture), the victims had been "causing [Godfrey] extreme emotional trauma," and he acknowledged his responsibility. The high court concluded that, in this case, the Georgia law was unconstitutionally vague. Moreover, the Georgia Supreme Court did not attempt to narrow the definition of "outrageously and wantonly vile." In a concurring opinion, Justice Thurgood Marshall, whom Justice Brennan joined, found this an example of the inherently "arbitrary [subject to individual judgment] and capricious [unpredictable]" nature of capital punishment, since even the prosecutor in Godfrey's case observed numerous times that there was no torture or abuse involved.

"COMPARATIVE PROPORTIONALITY REVIEW"

Robert Harris and his brother decided to steal a car they would need for a getaway in a planned bank robbery. Robert Harris approached two teenage boys eating hamburgers in a car. He forced them at gunpoint to drive to a nearby wooded area. The teenagers offered to delay telling the police of the car robbery and even to give the authorities misleading descriptions of the two robbers. When one of the boys appeared to be fleeing, Harris shot both of them. Harris and his brother later committed the robbery, were soon caught, and confessed to the robbery and murders.

Harris was found guilty. In California, a convicted murderer could be sentenced to death or life imprisonment without parole only if "special circumstances" existed and the murder had been "willful, deliberate, premeditated, and committed during the commission of kidnapping and robbery." This had to be proven during a separate sentencing hearing.

The state showed that Harris was convicted of manslaughter in 1975; he was found in possession of a makeshift knife and garrote (an instrument used for strangulation) while in prison; he and other inmates sodomized another inmate; and he threatened that inmate's life. Harris testified that he had a very unhappy childhood, had little education, and his father had sexually molested his sisters. The jury sentenced Harris to death, and the judge concurred.

Harris claimed the U.S. Constitution, as interpreted in previous capital punishment rulings, required the state of California to give his case "comparative proportionality review" to determine if his death sentence was not out of line with that of others convicted of similar crimes. In "comparative proportionality review," a court considers the seriousness of the offense, the severity of the penalty, the sentences imposed for other crimes, and the sentencing in other jurisdictions for the same crime. Courts have occasionally struck down punishments inherently disproportionate and, therefore, cruel and unusual. Georgia, by law, and Florida, by practice, had incorporated such reviews in their procedures. Other states, such as Texas and California, had not.

When the case reached the U.S. Ninth Circuit Court of Appeals, the court agreed with Harris and ordered California to establish proportionality or lift the death sentence. The U.S. Supreme Court (*Pulley v. Harris*, 465 U.S. 37, 1984), in a 7–2 decision, did not agree. The Court noted that the California procedure contained enough safeguards to guarantee a defendant a fair trial and those convicted, a fair sentence. The high court added,

> That some [state statutes] providing proportionality review are constitutional does not mean that such review is indispensable.... To endorse the statute as a whole is not to say that anything different is unacceptable. Examination of our 1976 cases makes clear that they do not establish proportionality review as a constitutional requirement.

Justice Brennan, joined by Justice Marshall, dissented. He noted that the Supreme Court had thrown out the existing death penalty procedures during the 1970s because they were deemed arbitrary and capricious. He believed they still were, but the introduction of "proportionality" might "eliminate some, if only a small part, of the irrationality that currently surrounds the imposition of the death penalty."

WHEN DOES THE RIGHT TO COUNSEL END?

Joseph Giarratano was a Virginia prisoner under sentence of death. He went to court, complaining that, because he was poor, the state of Virginia should provide him with a lawyer to help prepare conviction appeals. Virginia permitted the condemned prisoner the right to use the prison libraries to prepare an appeal, but it did not provide the condemned with his own personal attorney.

Virginia had "unit attorneys" who were assigned to help prisoners with prison-related legal matters. A unit attorney could give guidance to death row inmates, but could not act as the personal attorney for any one particu-

lar inmate. This case became a class action in which the federal district court certified a class comprising "all current and future Virginia inmates awaiting execution who do not have and cannot afford counsel to pursue postconviction proceedings."

The federal district court and the federal court of appeals agreed with Giarratano, but the U.S. Supreme Court, in *Murray v. Giarratano* (492 U.S. 1, 1989), disagreed. Writing for the majority (Justices Byron White, O'Connor, and Scalia, with Justice Anthony Kennedy filing a concurring opinion), Chief Justice William H. Rehnquist concluded that, while the Sixth and Fourteenth Amendments to the U.S. Constitution assured an indigent (poor) defendant the right to counsel at the trial stage of a criminal proceeding, they do not provide for counsel for postconviction proceedings, as they ruled in *Pennsylvania v. Finley* (481 U.S. 551, 1987). Since *Finley* had not specifically considered prisoners on death row, but all prisoners in general, the majority did not believe the decision needed to be reconsidered just because death row prisoners had more at stake.

Chief Justice Rehnquist agreed that those facing the death penalty had a right to counsel for the trial and during the initial appeal. During these periods, the defendant needed a heightened measure of protection because the death penalty was involved. Later appeals, however, involved more procedural matters that "serve a different and more limited purpose than either the trial or appeal."

In dissent, Justice John Stevens (joined by Justices Brennan, Marshall, and Harry A. Blackmun) indicated that he thought condemned prisoners in Virginia faced three critical differences from those considered in *Finley*. First, the Virginia prisoners had been sentenced to death, which made their condition different from a sentence of life imprisonment. Second, Virginia's particular judicial decision forbids certain issues to be raised during the direct review or appeal process and forces them to be considered only during later postconviction appeals. This means that very important issues may be considered without the benefit of counsel. Finally,

> Unlike the ordinary inmate, who presumably has ample time to use and reuse the prison library and to seek guidance from other prisoners experienced in preparing ... petitions, a grim deadline imposes a finite limit on the condemned person's capacity for useful research.... [As the district court concluded,] an inmate preparing himself and his family for impending death is incapable of performing the mental functions necessary to adequately pursue his claims.

DOES THE RIGHT TO COUNSEL EXTEND TO CRIMES THAT HAVE NOT BEEN CHARGED?

In 1994 Raymond Levi Cobb confessed to burglarizing the home of Lindsey Owings the previous year. He claimed no knowledge, however, of the disappearances of Owings's wife and infant at the time of the burglary. The court subsequently assigned Cobb a lawyer to represent him in the burglary offense. With his lawyer's permission, investigators twice questioned Cobb regarding the disappearance of the Owings family. Both times Cobb denied any knowledge of the missing pair.

In 1995, while free on bond for the burglary and living with his father, Cobb told his father he killed Margaret Owing and buried her baby, while still alive, with her. Cobb was convicted of murder and sentenced to death. On appeal, Cobb claimed that his confession, obtained in violation of his Sixth Amendment right to counsel, should have been suppressed.

The Texas Court of Criminal Appeals reversed Cobb's conviction, ordering a new trial. The court considered Cobb's confession to the murders inadmissible, holding that "once the right to counsel attaches to the offense charged [burglary], it also attaches to any other offense [in this case, murder] that is very closely related factually to the offense charged."

The state appealed to the U.S. Supreme Court. On April 2, 2001, in *Texas v. Cobb* (No. 99-1702), the Supreme Court, in a 5–4 decision, stated,

> The Sixth Amendment right to counsel is ... "offense specific." It cannot be invoked once for all future prosecutions, for it does not attach until a prosecution is commenced, that is, at or after the initiation of adversary judicial proceedings—whether by way of formal charge, preliminary hearing, indictment, information, or arraignment [citing *McNeil v. Wisconsin*, 501 U.S. 171, 1991].

This means that Cobb's right to counsel did not extend to crimes with which he had not been charged. Since this right did not prohibit investigators from questioning him about the murders without first notifying his lawyer, Cobb's confession was admissible.

FEDERAL JUDGES CAN DELAY EXECUTIONS TO ALLOW HABEAS CORPUS REVIEWS

A Texas jury found Frank McFarland guilty of stabbing to death a woman he had met in a bar. The appellate court upheld his conviction, and two lower federal courts refused his request for a stay (postponement) of execution. The federal courts ruled that they did not have jurisdiction to stop the execution until McFarland filed a *habeas corpus* (a prisoner's petition to be heard in federal court; also referred to as *habeas*). The inmate argued that without the stay, he would be executed before he could obtain a lawyer to prepare the petition.

The Supreme Court granted a stay of execution. In a 5–4 decision (*McFarland v. Scott*, 512 U.S. 849, 1994), the Supreme Court ruled that federal law required governments to supply lawyers for poor defendants on death row who wanted to have *habeas* review. Once a defendant requested counsel, the federal court could postpone execution so the lawyer would have time to prepare an appeal. Justice Blackmun stated that "by providing indigent capital defendants with a mandatory right to qualified legal counsel in these proceedings, Congress has recognized that Federal *habeas corpus* has a particularly important role to play in promoting fundamental fairness in the imposition of the death penalty."

This case illustrated a problem in many states. For example, in 1994 there were 386 inmates on death row and only 118 lawyers with the Texas Resource Center, a federally financed legal office that handled capital cases. In 1993 judges in Texas set 100 execution dates. (State policy dictated that an execution must be scheduled about 45 days after the death sentence had been upheld on direct review.) If McFarland had drafted his own *habeas* petition, it would probably have been rejected as inadequate.

HARMLESS ERROR

Coerced Confessions

Oreste C. Fulminante called the Mesa, Arizona, police to report the disappearance of his 11-year-old stepdaughter, Jeneane Michelle Hunt. Fulminante was caring for the child while his wife, Jeneane's mother, was in the hospital. Several days later Jeneane's body was found in the desert east of Mesa with two shots to the head, fired at close range by a large caliber weapon. There was a ligature (a cord used in tying or binding) around her neck. Because of the decomposed state of her body, it was not possible to determine whether she had been sexually assaulted.

Fulminante's statements about the child's disappearance and his relationship to her included inconsistencies that made him a suspect in her death. He was not, however, charged with the murder. Fulminante left Arizona for New Jersey, where he was eventually convicted on federal charges of unlawful possession of a firearm by a felon.

While incarcerated, he became friendly with Anthony Sarivola, a former police officer. Sarivola had been involved in loansharking for organized crime, but then became a paid informant for the Federal Bureau of Investigation. In prison he masqueraded as an organized crime figure. When Fulminante was getting some tough treatment from the other inmates, Sarivola offered him protection, but only on the condition that Fulminante tell him everything.

Fulminante was later indicted in Arizona for the first-degree murder of Jeneane. In a hearing prior to the trial Fulminante moved to suppress (remove from the record) the statement he had made to Sarivola in prison and then later to Sarivola's wife, Donna, following his release from prison. He maintained that the confession to Sarivola was coerced, and that the second confession was the "fruit" of the first one.

The trial court denied the motion to suppress, finding that, based on the specified facts, the confessions were voluntary. Fulminante was convicted of Jeneane's murder and subsequently sentenced to death.

In his appeal Fulminante argued, among other things, that his confession to Sarivola was coerced and that its use at the trial violated his rights of due process under the Fifth and Fourteenth Amendments to the U.S. Constitution. The Arizona Supreme Court ruled that the confession was coerced, but initially determined that the admission of the confession at the trial was a harmless error because of the overpowering evidence against Fulminante.

After Fulminante motioned for reconsideration, however, the Arizona Supreme Court ruled that the U.S. Supreme Court had set a precedent that prevented the use of harmless-error analysis in the case of a coerced confession. (The harmless-error standard, as stated in *Chapman v. California* [386 U.S. 18, 1967], held that an error is harmless if it appears "beyond a reasonable doubt that the error complained of did not contribute to the verdict obtained.") The Arizona Supreme Court reversed the conviction and ordered that Fulminante be retried without the use of his confession to Sarivola. Because of differences in the state and federal courts over the admission of a coerced confession with regard to harmless-error analysis, the U.S. Supreme Court agreed to hear the case.

In *Arizona v. Fulminante* (499 U.S. 279, 1991), Justice White, writing for the majority, stated that although the question was a close one, the Arizona Supreme Court was right in concluding that Fulminante's confession had been coerced. He further noted,

> The Arizona Supreme Court found a credible threat of physical violence unless Fulminante confessed. Our cases have [found] ... that a finding of coercion need not depend upon actual violence by a government agent; a credible threat is sufficient. As we have said, "coercion can be mental as well as physical, and ... the blood of the accused is not the only hallmark of an unconstitutional inquisition."

Justice White further argued that the state of Arizona had failed to meet its burden of establishing, beyond a reasonable doubt, that the admission of Fulminante's confession to Sarivola was harmless. He added,

> A defendant's confession is like no other evidence. Indeed, "the defendant's own confession is probably the most probative [providing evidence] that can be admitted against him.... [T]he admissions of a defendant come from the actor himself, the most knowledgeable and unimpeachable source of information about his past conduct. Certainly confessions have a profound impact on the jury, so much so that we may justifiably doubt its ability to put them out of mind even if told to do so" [From *Bruton v. United States*, 391 U.S. 123, 1968].

Presumption of Malice

Dale Robert Yates and Henry Davis planned to rob a country store in Greenville County, South Carolina. When they entered the store, only the owner, Willie Wood, was present. Yates and Davis showed their weapons and ordered Wood to give them money from the cash register. Davis handed Yates the three thousand dollars and ordered Wood to lie across the counter. Wood, who had a pistol beneath his jacket, refused.

Meanwhile, Yates was backing out of the store with his gun pointed at the owner. After being told to do so by Davis, Yates fired two shots. The first bullet caused flesh wounds in Wood; the second shot missed. Yates then jumped into the car and waited for Davis. When Davis did not appear, he drove off. Inside the store, although wounded, Wood pursued Davis. As the two struggled, Wood's mother came in and ran to help her son. During the struggle, Mrs. Wood was stabbed once in the chest and died at the scene. Wood then shot Davis five times, killing him.

After Yates was arrested and charged with murder, his primary defense was that Mrs. Wood's death was not the probable natural consequence of the robbery he had planned with Davis. He claimed that he had brought the weapon only to induce the owner to give him the cash and that neither he nor Davis intended to kill anyone during the robbery.

The prosecutor's case for murder hinged on the agreement between Yates and Davis to commit an armed robbery. He argued that they planned to kill any witnesses, thereby making homicide a probable or natural result of the robbery. The prosecutor concluded, "It makes no difference who actually struck the fatal blow, the hand of one is the hand of all."

In his instructions to the jury, the judge said,

> Malice is implied or presumed by the law from the willful, deliberate and intentional doing of an unlawful act without any just cause or excuse. In its general signification, malice means the doing of a wrongful act, intentionally, without justification or excuse.... I tell you, also, that malice is implied or presumed from the use of a deadly weapon.

The judge continued to instruct the jury on the theory of accomplice liability. The jury returned guilty verdicts on the murder charge and on all other counts in the indictment. Yates was sentenced to death.

Yates petitioned the South Carolina Supreme Court, asserting that the jury charge that "malice is implied or presumed from the use of a deadly weapon" was an unconstitutional burden-shifting instruction. The case was twice reviewed by the South Carolina Supreme Court, which agreed that the jury instructions were unconstitutional, but that allowing the jury to presume malice was a harmless error. The state found that the jury did not have to rely on presumptions of malice because Davis's "lunging" at Mrs. Wood and stabbing her were acts of malice.

The U.S. Supreme Court, in *Yates v. Evatt* (500 U.S. 391, 1991), reversed the decisions of the South Carolina Supreme Court and remanded the case (sent it back to the lower court for further proceedings). Justice David Souter, writing for the high court, ruled that the state supreme court failed to apply the proper harmless-error standard as stated in *Chapman*. "The issue under *Chapman* is whether the jury actually rested its verdict on evidence establishing the presumed fact beyond a reasonable doubt, independently of the presumption."

Souter concluded by stating that there was clear evidence of Davis's attempt to kill Wood because he could have left the store with Yates, but stayed to pursue Wood with a deadly weapon. The evidence that Davis intended to kill Mrs. Wood was not as clear. The record also showed that Yates heard a woman scream as he left the store, but did not attempt to return and kill her.

The jury could have interpreted Yates's behavior to confirm his claim that he and Davis had not originally intended to kill anyone. Even the prosecutor, in summation, conceded that Mrs. Wood could have been killed inadvertently by Davis.

DUE PROCESS AND ADVANCE NOTICE OF IMPOSING THE DEATH PENALTY

Robert and Cheryl Bravence were beaten to death at their campsite near Santiam Creek, Idaho. Two brothers, Bryan and Mark Lankford, were charged with two counts of first-degree murder. At the arraignment (a summoning before a court to hear and answer charges), the trial judge advised Bryan Lankford that, if convicted of either of the two charges (he was charged with both murders), the maximum punishment he might receive was either life imprisonment or death.

After the arraignment Bryan Lankford's attorney made a deal with the prosecutor. Bryan Lankford entered a plea bargain in which he agreed to take two lie-detector tests in exchange for a lesser sentence. Although the results were somewhat unclear, they convinced the prosecutor that Lankford's older brother, Mark, was primarily responsible for the crimes and was the actual killer of both victims. Bryan Lankford's attorney and the prosecutor agreed on an indeterminate sentence with a 10-year minimum in exchange for a guilty plea, subject to commitment from the trial judge that he would impose that sentence. The judge refused to make such a commitment, and the case went to trial.

The judge refused to instruct the jury that a specific intent to kill was required to support a conviction of first-degree murder. The jury found Bryan Lankford guilty on both counts. The sentencing hearing was postponed until after Mark's trial. (He was also charged with both murders.)

Before the sentencing trial, at Bryan Lankford's request, the trial judge ordered the prosecutor to notify the court and Lankford whether it would seek the death penalty and, if so, to file a statement of the aggravating circumstance on which the death penalty would be based. The prosecutor notified the judge that the state would not recommend the death penalty. Several proceedings followed, including Lankford's request for a new attorney, a motion for a new trial, and a motion for continuance of the sentencing hearing. At none of the proceedings was there any mention that Lankford might receive the death penalty.

At the sentencing hearing the prosecutor recommended a life sentence, with a minimum ranging between 10 and 20 years. The trial judge indicated that he considered Lankford's testimony unbelievable and that the seriousness of the crime warranted more severe punishment than recommended by the state. He sentenced Lankford to death.

Lankford appealed, asserting that the trial judge violated the Constitution by failing to give notice that he intended to impose the death penalty in spite of the state's earlier notice that it would not seek the death penalty. The judge maintained that the Idaho Code provided Lankford with sufficient notice. The judge added that the fact the prosecutor said he would not seek the death penalty had "no bearing on the adequacy of notice to petitioner [Lankford] that the death penalty might be sought." The Idaho Supreme Court agreed with the judge's decision.

In *Lankford v. Idaho* (500 U.S. 110, 1991), the U.S. Supreme Court reversed the state supreme court ruling and remanded the case for a new trial. Writing for the majority, Justice Stevens stated that the due process clause of the Fourteenth Amendment was violated. Stevens noted,

> If the defense counsel had been notified that the trial judge was contemplating a death sentence based on five specific aggravating circumstances, presumably she would have advanced arguments that addressed these circumstances; however, she did not make these arguments because they were entirely inappropriate in a discussion about the length of the petitioner's possible incarceration.

Stevens further indicated that the trial judge's silence, in effect, hid from Lankford and his attorney, as well as from the prosecutor, the principal issues to be decided.

In a dissenting opinion, Justice Scalia wrote that Lankford's due process rights were not violated because he knew that he had been convicted of first-degree murder, and the Idaho Code clearly states that "every person guilty of murder of the first degree shall be punished by death or by imprisonment for life." At the arraignment the trial judge told Lankford that he could receive either punishment. Scalia further noted that, in Idaho, the death penalty statute places full responsibility for determining the sentence on the judge.

EVIDENCE AND APPEALS

Newly Discovered Evidence Does Not Stop Execution

On an evening in late September 1981 the body of Texas Department of Public Safety Officer David Rucker was found lying beside his patrol car. He had been shot in the head. At about the same time, police officer Enrique Carrisalez saw a vehicle speeding away from the area where Rucker's body had been found. Carrisalez and his partner chased the vehicle and pulled it over. Carrisalez walked to the car. The driver opened his door and exchanged a few words with the police officer before firing at least one shot into Carrisalez's chest. The officer died nine days later.

Leonel Torres Herrera was arrested a few days after the shootings and charged with capital murder. In January 1982 he was tried and found guilty of murdering Carrisalez. In July 1982 he pleaded guilty to Rucker's murder.

At the trial Officer Carrisalez's partner identified Herrera as the person who fired the gun. He also testified that there was only one person in the car. In a statement by Carrisalez before he died, he also identified Herrera. The speeding car belonged to Herrera's girlfriend, and Herrera had the car keys in his pocket when he was arrested. Splatters of blood on the car and on Herrera's clothes were the same type as Rucker's. Strands of hair found in the car also belonged to Rucker. Finally, a handwritten letter, which strongly implied that he had killed Rucker, was found on Herrera when he was arrested

In 1992, 10 years after the initial trial, Herrera appealed to the federal courts, alleging that he was innocent of the murders of Rucker and Carrisalez and that his execution would violate the Eighth and Fourteenth Amendments. He presented affidavits (sworn statements) claiming that he had not killed the officers, but that his now dead brother had. The brother's attorney, one of Herrera's cellmates, and a school friend all swore that the brother had killed the police officers. The dead brother's son also said that he had witnessed his father killing the men.

The U.S. Supreme Court, in *Herrera v. Collins* (506 U.S. 390, 1993), in a 7–3 decision, ruled that executing Herrera would not violate the Eighth and Fourteenth Amendments. The high court said that the trial and not the appeals process judges guilt or innocence. Appeals courts determine only the fairness of the proceedings.

Writing for the majority, Chief Justice Rehnquist stated,

A person when first charged with a crime is entitled to a presumption of innocence and may insist that his guilt be established beyond a reasonable doubt.... Once a defendant has been afforded a fair trial and convicted of the offense for which he was charged, the presumption of innocence disappears.... Here, it is not disputed that the State met its burden of proving at trial that petitioner was guilty of the capital murder of Officer Carrisalez beyond a reasonable doubt. Thus, in the eyes of the law, petitioner does not come before the Court as one who is "innocent," but on the contrary as one who has been convicted by due process of two brutal murders.

Based on affidavits here filed, petitioner claims that evidence never presented to the trial court proves him innocent....

Claims of actual innocence based on newly discovered evidence have never been held to state a ground for [court] relief, absent an independent constitutional violation occurring in the underlying state criminal proceeding....

This rule is grounded in the principle that ... [appeals] courts sit to ensure that individuals are not imprisoned in violation of the Constitution—not to correct errors of fact.

Rehnquist continued that states all allow the introduction of new evidence. Texas was one of 17 states that require a new trial motion based on new evidence within 60 days. Herrera's appeal came 10 years later. The chief justice, however, emphasized that Herrera still had options, saying,

For under Texas law, petitioner may file a request for executive clemency. Executive clemency has provided the "fail safe" in our criminal justice system.... It is an unalterable fact that our judicial system, like the human beings who administer it, is fallible. But history is replete with examples of wrongfully convicted persons who have been pardoned in the wake of after-discovered evidence establishing their innocence.

The majority opinion found the information presented in the affidavits inconsistent with the other evidence. The justices questioned why the affidavits were produced at the very last minute. The justices also wondered why Herrera had pleaded guilty to Rucker's murder if he had been innocent. They did note that some of the information in the affidavits might have been important to the jury, "but coming 10 years after the ... trial, this showing of innocence falls far short of that which would have to be made in order to trigger the sort of constitutional claim [to decide for a retrial]."

Speaking for the minority, Justice Blackmun wrote,

We really are being asked to decide whether the Constitution forbids the execution of a person who has been validly convicted and sentenced but who, nonetheless, can prove his innocence with newly discovered evidence. Despite the State of Texas' astonishing protestation to the contrary ... I do not see how the answer can be anything but "yes."

The Eighth Amendment prohibits "cruel and unusual punishments." This proscription [prohibition] is not static [fixed] but rather reflects evolving standards of decency. I think it is crystal clear that the execution of an innocent person is "at odds with contemporary standards of fairness and decency." ... The protection of the Eighth Amendment does not end once a defendant has been validly convicted and sentenced.

Claim of Miscarriage of Justice

Lloyd Schlup, a Missouri prisoner, was convicted of participating in the murder of a fellow inmate and sentenced to death. He had filed one petition for *habeas corpus*, arguing that he had inadequate counsel. He filed a second petition, alleging that constitutional error at his trial deprived the jury of crucial evidence that would have established his innocence.

Using a previous U.S. Supreme Court ruling (*Sawyer v. Whitley*, 505 U.S. 333, 1992), the district court claimed that Schlup had not shown "by clear and convincing evidence that, but for a constitutional error, no reasonable juror would have found him guilty." Schlup's lawyers argued that the district court should have used another ruling (*Murray v. Carrier*, 477 U.S. 478, 1986), in which a petitioner need only to show that "a constitutional violation has probably resulted in the conviction of one who is actually innocent." The appellate court affirmed the district court's ruling, noting that Schlup's guilt, which had been proven at the trial, barred any consideration of his constitutional claim.

The U.S. Supreme Court, upon appeal, reviewed the case to determine whether the *Sawyer* standard provides enough protection from a miscarriage of justice that would result from the execution of an innocent person. In *Schlup v. Delo* (513 U.S. 298, 1995), the Court observed,

> If a petitioner such as Schlup presents evidence of innocence so strong that a court cannot have confidence in the outcome of the trial unless the court is also satisfied that the trial was free of non-harmless constitutional error, the petitioner should be allowed to ... argue the merits of his underlying claims.

The justices concluded that the *Carrier*, rather than *Sawyer*, standard focuses the investigation on the actual innocence, allowing the Court to review relevant evidence that might have been excluded or unavailable during the trial.

Suppressed Evidence Means a New Trial

Curtis Lee Kyles was convicted by a Louisiana jury of the first-degree murder of a woman in a grocery store parking lot in 1984. He was sentenced to death. It was revealed on review that the prosecutor had never disclosed certain evidence favorable to the defendant. The state supreme court, the federal district court, and the Fifth Circuit Court denied Kyles's appeals. The U.S. Supreme Court, in *Kyles v. Whitley* (514 U.S, 419, 1995), reversed the lower courts' decisions. The high court ruled,

> Favorable evidence is material, and constitutional error results from its suppression by the government, if there

is a "reasonable probability" that, had the evidence been disclosed to the defense, the result of the proceeding would have been different.... [The] net effect of the state-suppressed evidence favoring Kyles raises a reasonable probability that disclosure would have produced a different result at trial.

The conviction was overturned. Four mistrials followed. On February 18, 1998, after his fifth and final trial ended with a hung jury, Curtis Lee Kyles was released from death row.

VICTIM IMPACT STATEMENTS

First, They Are Not Constitutional

John Booth and Willie Reid stole money from elderly neighbors to buy heroin. Booth, knowing his neighbors could identify him, tied up the elderly couple and then repeatedly stabbed them in the chest with a kitchen knife. The couple's son found their bodies two days later. Booth and Reid were found guilty.

The state of Maryland permitted a victim impact statement (VIS) to be read to the jury during the sentencing phase of the trial. The VIS prepared in this case explained the tremendous pain caused by the murder of the parents and grandparents to the family. It revealed that not only had the murdered victims suffered, but their family also suffered severely in many ways, including sleepless nights, lack of trust, depression, and disorientation. A 5–4 Supreme Court, in *Booth v. Maryland* (482 U.S. 496, 1987), while recognizing the agony caused to the victim's family, ruled that victim impact statements, as required by Maryland's statute, were unconstitutional and could not be used during the sentencing phase of a capital murder trial.

Writing for the majority, Justice Lewis Powell indicated that a jury must determine whether the defendant should be executed, based on the circumstances of the crime and the character of the offender. These factors had nothing to do with the victim. The high court noted that it is the crime and the criminal that were at issue. Had Booth and Reid viciously murdered a drunken bum, the crime would have been just as horrible.

Furthermore, some families could express the pain and disruption they suffered as a result of the murder better than other families. Should a sentencing be dependent upon how well a family could express its grief? In addition, if the character of the victim should play a role in determining the sentence, then the prisoner should have the right to attack that character to show it was not as flawless as presented. This could likely lead to attacks on the character of the victim and more pain for the victim's family.

... And Then They Are

Pervis Tyronne Payne spent the morning and early afternoon injecting cocaine and drinking beer. Later, he drove around the town with a friend, each of them taking turns reading a pornographic magazine. In mid-afternoon, Payne went to his girlfriend's apartment across the hall from the apartment of Charisse Christopher. He entered Christopher's apartment and made sexual advances toward Christopher, who resisted. Payne became violent.

The first police officer to arrive at the scene saw Payne leaving the building so covered with blood that he appeared to be "sweating blood." Inside the apartment the police saw Christopher and her children lying on the kitchen floor. Blood covered the walls and floor throughout the apartment.

Christopher had 42 direct knife wounds and 42 defensive wounds on her arms and hands. Her two-year-old daughter had suffered stab wounds to the chest, abdomen, back, and head. The murder weapon, a butcher knife, was found at her feet. Christopher's three-year-old son, despite several stab wounds that went completely through his body, was still alive. Payne was arrested, and a Tennessee jury convicted Payne of the first-degree murders of Christopher and her daughter and of the first-degree assault, with intent to murder, of Christopher's son, Nicholas.

During the sentencing phase of the trial, Payne called his parents, his girlfriend, and a clinical psychologist to testify about the mitigating aspects of his background and character. The prosecutor, on the other hand, called Nicholas's grandmother, who testified how much the child missed his mother and baby sister. In arguing for the death penalty, the prosecutor commented on the continuing effects the crime had had on Nicholas and his family. The jury sentenced Payne to death on each of the murder counts. The state supreme court agreed, rejecting Payne's claim that the admission of the grandmother's testimony and the state's closing argument violated his Eighth Amendment rights under *Booth v. Maryland*.

On hearing the appeal (*Payne v. Tennessee*, 501 U.S. 808, 1991), a 6–3 U.S. Supreme Court upheld the death penalty and overturned both *Booth v. Maryland* and *South Carolina v. Gathers* (490 U.S. 805, 1989; in *Gathers*, the Court reversed the defendant's death sentence because of the prosecutor's statement about the victim being a religious man and a registered voter). In *Payne*, the Court ruled that the Eighth Amendment does not prohibit a jury from considering, at the sentencing phase of a capital trial, victim impact evidence relating to a victim's person-

al characteristics and the emotional impact of the murder on the victim's family. The Eighth Amendment also does not bar a prosecutor from arguing such evidence at the sentencing phase.

The Court reasoned that the assessment of harm caused by a defendant as a result of a crime has long been an important concern of criminal law in determining both the elements of the offense and the appropriate punishment. Victim impact evidence is simply another form or method of informing the sentencing jury or judge about the specific harm caused by the crime in question.

The *Booth* case unfairly weighted the scales in a capital trial. No limits were placed on the mitigating evidence the defendant introduced relating to his own circumstances. The state, however, was barred from offering a glimpse of the life of the victim, which the defendant chose to extinguish, or from showing the loss to the victim's family or to society. *Booth and Gathers* were decided by narrow margins, the Court continued, and had been questioned by members of the Supreme Court as well as by the lower courts.

Chief Justice Rehnquist, delivering the opinion of the Court, stated,

> The State has a legitimate interest in counteracting the mitigating evidence which the defendant is entitled to put in, by reminding the sentencer that just as the murderer should be considered as an individual, so too the victim is an individual whose death represents a unique loss to society and in particular to his family.

Justice Stevens, dissenting, stated,

> [A victim impact statement] sheds no light on the defendant's guilt or moral culpability [blameworthiness] and thus serves no purpose other than to encourage jurors to decide in favor of death rather than life on the basis of their emotions rather than their reason.

> Victim impact evidence, as used in this case, has two flaws. First, aspects of the character of the victim, unforeseeable to the defendant at the time of his crime, are irrelevant to the defendant's "personal responsibility and moral guilt" and therefore cannot justify a death sentence....

> Second, the quantity and quality of victim impact evidence sufficient to turn a verdict of life in prison into a verdict of death is not defined until after the crime has been committed and therefore cannot possibly be applied consistently in different cases.

CHAPTER 4

LEGAL DECISIONS—YOUTH, INSANITY, RACE, METHODS OF EXECUTION, AND *HABEAS CORPUS* REVIEW UNDER THE ANTITERRORISM ACT

CAN A MINOR BE SENTENCED TO DEATH?

On April 4, 1977, 16-year-old Monty Lee Eddings and several friends were pulled over by a police officer as they traveled in a car. Eddings had several guns in the car, which he had taken from his father. When the police officer approached the car, Eddings shot and killed him. Eddings was tried as an adult even though he was 16 at the time of the murder. He was convicted of first-degree murder for killing a police officer and was sentenced to death.

At the sentencing hearing following the conviction, Eddings's lawyer presented substantial evidence of a turbulent family history, beatings by a harsh father, and serious emotional disturbance. The judge refused, as a matter of law, to consider the mitigating circumstances of Eddings's unhappy upbringing and emotional problems. He ruled that the only mitigating circumstance was the petitioner's youth, which was insufficient to outweigh the aggravating circumstances. (Mitigating circumstances may lessen responsibility for a crime, while aggravating circumstances may add to responsibility for a crime.)

In *Eddings v. Oklahoma* (455 U.S. 104, 1982), the Supreme Court, in a 5-4 opinion, ordered the case remanded (sent back to the lower courts for further proceedings). The justices based their ruling on *Lockett v. Ohio* (438 U.S. 586, 1978), which required the trial court to consider and weigh all of the mitigating evidence concerning the petitioner's family background and personal history.

By implication, since the majority did not reverse the case on the issue of age, it let stand Oklahoma's decision to try Eddings as an adult. Meanwhile, Chief Justice Warren Burger, who filed the dissenting opinion in which Justices Byron White, Harry A. Blackmun, and William H. Rehnquist joined, observed,

> The Constitution does not authorize us to determine whether sentences imposed by state courts are sentences we consider "appropriate"; our only authority is to decide whether they are constitutional under the Eighth Amendment. The Court stops far short of suggesting that there is any constitutional proscription [prohibition] against imposition of the death penalty on a person who was under age 18 when the murder was committed.

Hence, while the high court did not directly rule on the question of minors being sentenced to death, the sense of the Court would appear to be that it would uphold such a sentencing.

Not at Fifteen Years Old

With three adults, William Thompson brutally murdered a former brother-in-law. Thompson was 15 at the time of the murder, but the state determined that Thompson, who had a long history of violent assault, had "virtually no reasonable prospects for rehabilitation ... within the juvenile system and ... should be held accountable for his acts as if he were an adult and should be certified to stand trial as an adult." Thompson was tried as an adult and found guilty. As in *Eddings*, his age was considered a mitigating circumstance, but the jury still sentenced him to death.

Thompson appealed, and while the Court of Criminal Appeals of Oklahoma upheld the decision, the U.S. Supreme Court, in *Thompson v. Oklahoma* (487 U.S. 815, 1988), did not. In a 5-3 majority vote, with Justice Sandra Day O'Connor agreeing to vacate (annul) the sentence, but not agreeing with the majority reasoning, the case was reversed. (Justice Anthony Kennedy took no part in the decision.)

Writing for the majority (Justices John Stevens, William J. Brennan, Thurgood Marshall, and Blackmun), Justice Stevens observed,

> Inexperience, less education, and less intelligence make the teenager less able to evaluate the consequences of his or her conduct, while at the same time he or she is much more apt to be motivated by mere emotion or peer pres-

sure than is an adult. The reasons why juveniles are not trusted with the privileges and responsibilities of an adult also explain why their irresponsible conduct is not as morally reprehensible (blameworthy) as that of an adult.

Justice Stevens noted that 18 states required the age of at least 16 years before the death penalty could be considered. Counting the 14 states prohibiting capital punishment, a total of 32 states did not execute people under 16.

Justice O'Connor agreed with the judgment of the Court that the appellate court's ruling should be reversed. O'Connor pointed out, however, that, although most 15-year-old criminals are generally less blameworthy than adults who commit the same crimes, some may fully understand the horrible deeds they have done. Individuals, after all, have different characteristics, including their capability to distinguish right from wrong.

Writing for the minority (Justices Antonin Scalia, Rehnquist, and White), Justice Scalia found no national consensus forbidding the execution of a person who was 16 at the commission of the murder. The justice could not understand the majority's calculations establishing a "contemporary standard" that forbade the execution of young minors. Abolitionist states (those states that did not have the death penalty) should not be considered in the issue of executing minors since they did not have executions in the first place. Rather, the 18 states that prohibited the execution of offenders who were younger than 16 when they murdered should be compared to the 19 states that applied the death penalty to young offenders.

But It May Be Done at 16

A majority of the Court, with Justice O'Connor straddling the fence, found the death penalty unacceptable for an offender who was less than 16 when he or she committed murder. A majority of the Court, however, found the death sentence acceptable for a minor who was 16 or 17 during the commission of murder. The Supreme Court, in two jointly considered cases, *Stanford v. Kentucky* and *Wilkins v. Missouri* (492 U.S. 361, 1989), ruled that juveniles ages 16 and 17 could be executed for murder.

When he was 17 years old, Kevin Stanford and an accomplice raped the attendant at a gas station they were robbing. They then took the woman to a secluded area near the station, where Stanford shot her in the face and in the back of her head. Stressing the seriousness of the offense and Stanford's long history of criminal behavior, the Court certified him as an adult. He was tried, found guilty, and sentenced to death.

When he was 16 years old, Heath Wilkins stabbed Nancy Allen to death while he was robbing the convenience store where she worked. Wilkins indicated he murdered Allen because "a dead person can't talk." Based on his long history of juvenile delinquency, the Court

ordered Wilkins tried as an adult. He was found guilty and sentenced to die.

Writing for the majority (Justices Scalia, Rehnquist, White, and Kennedy), Justice Scalia could find no national consensus that executing minors ages 16 and 17 constituted cruel and unusual punishment. Scalia observed that of the 37 states whose statutes allowed the death penalty, just 12 refused to impose it on 17-year-old offenders and in addition to those 12, only 3 additional states refused to impose it on 16-year-old offenders.

Further, Justice Scalia saw no connection between the defendant's argument that those under 18 were denied the right to drive, drink, or vote because they were not considered mature enough to do so responsibly and whether this standard of maturity should be applied to a minor's understanding that murder is terribly wrong. Scalia added,

> Even if the requisite degrees of maturity were comparable, the age statutes in question would still not be relevant. These laws set the appropriate ages for the operation of a system that makes its determinations in gross, and that does not conduct individualized maturity tests for each driver, drinker, or voter. The criminal justice system, however, does provide individualized testing. In the realm of capital punishment in particular, "individualized consideration [is] a constitutional requirement," and one of the individualized mitigating factors that sentencers must be permitted to consider is the defendant's age.

Justice O'Connor also concluded that no national consensus prohibited the imposition of the death penalty on Stanford and Wilkins. O'Connor, however, believed that the high court had the constitutional obligation to determine whether the punishment imposed was proportional to the defendants' blameworthiness.

Writing for the minority (Justices Brennan, Marshall, Blackmun, and Stevens), Justice Brennan found a national consensus among 30 states when he added the 12 states forbidding the execution of a person who was 16 years during the commission of the crime to those with no capital punishment, and the states that, in practice if not in law, did not execute minors. Justice Brennan, taking serious exception to the majority's observation that they had to find a national consensus in the laws passed by the state legislatures, stated,

> Our judgment about the constitutionality of a punishment under the Eighth Amendment is informed, though not determined ... by an examination of contemporary attitudes toward the punishment, as evidenced in the actions of legislatures and of juries. The views of organizations with expertise in relevant fields and the choices of governments elsewhere in the world also merit our attention as indicators whether a punishment is acceptable in a civilized society.

Youth—A Mitigating Circumstance

Dorsie Lee Johnson Jr., age 19, and an accomplice staked out a convenience store, with the intention of robbing it. They found out that only one employee worked during the predawn hours. Agreeing to leave no witnesses to their crime, Johnson shot and killed the clerk, Jack Huddleston. They then emptied the cash register and stole some cigarettes.

The following month Johnson was arrested and subsequently confessed to the murder and the robbery. During the jury selection the defense attorneys asked potential jurors whether they believed that people were capable of change and whether they, the potential jurors, had ever done things in their youth that they would not now do.

The only witness the defense called was Johnson's father, who told of his son's drug use, grief over the death of his mother two years before the crime, and the murder of his sister the following year. He spoke of his son's youth and the fact that, at age 19, he did not evaluate things the way a person of 30 or 35 would.

Johnson was tried and convicted of capital murder. Under Texas law, the homicide qualified as a capital offense because Johnson intentionally or knowingly caused Huddleston's death. Moreover, the murder was carried out in the course of committing a robbery.

In the sentencing phase of the trial, the judge instructed the jury to answer two questions: (1) whether Johnson's actions were deliberate and intended to kill, and (2) whether there was a possibility that he would continue to commit violent crimes and be a threat to society. If the jury answered "yes" to both questions, Johnson would be sentenced to death. If the jury returned a "no" answer to either question, the defendant would be sentenced to life in prison. The jury was not to consider or discuss the possibility of parole.

Of equal importance was the instruction that the jury could consider all the evidence, both aggravating and mitigating, in either phase of the trial. The jury unanimously answered yes to both questions, and Johnson was sentenced to death.

Five days after the state appellate court denied Johnson's motions for a rehearing, the U.S. Supreme Court issued its opinion in another case, *Penry v. Lynaugh* (492 U.S. 302, 1989; see below). Based on the *Penry* ruling, Dorsie Lee Johnson Jr. claimed that a separate instruction should have been given to the jury that would have allowed them to consider his youth. Again, the appellate court rejected Johnson's petition.

Affirming the Texas appellate court decision, Justice Kennedy delivered the opinion of the Supreme Court in *Johnson v. Texas* (509 U.S. 350, 1993). He was joined by Justices Rehnquist, White, Scalia, and Clarence Thomas.

Kennedy noted that the Texas special-issues system (two questions asked of the jury and instruction to consider all evidence) allowed for adequate consideration of Johnson's youth. Justice Kennedy stated,

> Even on a cold record, one cannot be unmoved by the testimony of petitioner's father urging that his son's actions were due in large part to his youth. It strains credulity to suppose that the jury would have viewed the evidence of petitioner's youth as outside its effective reach in answering the second special issue. The relevance of youth as a mitigating factor derives from the fact that the signature qualities of youth are transient; as individuals mature, the impetuousness and recklessness that may dominate in younger years can subside.... As long as the mitigating evidence is within "the effective reach of the sentencer," the requirements of the Eighth Amendment are satisfied.

Justice O'Connor, in a dissenting opinion joined by Justices Blackmun, Stevens, and David Souter, stated that the jurors were not allowed to give "full effect to his strongest mitigating circumstance: his youth." Hearing of his less than exemplary youth, a jury might easily conclude, as Johnson's did, that he would continue to be a threat to society.

ROLE OF PSYCHIATRISTS

Validity of a Psychiatrist's Testimony

In 1978 Thomas Barefoot was convicted of murdering a police officer. During the sentencing phase of the trial, the prosecution put two psychiatrists on the stand. Neither psychiatrist had actually interviewed Barefoot nor did either ask to do so. Both psychiatrists agreed that an individual with Barefoot's background and who had acted as Barefoot had in murdering the policeman represented a future threat to society. Partially based on their testimony, the jury sentenced Barefoot to death.

Barefoot's conviction and sentence were appealed numerous times, and in 1983 his case was argued before the U.S. Supreme Court. Among the issues debated was the validity of the testimony of psychiatrists. Barefoot's lawyers questioned whether it was necessary for the psychiatrists to have interviewed Barefoot or if it was enough for them to answer hypothetical questions that pertained to a hypothetical individual who acted like Barefoot.

Barefoot's attorneys claimed that psychiatrists could not reliably predict that a particular offender would commit other crimes in the future and be a threat to society. They further argued that psychiatrists should also not be allowed to testify about an offender's future dangerousness in response to hypothetical situations presented by the prosecutor and without having first examined the offender.

In *Barefoot v. Estelle* (463 U.S. 880, 1983), the Supreme Court ruled 6-3 that local juries were in the best position to decide guilt and impose a sentence. The Court referred to *Jurek v. Texas* (428 U.S. 262, 1976), an earlier case that, among other things, upheld the testimony of laypersons concerning a defendant's possible future actions. The Court, therefore, looked upon psychiatrists as just another group of people presenting testimony to the jury for consideration. Like all evidence presented to the jury, the Court claimed,

> [A psychiatric observation] should be admitted and its weight left to the fact finder, who would have the benefit of cross examination and contrary evidence by the opposing party. Psychiatric testimony predicting dangerousness may be countered not only as erroneous in a particular case but as generally so unreliable that it should be ignored. If the jury may make up its mind about future dangerousness unaided by psychiatric testimony, jurors should not be barred from hearing the views of the State's psychiatrists along with opposing views of the defendant's doctors.

The high court dismissed the *amicus curiae* brief (a friend-of-the-court brief prepared to enlighten the court) presented by the American Psychiatric Association (APA), indicating that psychiatric testimony was "almost entirely unreliable" in determining future actions. The Court countered that such testimony had been traditionally accepted. The Court also observed that arguments, such as the APA brief, were founded "on the premise that a jury will not be able to separate the wheat from the chaff," a sentiment the Court did not agree with.

The high court also dismissed Barefoot's contention that the psychiatrists should have personally interviewed him. Such methods of observation and conclusion were quite normal in courtroom procedures and the psychiatric observations had been based on established facts. Barefoot's appeal was denied.

Justice Blackmun strongly dissented from the majority decision. He declared,

> In the present state of psychiatric knowledge, this is too much for me. One may accept this in a routine lawsuit for money damages, but when a person's life is at stake—no matter how heinous his offense—a requirement of greater reliability should prevail. In a capital case, the specious [seemingly fair but not so] testimony of a psychiatrist, colored in the eyes of an impressionable jury by the inevitable untouchability of a medical specialist's words, equates with death itself.

A Prisoner Maintains Rights During Psychiatric Examination

During the commission of a robbery Ernest Smith's accomplice fatally shot a grocery clerk (Smith had tried to shoot the clerk, but his weapon had jammed). The state of Texas sought the death penalty against Smith based on the Texas law governing premeditated murder.

Thereafter, the judge ordered a psychiatric examination of Smith by Dr. James Grigson to determine if Smith was competent to stand trial. Without permission from Smith's lawyer, Dr. Grigson interviewed Smith in jail for about 90 minutes and found him competent. Dr. Grigson then discussed his conclusions and diagnosis with the state attorney. Smith was found guilty. During the sentencing phase of the trial, over the protests of the defendant's lawyers, Dr. Grigson testified that Smith was a "very severe sociopath," who would continue his previous behavior, which would get worse. The jury sentenced Smith to death.

Smith appealed his sentence, claiming he was not informed of his rights. Both the federal district court and the appeals court agreed. So did a unanimous 9-0 Supreme Court. In *Estelle v. Smith* (451 U.S. 454, 1981), the Court ruled that the trial court had the right to determine if Smith was capable of standing trial. It had no right, however, to use the information gathered without first advising him of his Fifth Amendment right against self-incrimination. According to the Court, the psychiatrist was "an agent of the state" about whom the defendant had not been warned, but who was reporting about the defendant. Noting *Miranda v. Arizona* (384 U.S. 436, 1966), the Court continued,

> The Fifth Amendment privilege is available outside of criminal court proceedings and serves to protect persons in all settings in which their freedom of action is curtailed in any significant way from being compelled to incriminate themselves.... The prosecution may not use statements, whether exculpatory [proving innocence] or inculpatory [incriminating], stemming from custodial [while under arrest] interrogation of the defendant unless it demonstrates the use of procedural safeguards effective to secure the privilege against self-incrimination.

Needing a Psychiatrist to Prove Insanity

In 1979 Glen Burton Ake and Steven Hatch shot and killed the Reverend and Mrs. Richard Douglass and wounded their children, Brooks and Leslie. Before the trial, due to Ake's bizarre behavior, the trial judge ordered him examined by a psychiatrist to determine if he should be put under observation. The psychiatrist diagnosed Ake as a probable paranoid schizophrenic and recommended a long-term psychiatric examination to determine his competency to stand trial.

Ake's psychiatric evaluation confirmed his paranoid schizophrenia. Consequently, the court pronounced him incompetent to stand trial and ordered him committed to the state mental hospital.

Six weeks later the hospital psychiatrist informed the court that Ake had become competent to stand trial. Under daily treatment with an antipsychotic drug, he could stand trial. The state of Oklahoma resumed proceedings against the accused murderer.

Prior to the trial Ake's lawyer told the Court of his client's insanity defense. He also informed the court that in order for him to adequately defend Ake, he needed to have Ake examined by a psychiatrist to determine his mental condition at the time he committed murder. During his stay at the mental hospital, Ake was evaluated as to his "present sanity" to stand trial but not his mental state during the murder. Since Ake could not afford a psychiatrist, his counsel asked the court to provide a psychiatrist or the money to hire one. The trial judge refused his request, claiming the state is not obligated to provide a psychiatrist, even to poor defendants in capital cases.

Ake was tried for two counts of first-degree murder and for two counts of shooting with intent to kill. During the trial Ake's only defense was insanity; none of the psychiatrists at the state mental hospital, however, could testify to his mental state at the time of the crime.

The judge instructed the jurors that Ake could be found not guilty by reason of insanity if he could not distinguish right from wrong when he committed murder. The jurors were told they could presume Ake sane at the time of the crime unless he presented sufficient evidence to raise a reasonable doubt about his sanity during the crime. The jury found him guilty on all counts. The jury sentenced Ake to death based on the earlier testimony of the psychiatrist who concluded he was a threat to society. Upon appeal, the Oklahoma Court of Appeals agreed with the trial court that the state did not have the responsibility to provide an indigent (poor) defendant with a psychiatrist to help with his defense.

The U.S. Supreme Court disagreed. In an 8-1 ruling, the Court, in *Ake v. Oklahoma* (470 U.S. 68, 1985), reversed the lower court's ruling, finding that "there was no expert testimony for either side on Ake's sanity at the time of the offense." The high court further observed:

> This Court has long recognized that when a State brings its judicial power to bear on an indigent defendant in a criminal proceeding, it must take steps to assure that the defendant has a fair opportunity to present his defense. This elementary principle, grounded in significant part on the Fourteenth Amendment's due process guarantee of fundamental fairness, derives from the belief that justice cannot be equal where, simply as a result of his poverty, a defendant is denied the opportunity to participate meaningfully in a judicial proceeding in which his liberty is at stake.

CAN AN INSANE PERSON BE EXECUTED?

In 1974 Alvin Ford was convicted of murder and sentenced to death. There was no question that he was completely sane at the time of his crime, at the trial, and at the sentencing. Eight years later, Ford began to show signs of delusion—from thinking that people were conspiring to force him to commit suicide to believing that family members were being held hostage in prison.

Ford's lawyers had a psychiatrist examine their client. After 14 months of evaluation and investigation the doctor concluded that Ford suffered from a severe mental disorder that would preclude him from assisting in the defense of his life. A second psychiatrist concluded that Ford did not understand why he was on death row.

Florida law required the governor to appoint a panel of three psychiatrists to determine whether Ford was mentally capable of understanding the death penalty and the reasons he was being sentenced to death. The three state-appointed doctors met with Ford once for about 30 minutes and then filed separate reports. Ford's lawyers were present but were ordered by the judge not to participate in the examination "in any adversarial manner."

The three psychiatrists submitted different diagnoses, but all agreed that Ford was sane enough to be executed. Ford's lawyers attempted to submit the reports of the first two psychiatrists along with other materials. The governor, refusing to inform the lawyers whether he would consider these reports, proceeded to sign Ford's death warrant.

Ford's appeals were denied in state and federal courts, but a 7-2 Supreme Court, in *Ford v. Wainwright* (477 U.S. 399, 1986), reversed the earlier judgments. Writing for the majority, Justice Marshall observed that, while the reasons appear unclear, English common law forbade the execution of the insane. The English jurist Sir William Blackstone (1723–80) had labeled such a practice "savage and inhuman." Likewise, the other noted English judicial resource, Sir Edward Coke (1552–1634), observed that, while the execution of a criminal was to serve as an example, the execution of a madman was considered "of extreme inhumanity and cruelty, and can be no example to others." Consequently, since the Eighth Amendment forbidding cruel and unusual punishment was prepared by men who accepted English common law, there could be no question that the Eighth Amendment prohibited the execution of the insane.

The issue then became the method the state used to determine Ford's insanity. The high court noted that Florida did not allow the submission of materials that might be relevant to the decision whether or not to execute the condemned man. In addition, Ford's lawyers were not given the chance to question the state-appointed psychiatrists about the basis for finding their client competent. Questions the defense could have asked included the possibility of personal bias on the doctors' part toward the death penalty, any history of error in their judgment, and their degree of certainty in reaching their conclusions. Finally, the justices pointed out that the greatest defect in Florida's practice is its entrusting the ultimate decision of the execution entirely within the executive branch. The high court observed,

> Under this procedure, the person who appoints the experts and ultimately decides whether the State will be

able to carry out the sentence that it has long sought is the Governor, whose subordinates have been responsible for initiating every stage of the prosecution of the condemned from arrest through sentencing. The commander of the State's corps of prosecutors cannot be said to have the neutrality that is necessary for reliability in the fact-finding proceeding.

The high court further observed that, even though a prisoner has been sentenced to death, he is still protected by the Constitution. Therefore, ascertaining his sanity as a basis for a legal execution is as important as other proceedings in a capital case.

In dissent, Justice Rehnquist, joined by Chief Justice Burger, thought the Florida procedure consistent with English common law, which had left the decision to the executive branch. Rehnquist warned,

> A claim of insanity may be made at any time before sentence and, once rejected, may be raised again; a prisoner found sane two days before execution might claim to have lost his sanity the next day, thus necessitating another judicial determination of his sanity and presumably another stay of his execution.

CAN A MENTALLY RETARDED PERSON BE EXECUTED?

Penry I

In 1979 Pamela Carpenter was brutally raped, beaten, and stabbed with a pair of scissors. Before she died, she was able to describe her attacker, and as a result, Johnny Penry was arrested for, and later confessed to, the crime. He was found guilty and sentenced to die.

Among the issues considered in his appeal was whether the state of Texas could execute a mentally retarded person. At Penry's competency hearing a psychiatrist testified that the defendant had an intelligence quotient (IQ) of 54. (Penry had been tested in the past as having an IQ between 50 and 63, indicating mild to moderate retardation.) According to the psychiatrist, during the commission of the crime, 22-year-old Penry had the mental age of a child six and one-half years old and the social maturity of a 9 to 10 year old. Penry's attorneys argued,

> Because of their mental disabilities, mentally retarded people do not possess the level of moral culpability [blameworthiness] to justify imposing the death sentence.... [T]here is an emerging national consensus [majority view] against executing the retarded.

Writing for the five-person majority (Justices O'Connor, Rehnquist, White, Scalia, and Kennedy) regarding the execution of mentally retarded persons, Justice O'Connor, in *Penry v. Lynaugh* (492 U.S. 302, 1989), found no emerging national consensus against such execution. Furthermore, while, historically, idiots and profoundly retarded persons had not been executed for murder, Penry did not fall into this group.

Justice O'Connor noted that Penry was found competent to stand trial. He was able to rationally consult with his lawyer and understood the proceedings against him. Justice O'Connor thought that the defense was guilty of lumping all mentally retarded persons together, ascribing, among other things, a lack of moral capacity to be culpable for actions that call for the death punishment. Justice O'Connor wrote,

> Mentally retarded persons are individuals whose abilities and experiences can vary greatly. If the mentally retarded were not treated as individuals, but as an undifferentiated group, a mildly mentally retarded person could be denied the opportunity to enter into contracts or to marry by virtue of the fact that he had a "mental age" of a young child. In light of the diverse capacities and life experiences of mentally retarded persons, it cannot be said on the record before us today that all mentally retarded people, by definition, can never act with the level of culpability associated with the death penalty.

Further, the majority could find no national movement toward any type of consensus on this issue. While *Penry* produced several public opinion polls that indicated strong public opposition to executing the retarded, almost none of these public opinions was reflected in death penalty legislation. Only the federal Anti-Drug Abuse Act of 1988 (Public Law 100-690) and the states of Georgia and Maryland at the time banned the execution of retarded persons found guilty of a capital crime.

Justice Brennan disagreed. While he agreed that lumping mentally retarded people together might result in stereotyping and discrimination, there are characteristics that fall under the clinical definition of mental retardation. Citing the *amicus curiae* brief prepared by the American Association on Mental Retardation, Justice Brennan noted,

> Every individual who has mental retardation—irrespective of her precise capacities or experiences—has a substantial disability in cognitive ability and adaptive behavior.... Though individuals, particularly those who are mildly retarded, may be quite capable of overcoming these limitations to the extent of being able to "maintain themselves independently or semi-independently in the community," nevertheless, the mentally retarded, by definition, "have a reduced ability to cope with and function in the everyday world."

Justice Brennan did not believe that executing a person not fully responsible for his or her actions would serve the "penal goals of retribution or deterrence." What is the point of executing someone who did not fully recognize the terrible evil that he or she had done? Furthermore, executing a mentally retarded person would not deter nonretarded people, those who would be aware of the possibility of an execution.

Although the Supreme Court held that executing persons with mental retardation was not a violation of the

Eighth Amendment, it ruled that Penry's Eighth Amendment right was violated because the jury was not instructed that it could consider mental retardation as a mitigating factor during sentencing. In 1990 Texas retried Penry, and he was again found guilty of capital murder. During the sentencing phase the prosecution used a specific portion of a psychiatric report to point out the doctor's opinion that, if released from custody, Penry would be a threat to society. Penry appealed his case all the way to the Supreme Court. Ten years later, in November 2000, with Penry less than three hours from being put to death, the Supreme Court granted a stay of execution in order to hear Penry's claims.

Penry II

In his appeal to the Supreme Court, Penry argued that the use of a portion of a psychiatric report (unrelated to the Pamela Carpenter case) violated his Fifth Amendment right against self-incrimination. In 1977, during another rape case trial, the state of Texas provided Penry with a psychiatrist at the request of his lawyer. The psychiatrist was to determine the defendant's competency to stand trial. In 2000 Penry argued that the psychiatrist was an "agent of the state," and the prosecution's use of his report violated Penry's right against self-incrimination. Penry also claimed jury instructions were inadequate.

On June 4, 2001, the Supreme Court, in *Penry v. Johnson* (No. 00-6677), voted 6-3 that the admission of the psychiatrist's report did not violate Penry's Fifth Amendment right. The Court held that this case was different from *Estelle v. Smith* (see above), in which the justices found that the psychiatrist's testimony about the defendant's future dangerousness based on the defendant's statements without his lawyer present violated his Fifth Amendment right. The justices emphasized that *Estelle* was restricted to that particular case.

The justices, however, remanded (sent back) the case to the trial court for resentencing because, as in *Penry I*, the state did not give the sentencing jury adequate instructions about how to weigh mental retardation as a mitigating factor.

COMPETENCY STANDARD

On August 2, 1984, Richard Allen Moran fatally shot a bartender and a patron four times each, and several days later, his former wife. Failing a suicide attempt, Moran confessed to his crime. Later on the defendant pleaded not guilty to three counts of first-degree murder. Two psychiatrists examined Moran and concluded that he was competent to stand trial. Approximately 10 weeks after the evaluations, the defendant decided to dismiss his attorneys and change his plea to guilty. After review of the psychiatric reports the trial court accepted the waiver for counsel and the guilty plea. The defendant was later sentenced to death.

Seven months later Moran appealed his case, claiming that he had been "mentally incompetent to represent himself." The appellate court reversed the conviction, ruling that "competency to waive constitutional rights requires a higher level of mental functioning than that required to stand trial." A defendant is considered competent to stand trial if he can understand the proceedings and help in his defense. On the other hand, for a defendant to be considered competent to waive counsel or to plead guilty, he has to be capable of "'reasoned choice' among the alternatives available to him." The appellate court found Moran mentally incapable of the reasoned choice needed to be in a position to waive his constitutional rights.

In a 7-2 decision, the Supreme Court, in *Godinez v. Moran* (509 U.S. 389, 1993), reversed the judgment of the court of appeals, holding that the standard for measuring a criminal defendant's competency to plead guilty or to waive his right to counsel is not higher than the standard for standing trial. The high court then sent the case back to the lower courts for further proceedings.

RACE AS A CONSIDERATION

In 1978 Willie Lloyd Turner, a black man, robbed a jewelry store in Franklin, Virginia. Angered because the owner had set off a silent alarm, Turner first shot the owner in the head, wounding him, and then shot him twice in the chest, killing him for "snitching." Turner's lawyer included the following question for the jurors:

> The defendant, Willie Lloyd Turner, is a member of the Negro race. The victim, W. Jack Smith, Jr., was a white Caucasian. Will these facts prejudice you against Willie Lloyd Turner or affect your ability to render a fair and impartial verdict based solely on the evidence?

The judge refused to allow this question to be asked. A jury of eight whites and four blacks convicted Turner and then, in a separate sentencing hearing, recommended the death sentence, which the judge imposed.

Turner appealed his conviction, claiming that the judge's refusal to ask prospective jurors about their racial attitudes deprived him of his right to a fair trial. Although his argument failed to convince state and federal appeals courts, the U.S. Supreme Court heard his case. In *Turner v. Murray* (476 U.S. 28, 1986), the high court, in a 7-2 decision, overturned Turner's death sentence, but not his conviction.

Writing for the majority, Justice White noted that, in considering a death sentence, the jury makes a subjective decision that is uniquely his or her own regarding what punishment should be meted out to the offender. Justice White further stated,

> Because of the range of discretion entrusted to a jury in a capital sentencing hearing, there is a unique opportunity for racial prejudice to operate but remain undetected. On

the facts of this case, a juror who believes that blacks are violence-prone or morally inferior might well be influenced by that belief in deciding whether petitioner's crime involved the aggravating factors specified under Virginia law. Such a juror might also be less favorably inclined toward petitioner's evidence of mental disturbance as a mitigating circumstance. More subtle, less consciously held racial attitudes could also influence a juror's decision in this case. Fear of blacks, which could easily be stirred up by the violent facts of petitioner's crime, might incline a juror to favor the death penalty.

The high court recognized that the death sentence differs from all other punishments and, therefore, requires a more comprehensive examination of how it is imposed. The lower court judge, by not asking prospective jurors about their racial attitudes, had not exercised this thorough examination. Consequently, the Supreme Court reversed Turner's death sentence. Justice Lewis Powell, in his dissent, observed,

> [The Court ruling seemed to be] based on what amounts to a constitutional presumption that jurors in capital cases are racially biased. Such presumption unjustifiably suggests that criminal justice in our courts of law is meted out on racial grounds.

Limits to Consideration of Racial Attitudes

Warren McCleskey and three armed men robbed a furniture store in Fulton County, Georgia. A police officer, responding to a silent alarm, entered the store, was shot twice, and died. McCleskey was black; the officer was white. McCleskey admitted taking part in the robbery, but denied shooting the policeman. The state proved that at least one shot came from the weapon McCleskey was carrying and produced two witnesses who had heard McCleskey admit to the shooting. A jury found him guilty and McCleskey, offering no mitigating circumstances during the sentencing phase, received the death penalty.

McCleskey eventually appealed his case all the way to the U.S. Supreme Court. Part of his appeal was based upon two major statistical studies of over two thousand Georgia murder cases that occurred during the 1970s. Prepared by Professors David C. Baldus, George Woodworth, and Charles Pulanski, the statistical analyses were referred to as the Baldus study. (The two studies were "Comparative Review of Death Sentences: An Empirical Study of the Georgia Experience," *Journal of Criminal Law and Criminology*, Volume 74, pages 661-753, 1983, and "Monitoring and Evaluating Contemporary Death Sentencing Systems: Lessons from Georgia," *University of California Davis Law Review*, Volume 18, pages 1375-1407, 1985.)

The Baldus study found that defendants charged with killing white persons received the death penalty in 11 percent of cases, but defendants charged with killing blacks received the death penalty in only 1 percent of the cases.

Interestingly, the study also found a reverse racial difference, based on the defendant's race—4 percent of the black defendants received the death penalty, as opposed to 7 percent of the white defendants.

Furthermore, the Baldus study reported on the cases based on the combination of the defendant's race and that of the victim. The death penalty was imposed in 22 percent of the cases involving black defendants and white victims, in 8 percent of the cases involving white defendants and white victims, in 3 percent of the cases involving white defendants and black victims, and in 1 percent of the cases involving black defendants and black victims.

The Baldus study also found that prosecutors sought the death penalty in 70 percent of the cases involving black defendants and white victims, in 32 percent of the cases involving white defendants and white victims, in 19 percent of the cases involving white defendants and black victims, and in 15 percent of the cases involving black defendants and black victims.

Finally, after taking account of variables that could have explained the differences on nonracial grounds, the study concluded that defendants charged with killing white victims were 4.3 times as likely to receive the death penalty as defendants charged with killing blacks. In addition, black defendants were 1.1 times as likely to get a death sentence as other defendants were. Therefore, McCleskey, who was black and killed a white victim, had the greatest likelihood of being sentenced to death.

In court testimony Dr. Baldus testified that, in really brutal cases where there is no question the death penalty should be imposed, racial discrimination on the part of the jurors tends to disappear. The racial factors usually come into play in mid-range cases, such as McCleskey's, where the jurors were faced with choices.

While the federal district court did not accept the Baldus study, both the court of appeals and the U.S. Supreme Court accepted the study as valid. A 5-4 Supreme Court, however, in *McCleskey v. Kemp* (481 U.S. 279, 1987), rejected McCleskey's appeal. McCleskey had to show that the state of Georgia had acted in a discriminatory manner in his case, and the Baldus study was not enough to support the defendant's claim that any of the jurors had acted with discrimination.

Judge Powell noted that statistics, at most, may show that a certain factor might likely enter some decision-making processes. The Court recognized that jury decision could be influenced by racial prejudice, but the majority believed previous rulings had built in enough safeguards to guarantee equal protection for every defendant. The Court declared,

> At most, the Baldus study indicates a discrepancy that appears to correlate with race. Apparent disparities in

sentencing are an inevitable part of our criminal justice system.... Where the discretion that is fundamental to our criminal process is involved, we decline to assume that what is unexplained is invidious [unfairly discriminatory].... We hold that the Baldus study does not demonstrate a constitutionally significant risk of racial bias affecting the Georgia capital-sentencing process.

The Court expressed concern that if they found that Baldus's findings did represent a risk, it might well be applied to lesser cases. It further noted that it is the job of the legislative branch to consider these findings and incorporate them into the laws to guarantee equal protection in courts of law.

Justice Brennan, who, along with Justice Marshall, believed capital punishment constitutes cruel and unusual punishment and, therefore, is unconstitutional, thought the Baldus study powerfully showed that it is impossible to eliminate arbitrariness in the imposition of the death penalty. Therefore, it must be abolished altogether because the Court cannot rely on legal safeguards to guarantee a black defendant a fair sentencing. While the Baldus study did not show that racism necessarily led to McCleskey's death sentence, it had surely shown that McCleskey faced a considerably greater likelihood of being sentenced to death because he was a black man convicted of killing a white man.

Also writing in dissent, Justice Blackmun thought the Court majority had concentrated too much on the potential racial attitudes of the jury. As important, he thought, were the racial attitudes of the prosecutor's office, which the Baldus study found to be much more likely to seek the death penalty for a black who had killed a white than other categories.

The district attorney for Fulton County had testified that no county policy existed on how to prosecute capital cases. Decisions to seek the death penalty were left to the judgment of the assistant district attorneys who handled the cases. Blackmun thought that such a system was certainly open to abuse. Without guidelines, the prosecutors could let their racial prejudices influence their decisions.

Blackmun also noted that the Court majority had totally dismissed Georgia's history of racial prejudice as past history. While it should not be the overriding factor, it should be considered in any case presented to the high court. Justice Blackmun found most disturbing the Court's concern that, if the Baldus findings were upheld, they might be applied to other cases, leading to constitutional challenges. Blackmun thought that a closer scrutiny of the effects of racial discrimination would benefit the criminal justice system and, ultimately, society.

The Race of Jurors and Equal Protection

James A. Ford, a black man, was charged with the kidnapping, rape, and murder of a white woman. The state informed Ford that it planned to seek the death penalty. Before the trial, Ford filed a "Motion to Restrict Racial Use of Peremptory Challenges," claiming that the prosecutor had consistently excluded black persons from juries where the victim was white.

At a hearing on the defendant's motion, Ford's lawyer noted that it had been his experience that the district attorney and his assistants had used their peremptory challenges (the right to reject a juror without giving a reason) to excuse potential black jurors. Ford's lawyer asked the trial judge to prevent this by ordering the district attorney to justify on the record his reasons for excusing potential black jurors.

The prosecutor denied any discrimination on his part. He referred to the U.S. Supreme Court decision in *Swain v. Alabama* (380 U.S. 202, 1965), which said, in part, "It would be an unreasonable burden to require an attorney for either side to justify his use of peremptory challenges." The judge denied Ford's attorney's motion because he had previously seen the district attorney passing over prospective white jurors in favor of potential black jurors.

During jury selection the prosecutor used 9 of his 10 peremptory challenges to dismiss prospective black jurors, leaving only one black member seated on the jury. In closed sessions, the judge allowed Ford's attorney's observation, for the record, that 9 of the 10 black prospective members had been dismissed on peremptory challenges by the prosecutor. The judge, however, told the prosecutor that he did not have to offer any reasons for his peremptory actions.

Ford was convicted on all counts and was sentenced to death. His attorney called for a new trial and claimed that Ford's "right to an impartial jury as guaranteed by the Sixth Amendment [calling for a fair cross section of the community] of the United States Constitution was violated by the prosecutor's exercise of his peremptory challenges on a racial basis." On appeal, the Supreme Court of Georgia affirmed the conviction.

Ford appealed to the U.S. Supreme Court. In *Ford v. Georgia* (498 U.S. 411, 1991), the high court reversed the decision of the Georgia Supreme Court. The Court vacated (annulled) Ford's conviction and ruled that its decision on *Batson v. Kentucky* (476 U.S. 79, 1986) could be applied retroactively to Ford's case. In 1986 the high court had ruled in *Batson*, which dropped the *Swain* requirement of proof of prior discrimination, that a black defendant could make a case claiming the denial of equal protection of the laws. The defendant could do so solely on evidence that the prosecutor had used peremptory challenges to exclude members of the defendant's race from the jury.

Delivering the opinion for a unanimous Court, Justice Souter held that the Georgia Supreme Court had erred when it ruled that Ford had failed to present a proper equal protection claim. Although Ford's pretrial motion did not mention the Equal Protection Clause (of the Fourteenth Amendment), and his new trial motion had cited the Sixth Amendment rather than the Fourteenth, the motion referring to a pattern of excluding black members "over a long period of time asserts an equal protection claim."

Using Race to Obtain a Death Sentence

On June 5, 2000, the Supreme Court, in a summary disposition, ordered the Texas Court of Criminal Appeals to hold a new sentencing hearing for Victor Saldano, an Argentine national on death row. (In a summary disposition, the Court decides a case in a simple proceeding without the aid of a jury.) In *Saldano v. Texas* (99-8119), the Court cited the confession of error by Texas Attorney General John Cornyn regarding the use of race as a factor in sentencing the defendant.

Texas death penalty statutes require that the jury consider a defendant's future dangerousness to determine whether or not to impose the death penalty. At the sentencing hearing court-appointed psychologist Dr. Walter Quijano testified that Saldano was "a continuing threat to society" because he is Hispanic. Dr. Quijano told the jury that because Hispanics are "over-represented" in prisons they are more likely to be dangerous. Since then the attorney general announced that the psychiatrist had given similar testimony in six other cases of death row inmates sentenced to death.

METHODS OF EXECUTION

Lethal Injection May Be Used for Executions

The injection of a deadly combination of drugs has become the method of execution in most states permitting capital punishment. Condemned prisoners from Texas and Oklahoma, two of the first states to introduce this method, brought suit claiming that, while the drugs used had been approved by the U.S. Food and Drug Administration (FDA) for medical purposes, they had never been approved for use in nor tested for human executions.

The petitioners further claimed that, since the drugs would likely be administered by untrained personnel, they might not cause the quick and painless death intended. They alleged these drugs had been "misbranded," a violation of 21 U.S.C. para. 352 (f), which states, "A drug or device shall be deemed to be misbranded ... unless its labeling bears (1) adequate directions for use." In addition, since the drugs were being put to a new use, they had to be reapproved by the FDA to determine if they were "safe and effective" for human execution.

The FDA commissioner refused to act, claiming serious questions as to whether the agency had jurisdiction in the area. He further noted,

Generally, enforcement proceedings in this area are initiated only when there is a serious danger to the public health or a blatant scheme to defraud. We cannot conclude that those dangers are present under State lethal injections laws, which are duly authorized statutory enactments in furtherance of proper State [goals].

The U.S. District Court for the District of Columbia disagreed with the condemned prisoners that the FDA had a responsibility to determine if the lethal mixture used during execution was safe and effective. The court noted that decisions by a federal agency not to take action were not reviewable in court.

A divided Court of Appeals for the District of Columbia reversed the lower court ruling, noting that the FDA's own policy required the FDA to investigate the unapproved use of an approved drug when such use became "widespread" or "endanger[ed] the public health." Therefore, the prisoners who risked a "cruel and protracted" death were entitled to a more thorough investigation of the drugs used in their execution.

A generally irritated U.S. Supreme Court agreed to hear the case "to review the implausible result that the FDA is required to exercise its enforcement power to ensure that States use only drugs that are 'safe and effective' for human execution."

In *Heckler v. Chaney* (470 U.S. 821, 1985), the unanimous Court agreed that, in this case, the FDA did not have jurisdiction, although Justices Brennan and Marshall indicated that the limitation on court jurisdiction should not apply to all agency decisions not to intervene. The remaining justices, on the other hand, thought the courts had no right to question any agency decision not to take action.

Writing for all but Justices Marshall and Brennan, Justice Rehnquist explained why the majority of justices concluded that the FDA decision not to investigate the prisoner's request was simply not the high court's business:

First, an agency decision not to enforce often involves a complicated balancing of a number of factors which are peculiarly within its expertise. Thus, the agency must not only assess where a violation has occurred, but whether agency resources are best spent on this violation or another, whether the agency is likely to succeed if it acts, whether the particular enforcement action requested best fits the agency's overall policies, and indeed, whether the agency has enough resources to undertake the action at all. An agency generally cannot act against each technical violation of the statute it is charged with enforcing. The agency is better equipped than the courts to deal with the many variables involved in the proper ordering of its priorities.

Is Execution by Hanging Constitutional?

Washington state law imposes capital punishment either by "hanging by the neck" or, if the condemned chooses, by lethal injection. Charles Rodham Campbell was convicted of three counts of murder in 1982 and sentenced to death. Campbell, in challenging the constitutionality of hanging under the Washington statute, claimed that execution by hanging violated his Eighth Amendment right because it was cruel and unusual punishment. Furthermore, the direction that he be hanged unless he chose lethal injection was cruel and unusual punishment. He claimed that such instruction further violated his First Amendment right by forcing him to participate in his own execution to avoid hanging.

In *Campbell v. Wood* (18 F.3d. 662, 9th Cir. 1994), the U.S. Court of Appeals for the Ninth Circuit noted,

> We do not consider hanging to be cruel and unusual simply because it causes death, or because there may be some pain associated with death.... As used in the Constitution, "cruel" implies "something inhuman and barbarous, something more than the mere extinguishment of life." ... Campbell is entitled to an execution free only of "the unnecessary and wanton infliction of pain."

According to the Court, just because the defendant was given a choice of a method of execution did not mean that he was being subjected to cruel and unusual punishment:

> We believe that benefits to prisoners who may choose to exercise the option and who may feel relieved that they can elect lethal injection outweigh the emotional costs to those who find the mere existence of an option objectionable.

Campbell argued that the state was infringing on his First Amendment right of free exercise of his religion. He claimed that it was against his religion to participate in his own execution by being allowed to elect lethal injection over hanging.

The Court contended that Campbell did not have to choose an execution method or participate in his own execution. "He may remain absolutely silent and refuse to participate in any election." The death penalty statute does not require him to choose the method of execution; it simply offers a choice. Upon appeal (*Campbell v. Wood*, 511 U.S. 1119, 1994), the U.S. Supreme Court decided not to hear the case.

Is Execution by Lethal Gas Constitutional?

On April 17, 1992, three California death row inmates (David Fierro, Alejandro Gilbert Ruiz, and Robert Alton Harris) filed a suit on behalf of themselves and all others under sentence of execution by lethal gas. In *Fierro v. Gomez* (790 F. Supp. 966 [N.D. Cal. 1992], also referred to as *Fierro I*), the inmates alleged that California's method of execution by lethal gas violated the Eighth and Fourteenth Amendments. Harris was scheduled to be executed four days later, on April 21, 1992.

The district court prohibited James Gomez, director of the California Department of Corrections, and Arthur Calderon, warden of San Quentin Prison, from executing any inmate until a hearing was held. On appeal from Gomez and Calderon, the U.S. Court of Appeals for the Ninth Circuit vacated the district court's ruling. On his execution day Harris had filed a *habeas corpus* petition with the California Supreme Court, challenging the constitutionality of the gas chamber. The court declined to review the case. Harris was put to death that day. In the aftermath of Harris's execution, the California legislature, in 1993, amended its death penalty statute, providing that, if lethal gas "is held invalid, the punishment of death shall be imposed by the alternative means," lethal injection.

In October 1994 a federal district judge, Marilyn Hall Patel, ruled that execution by lethal gas "is inhumane and has no place in civilized society" (865 F. Supp. at 1415; also referred to as *Fierro II*). She then ordered California's gas chamber closed and that lethal injection be used instead. This was the first time a federal judge had ruled that any method of execution violated the Eighth and Fourteenth Amendments. While the state of California maintained that cyanide gas caused almost instant unconsciousness, the judge referred to doctors' reports and witnesses' accounts of gas chamber executions, which indicated that the dying inmates stayed conscious for 15 seconds to a minute or longer and suffered "intense physical pain."

Gomez and Calderon appealed Judge Patel's ruling on the unconstitutionality of the gas chamber before the U.S. Court of Appeals for the Ninth Circuit. They also appealed the permanent injunction against the use of lethal gas as a method of execution. In February 1996, in *Fierro v. Gomez* (77 F. 3d. 301, 9th Cir.), the appellate court affirmed Judge Patel's ruling.

Gomez and Calderon appealed the case to the U.S. Supreme Court. In October 1996 the 7-2 Supreme Court, in *Gomez v. Fierro* (No. 95-1830), vacated the appellate court's ruling and returned the case to the appellate court for additional proceedings, citing the death penalty statute amended in 1993 (lethal injection as an alternative to lethal gas).

Does Electrocution Constitute a Cruel and Unusual Punishment?

In the 1990s, although Florida had three botched executions using the electric chair, the state supreme court ruled each time that electrocution does not constitute cruel or unusual punishment. In 1990 and 1997 flames shot out from the headpiece worn by the condemned man. On July 8, 1999, Allen Lee Davis developed a nosebleed.

Thomas Provenzano, scheduled to be electrocuted after Davis, challenged the use of the electric chair as

Florida's sole method of execution. In *Provenzano v. Moore* (No. 95,973, September 24, 1999), the Florida Supreme Court, in a 4-3 decision, ruled that the electric chair was not cruel and unusual punishment. The court further reported that Davis's nosebleed occurred prior to the execution and did not result from the electrocution.

Subsequently, the court, as it routinely does with all its rulings, posted the *Provenzano* decision on the Internet. Three photographs of Davis, covered with blood, were posted as part of Justice Leander Shaw's dissenting opinion. The photographs brought public outcry worldwide. Justice Shaw claimed that Davis was "brutally tortured to death."

In October 1999, for the first time, the U.S. Supreme Court agreed to consider the constitutionality of electrocution. Death row inmate Anthony Braden Bryan asked the U.S. Supreme Court to review his case, based on the unreliability of the electric chair. Before the high court could hear the case, however, the Florida legislature, in a special session, voted to replace electrocution with lethal injection as the primary method of execution. A condemned person, however, may choose the electric chair.

On January 24, 2000, the Supreme Court dismissed *Bryan v. Moore* (No. 99-6723) as moot or irrelevant, based on Florida's new legislation. Governor Jeb Bush agreed to sign the bill in conjunction with a second bill that limits, in most cases, death row inmates to two appeals in state courts, with the second appeal to be filed within six months of the first. This provision cut in half the time limit for the second appeal. As of November 2001 just two states—Alabama and Nebraska—authorized electrocution as the only means of execution.

On October 5, 2001, the Georgia Supreme Court, voting 4-3, ruled that use of the electric chair was cruel and unusual punishment, in violation of the Eighth Amendment. According to the court, electrocution "inflicts purposeless physical violence and needless mutilation that makes no measurable contribution to accepted goals of punishment." Georgia last used electrocution in June 1998. In 2000 the legislature passed a law making lethal injection the sole method of execution. This applied, however, only to those sentenced after May 1, 2000.

CHALLENGING THE ANTITERRORISM ACT OF 1996

The Antiterrorism and Effective Death Penalty Act (AEDPA; Public Law 104-132) became law on April 24, 1996, around the first anniversary of the Oklahoma City bombing. AEDPA aims in part to "deter terrorism, provide justice for victims, and provide for an effective death penalty." Since passage of the law the lower courts had differed in their interpretations of certain core provisions. For the first time, on October 18, 2000, the U.S. Supreme Court addressed these problems. Interestingly, the defendants in the two cases share the same last name.

Federal *Habeas Corpus* Relief and the AEDPA

The AEDPA restricts the power of federal courts to grant writs of *habeas corpus* to state inmates. Through the writ of *habeas corpus,* an inmate could have a federal court review his or her conviction or sentencing. The AEDPA bars a federal court from granting an application for a writ of *habeas corpus* unless the state court's decision "was contrary to, or involved an unreasonable application of, clearly established federal law, as determined by the Supreme Court of the United States."

In 1986 Terry Williams, while incarcerated in a Danville, Virginia, city jail, wrote to police that he had killed two people and that he was sorry for his acts. He also confessed to stealing money from one of the victims. He was subsequently convicted of robbery and capital murder.

During the sentencing hearing the prosecutor presented numerous crimes Williams had committed in addition to the murder for which he was convicted. Two state witnesses also testified to the defendant's future dangerousness.

Williams's lawyer, on the other hand, called on his mother to testify to his being a nonviolent person. The defense also played a taped portion of a psychiatrist's statement, saying that Williams told the psychiatrist he had removed bullets from a gun used during robbery so as not to harm anyone. During his closing statement, however, the lawyer noted that the jury would probably find it hard to give his client mercy because he did not show mercy to his victims. The jury sentenced Williams to death, and the trial judge imposed the sentence.

Williams appealed to the Virginia Supreme Court, claiming that the trial judge did not consider the mitigating factor that he had turned himself in. The court refused to review the case, affirming the conviction and sentence.

In 1988 Williams filed a state *habeas corpus* petition. The Danville Circuit Court found Williams's conviction valid. The court found, however, that the defense lawyer's failure to present several mitigating factors at the sentencing phase violated Williams's right to effective assistance of counsel as prescribed by *Strickland v. Washington* (466 U.S. 668, 1984). The mitigating circumstances included early childhood abuse and borderline mental retardation. The *habeas corpus* hearing further revealed that the state expert witnesses had testified that if Williams were kept in a "structured environment," he would not be a threat to society. The circuit court recommended a new sentencing hearing.

While Williams's petition was pending, a new state law gave the Virginia Supreme Court the exclusive power to grant *habeas corpus* review. In 1997 the state supreme court rejected the district court's recommendation for a new sentencing hearing, concluding that the omitted evidence would not have affected the sentence.

Next, Williams filed a federal *habeas corpus*. The federal trial judge not only ruled that the death sentence was "constitutionally infirm," but that defense counsel was ineffective. The Fourth Circuit Court of Appeals, however, reversed the federal trial judge's decision, holding that the AEDPA prohibits a federal court from granting *habeas corpus* relief unless the state courts "decided the question by interpreting or applying the relevant precedent in a manner that reasonable jurists would all agree is unreasonable."

On April 18, 2000, the U.S. Supreme Court, in *(Terry) Williams v. Taylor* (529 U.S. 362, 2000), reversed the Fourth Circuit Court's ruling by a 6-3 decision. The Court concluded that the Virginia Supreme Court's decision rejecting Williams's claim of ineffective assistance was contrary to a Supreme Court established precedent (*Strickland v. Washington*), as well as an unreasonable application of that precedent. This was the first time the Supreme Court had granted relief on such a claim.

Federal Evidentiary Hearings for Constitutional Claims

Under an AEDPA provision, if the petitioner has failed to develop the facts of his or her challenges of a constitutional claim in state court proceedings, the (federal) court shall not hold an evidentiary hearing on the claim unless the facts involve an exception listed by the AEDPA.

In 1993, after robbing the home of Morris Keller Jr. and his wife, Mary Elizabeth, Michael Wayne Williams and his friend Jeffrey Alan Cruse raped the woman and then killed the couple. In exchange for the state's promise not to seek capital punishment, Cruse described details of the crimes. Williams received the death sentence for the capital murders. The prosecution told the jury about the plea agreement with Cruse. The state later revoked the plea agreement after discovering that Cruse had also raped the wife and failed to disclose it. After Cruse's court testimony against Williams, however, the state gave Cruse a life sentence.

Williams filed a *habeas* petition in state court, claiming he was not told of the second plea agreement between the state and his codefendant. The Virginia Supreme Court dismissed the petition (1994), and the U.S. Supreme Court refused to review the case (1995).

In 1996, upon appeal, a federal district court agreed to an evidentiary hearing of Williams's claims of the undisclosed second plea agreement. The defendant had also claimed that a psychiatric report about Cruse, which was not revealed by prosecution, could have shown that Cruse was not credible. Moreover, a certain juror might have had possible bias, which the prosecution failed to disclose. Before the hearing could be held, the state concluded that the AEDPA prohibited such hearing. Consequently, the federal district court dismissed Williams's petition.

When the case was brought before the U.S. Court of Appeals for the Fourth Circuit, the court, interpreting the AEDPA, concluded that the defendant had failed to develop the facts of his claims. On April 18, 2000, in *(Michael) Williams v. Taylor* (529 U.S. 420), a unanimous U.S. Supreme Court did not address Williams's claim of the undisclosed plea agreement between Cruse and the state. Instead, the high court held that the defendant was entitled to a federal district court evidentiary hearing regarding his other claims. According to the Court,

> Under the [AEDPA], a failure to develop the factual basis of a claim is not established unless there is lack of diligence, or some greater fault, attributable to the prisoner or the prisoner's counsel. We conclude petitioner has met the burden of showing he was diligent in efforts to develop the facts supporting his juror bias and prosecutorial misconduct claims in collateral proceedings before the Virginia Supreme Court.

CHAPTER 5
DEATH PENALTY STATUTES AND METHODS

CAPITAL OFFENSES

Most death penalty statutes in force prior to the *Furman v. Georgia* (408 U.S. 238) decision of June 29, 1972, provided for the imposition of the death penalty for capital murder and, in some states, for other crimes. In *Furman,* however, the U.S. Supreme Court found that the death penalty, as then being administered, was cruel and unusual punishment in violation of the Eighth Amendment to the U.S. Constitution. Many states revised their laws to conform to standards set by the *Furman* decision. Since *Furman,* review of individual state statutes has continued as appeals of capital sentences reach state courts or the U.S. Supreme Court.

Under revised state laws, different types of capital murder have been specifically defined. Although varying somewhat from one jurisdiction to another, the types of homicide most commonly specified are murder carried out during the commission of a felony; murder of a peace officer, corrections employee, or firefighter engaged in the performance of official duties; murder by an inmate serving a life sentence; and murder for hire (contract murder). Different statutory terminology may be used by different states to designate basically identical crimes. In some states, such terms as "capital murder," "first-degree murder," "capital felony," or "murder Class 1 felony" may indicate the same capital offense. At year-end 1999 the death penalty was authorized for certain cases of homicide by the statutes of 38 states (see Table 5.1) and by the federal government (see Table 5.2).

While other offenses (most notably, treason and air piracy, or hijacking) also carry the death penalty, most have not yet had their constitutionality tested. The Supreme Court has held, in *Everheart v. Georgia* (433 U.S. 917, 1977) and *Coker v. Georgia* (433 U.S. 584, 1977), that rape and kidnapping, as horrible as they are, do not result in death and, therefore, do not warrant the death penalty. Nonetheless, in 1995 the Louisiana legislature amended statute La. R.S. 14:42(C) to allow for the death penalty when the victim of rape is less than 12 years old.

STATUTORY CHANGES

In 1999 no state enacted new legislation authorizing capital punishment. As in the past, states continued to revise their statutory provisions relating to the death penalty. In 1999 most statutory changes involved aggravating circumstances (factors that may add to responsibility for a crime) and procedural amendments. In 1999 nine states revised their laws that related to the death penalty.

Among the statutory changes, Colorado added to its aggravating circumstances the murder of a person because of his or her race, color, ancestry, religion, or national origin. Kansas required keeping confidential the identity of executioners. The law also mandated that drugs used in executions will "result in death in a swift and humane manner."

Effective October 1, 1999, Nevada added another aggravating circumstance to the list of those constituting first-degree murder—murder that is committed on school property or any place where school-related activities occur when the offender "intended to cause death or substantial bodily harm to more than one person" through his or her action or through the use of a weapon. To its felony murder law, New Jersey added as an aggravating circumstance any murder in which the victim had filed a domestic violence restraining order against the murderer.

Among several amendments to its death penalty statute, Oregon granted health care professionals protection against disciplinary action if they participated in an execution. Starting September 1999, defense counsel in Texas may request in writing that during the sentencing phase the court instructs the jury that any person not sentenced to death will serve a life sentence with no parole eligibility for 40 years. Murder while abusing a child under age 16 was added to the list of Wyoming's aggravating circumstances for capital felony murder.

TABLE 5.1

Capital offenses, by state, 1999

Alabama. Capital murder with a finding of at least 1 of 10 aggravating circumstances (Ala. Code § 13A-5-40 and § 13A-5-49).

Arizona. First-degree murder accompanied by at least 1 of 10 aggravating factors.

Arkansas. Capital murder (Ark. Code Ann. 5-10-101) with a finding of at least 1 of 10 aggravating circumstances; treason.

California. First-degree murder with special circumstances; train wrecking; treason; perjury causing execution.

Colorado. First-degree murder with at least 1 of 14 aggravating factors; treason. Capital sentencing excludes persons determined to be mentally retarded.

Connecticut. Capital felony with 9 categories of aggravated homicide (C.G.S. 53a-54b).

Delaware. First-degree murder with aggravating circumstances.

Florida. First-degree murder; felony murder; capital drug trafficking.

Georgia. Murder; kidnaping with bodily injury or ransom where the victim dies; aircraft hijacking; treason.

Idaho. First-degree murder; aggravated kidnaping.

Illinois. First-degree murder with 1 of 15 aggravating circumstances.

Indiana. Murder with 16 aggravating circumstances (IC 35-50-2-9). Capital sentencing excludes persons determined to be mentally retarded.

Kansas. Capital murder with 7 aggravating circumstances (KSA 21-3439). Capital sentencing excludes persons determined to be mentally retarded.

Kentucky. Murder with aggravating factors; kidnaping with aggravating factors.

Louisiana. First-degree murder; aggravated rape of victim under age 12; treason (La. R.S. 14:30, 14:42, and 14:113).

Maryland. First-degree murder, either premeditated or during the commission of a felony, provided that certain death eligibility requirements are satisfied.

Mississippi. Capital murder (97-3-19(2) MCA); aircraft piracy (97-25-55(1) MCA).

Missouri. First-degree murder (565.020 RSMO).

Montana. Capital murder with 1 of 9 aggravating circumstances (46-18-303 MCA); capital sexual assault (45-5-503 MCA).

Nebraska. First-degree murder with a finding of at least 1 statutorily-defined aggravating circumstance.

Nevada. First-degree murder with 14 aggravating circumstances.

New Hampshire. Six categories of capital murder (RSA 630:1 and RSA 630:5).

New Jersey. Purposeful or knowing murder by one's own conduct; contract murder; solicitation by command or threat in furtherance of a narcotics conspiracy (NJSA 2C:11-3C).

New Mexico. First-degree murder in conjunction with a finding of at least 1 of 7 aggravating circumstances (Section 30-2-1 A, NMSA).

New York. First-degree murder with 1 of 12 aggravating factors. Capital sentencing excludes persons determined to be mentally retarded.

North Carolina. First-degree murder (N.C.G.S. 14-17).

Ohio. Aggravated murder with at least 1 of 8 aggravating circumstances. (O.R.C. secs. 2903.01, 2929.01, and 2929.04).

Oklahoma. First-degree murder in conjunction with a finding of at least 1 of 8 statutorily defined aggravating circumstances.

Oregon. Aggravated murder (ORS 163.095).

Pennsylvania. First-degree murder with 18 aggravating circumstances.

South Carolina. Murder with 1 of 10 aggravating circumstances (§ 16-3-20(C)(a)). Mental retardation is a mitigating factor.

South Dakota. First-degree murder with 1 of 10 aggravating circumstances; aggravated kidnaping.

Tennessee. First-degree murder.

Texas. Criminal homicide with 1 of 8 aggravating circumstances (TX Penal Code 19.03).

Utah. Aggravated murder (76-5-202, Utah Code annotated).

Virginia. First-degree murder with 1 of 12 aggravating circumstances (VA Code § 18.2-31).

Washington. Aggravated first-degree murder.

Wyoming. First-degree murder.

SOURCE: Tracy L. Snell, "Table 1. Capital offenses, by State, 1999," in *Capital Punishment 1999*, U.S. Department of Justice, Bureau of Justice Statistics, Washington, DC, December 2000

CHALLENGES TO STATE DEATH PENALTY LAWS

Louisiana

In August 1995 Louisiana became the first state to allow the death penalty for rape victims under age 12. In December 1995 Anthony Wilson was charged by a grand jury with the aggravated rape of a five-year-old girl. Patrick Dwayne Bethley was charged with raping three girls, one of whom was his daughter. At the time of the rape, the girls were five, seven, and nine years old. The two defendants moved to quash their indictments. They claimed that the death penalty, when imposed for rape, constitutes "cruel and unusual punishment" and, therefore, is unconstitutional under the Eighth Amendment and Article I, Section 20 of the Louisiana Constitution. On December 13, 1996, the Louisiana Supreme Court, in *Louisiana v. Wilson* (1996 W.L. 718217), held that the state death penalty statute was constitutional. The Louisiana Supreme Court concluded,

> Given the appalling nature of the crime, the severity of the harm inflicted upon the victim, and the harm imposed on society, the death penalty is not an excessive penalty for the crime of rape when the victim is a child under the age of twelve years old.

In 1998 Bethley entered into a plea agreement with prosecution in which he received a life sentence for rape in place of the state of Louisiana seeking the death penalty against him. In 1999, upon appeal, Wilson was found mentally retarded and, therefore, unable to assist in his defense.

New York

Until 1998 New York's death penalty statute prohibited the imposition of a death sentence when a defendant entered a guilty plea, while a defendant who pleaded not guilty would have to stand trial and face the possibility of a death sentence. The maximum penalty in the first case would be life imprisonment without parole. In other words, the law provided two levels of penalty for the same offense, imposing the death penalty only on those who claimed innocence.

Defendants in two capital cases challenged the plea provisions of New York's death penalty statute, claiming these provisions violated their Fifth Amendment right against self-incrimination and Sixth Amendment right to a jury trial. This was the first major constitutional challenge to New York's death penalty law. On December 22, 1998, the New York Court of Appeals, in *Hynes v. Tomei* (including *Relin v. Mateo,* 92 N.Y. 2d. 613, 706 N.E. 2d. 1201, 684 N.Y.S. 2d. 177), unanimously agreed, striking down these plea-bargaining provisions as unconstitutional. The court, relying on the U.S. Supreme Court decision in *United States v. Jackson* (390 U.S. 570, 1968), observed that "the Supreme Court in *Jackson* prohibited statutes that 'needlessly' encourage guilty pleas, which are not constitutionally protected, by impermissibly burdening constitutional rights."

TABLE 5.2

Federal laws providing for the death penalty, 1999

8 U.S.C. 1342 — Murder related to the smuggling of aliens.

18 U.S.C. 32-34 — Destruction of aircraft, motor vehicles, or related facilities resulting in death.

18 U.S.C. 36 — Murder committed during a drug-related drive-by shooting.

18 U.S.C. 37 — Murder committed at an airport serving international civil aviation.

18 U.S.C. 115(b)(3) [by cross-reference to 18 U.S.C. 1111] — Retaliatory murder of a member of the immediate family of law enforcement officials.

18 U.S.C. 241, 242, 245, 247 — Civil rights offenses resulting in death.

18 U.S.C. 351 [by cross-reference to 18 U.S.C. 1111] — Murder of a member of Congress, an important executive official, or a Supreme Court Justice.

18 U.S.C. 794 — Espionage.

18 U.S.C. 844(d), (f), (i) — Death resulting from offenses involving transportation of explosives, destruction of government property, or destruction of property related to foreign or interstate commerce.

18 U.S.C. 924(i) — Murder committed by the use of a firearm during a crime of violence or a drug-trafficking crime.

18 U.S.C. 930 — Murder committed in a Federal Government facility.

18 U.S.C. 1091 — Genocide.

18 U.S.C. 1111 — First-degree murder.

18 U.S.C. 1114 — Murder of a Federal judge or law enforcement official.

18 U.S.C. 1116 — Murder of a foreign official.

18 U.S.C. 1118 — Murder by a Federal prisoner.

18 U.S.C. 1119 — Murder of a U.S. national in a foreign country.

18 U.S.C. 1120 — Murder by an escaped Federal prisoner already sentenced to life imprisonment.

18 U.S.C. 1121 — Murder of a State or local law enforcement official or other person aiding in a Federal investigation; murder of a State correctional officer.

18 U.S.C. 1201 — Murder during a kidnaping.

18 U.S.C. 1203 — Murder during a hostage taking.

18 U.S.C. 1503 — Murder of a court officer or juror.

18 U.S.C. 1512 — Murder with the intent of preventing testimony by a witness, victim, or informant.

18 U.S.C. 1513 — Retaliatory murder of a witness, victim, or informant.

18 U.S.C. 1716 — Mailing of injurious articles with intent to kill or resulting in death.

18 U.S.C. 1751 [by cross-reference to 18 U.S.C. 1111] — Assassination or kidnaping resulting in the death of the President or Vice President.

18 U.S.C. 1958 — Murder for hire.

18 U.S.C. 1959 — Murder involved in a racketeering offense.

18 U.S.C. 1992 — Willful wrecking of a train resulting in death.

18 U.S.C. 2113 — Bank-robbery-related murder or kidnaping.

18 U.S.C. 2119 — Murder related to a carjacking.

18 U.S.C. 2245 — Murder related to rape or child molestation.

18 U.S.C. 2251 — Murder related to sexual exploitation of children.

18 U.S.C. 2280 — Murder committed during an offense against maritime navigation.

18 U.S.C. 2281 — Murder committed during an offense against a maritime fixed platform.

18 U.S.C. 2332 — Terrorist murder of a U.S. national in another country.

18 U.S.C. 2332a — Murder by the use of a weapon of mass destruction.

18 U.S.C. 2340 — Murder involving torture.

18 U.S.C. 2381 — Treason.

21 U.S.C. 848(e) — Murder related to a continuing criminal enterprise or related murder of a Federal, State, or local law enforcement officer.

49 U.S.C. 1472-1473 — Death resulting from aircraft hijacking.

SOURCE: Tracy L. Snell, "Table 2. Federal laws providing for the death penalty, 1999," in *Capital Punishment 1999*, Bureau of Justice Statistics, Washington, DC, December 2000

MINIMUM AGE FOR EXECUTION

Under state laws, the term "juvenile" refers to persons below the age of 18. Literature on the death penalty typically considers "juvenile offenders" as persons younger than 18 at the time of their crimes. Professor Victor L. Streib traced the first execution of a juvenile, Thomas Graunger, to Plymouth Colony, Massachusetts, in 1642 (*The Juvenile Death Penalty Today: Death Sentences and Executions for Juvenile Crimes, January 1, 1973–December 31, 2000*, Claude W. Pettit College of Law, Ohio Northern University, February 2001). Professor Streib reported that the United States has since executed an estimated 361 persons (as of year-end 2000) who were juveniles during the commission of the crime. The time spent on death row prior to execution was between 6 and 20 years.

According to Professor Streib, in the modern death penalty era (1973–2000), 17 inmates who were juveniles at the time of their crimes were executed. Nine offenders were from Texas, followed by Virginia (three), and one each from Georgia, Louisiana, Missouri, Oklahoma, and South Carolina. In 2000 the United States put to death four death row inmates who were all 17 years old at the commission of the crime—Douglas Christopher Thomas (Virginia), Steve Roach (Virginia), Glen McGinnis (Texas), and Gary Graham (Texas). They were ages 26, 23, 27, and 36, respectively, at the time of their deaths. An inmate from Texas, Gerald Mitchell, who was 17 at the time of the crime, was executed in October 2001. He was 33 years old.

The International Covenant on Civil and Political Rights, the United Nations Convention on the Rights of the

TABLE 5.3

Minimum age authorized for capital punishment, 1999

Age 16 or less	Age 17	Age 18	None specified
Alabama (16)	Georgia	California	Arizona
Arkansas (14)[a]	New Hampshire	Colorado	Idaho
Delaware (16)	North Carolina[b]	Connecticut[c]	Louisiana
Florida (16)	Texas	Federal system	Montana[d]
Indiana (16)		Illinois	Pennsylvania
Kentucky (16)		Kansas	South Carolina
Mississippi (16)[e]		Maryland	South Dakota[f]
Missouri (16)		Nebraska	
Nevada (16)		New Jersey	
Oklahoma (16)		New Mexico	
Utah (14)		New York	
Virginia (14)[g]		Ohio	
Wyoming (16)		Oregon	
		Tennessee	
		Washington	

Note: Reporting by States reflects interpretations by offices of State attorneys general and may differ from previously reported ages.

[a] See Ark. Code Ann. 9-27-318(c)(2)(Supp. 1999).
[b] Age required is 17 unless the murderer was incarcerated for murder when a subsequent murder occurred; then the age may be 14.
[c] See Conn. Gen. Stat. 53a-46a(g)(1).
[d] Montana law specifies that offenders tried under the capital sexual assault statute be 18 or older. Age may be a mitigating factor for other capital crimes.
[e] The minimum age defined by statute is 13, but the effective age is 16 based on interpretation of U.S. Supreme Court decisions by the Mississippi Supreme Court.
[f] Juveniles may be transferred to adult court. Age can be a mitigating factor.
[g] The minimum age for transfer to adult court by statute is 14, but the effective age is 16 based on interpretation of U.S. Supreme Court decisions by the State attorney general's office.

SOURCE: Tracy L. Snell, "Table 4. Minimum age authorized for capital punishment, 1999," in *Capital Punishment 1999,* Bureau of Justice Statistics, Washington, DC, December 2000

Child, and the American Convention on Human Rights forbid the imposition of the death penalty on offenders who committed their crimes while under the age of 18. Although the United States ratified (became party to) the International Covenant on Civil and Political Rights in 1992, it has reserved the right to execute juveniles. The United States is the only ratifying country that has reserved this right. The United States has signed (intended to be a party to) but not ratified the latter two agreements.

In 1999 only seven states did not specify a minimum age for which the death penalty may be imposed. Fourteen states and the federal government required a minimum age of 18, four states authorized a minimum age of 17, and 13 states required an age of eligibility between 14 and 16. (See Table 5.3.) In some states the minimum age is determined by state laws that define the age at which a juvenile may be transferred to the criminal court for trial as an adult. Once a minor is tried as an adult, he or she could then face the same penalties (including death) to which an adult may be sentenced. The Supreme Court, in *Stanford v. Kentucky* and *Wilkins v. Missouri* (492 U.S. 361, 1989), ruled that a minor as young as 16 years old may be executed.

In February 1999, for the first time in 40 years, the United States executed an offender who was 16 during the commission of the crime. Sean Sellers of Oklahoma was 29 years old at the time of execution. He was convicted for the murders of his mother, stepfather, and a convenience-store clerk. His supporters claimed Sellers suffered from multiple personality disorder, which was diagnosed after his conviction. The last execution of a person who was 16 at the time of his crime occurred in 1959, when Maryland executed Leonard Shockley.

EXECUTING MENTALLY RETARDED PERSONS

According to the Death Penalty Information Center (Washington, D.C.), which opposes the death penalty, as of November 2001, 34 mentally retarded offenders have been executed since 1976. In 1988 Georgia became the first state to prohibit the execution of murderers found "guilty but mentally retarded." The legislation resulted from the 1986 execution of Jerome Bowden, who had an IQ of 65 (normal IQ is considered 90 and above).

As of November 2001 the federal government and 18 states—Arizona, Arkansas, Colorado, Connecticut, Florida, Georgia, Indiana, Kansas, Kentucky, Maryland, Missouri, Nebraska, New Mexico, New York (except for murder by a prisoner), North Carolina, South Dakota, Tennessee, and Washington—forbade the execution of offenders with mental retardation. Among these states, Arizona, Florida, Missouri, Connecticut, and North Carolina passed such legislation between April and November 2001. On June 17, 2001, Governor Rick Perry of Texas vetoed a bill that would have banned execution of the mentally retarded.

In March 2001 the U.S. Supreme Court agreed to review the case of North Carolina death row inmate Ernest McCarver to consider whether it is cruel and unusual, and therefore, unconstitutional, to execute inmates with mental retardation. The passage of a bill banning the execution of inmates with mental retardation, however, had rendered that case moot. In September 2001 the Supreme Court agreed to hear, in the near future, the case of Daryl Atkins, a Virginia death row inmate with mental retardation.

The federal government, in the Anti-Drug Abuse Act of 1988 (Public Law 100-690), permits the death penalty for any person working "in furtherance of a continuing criminal enterprise or any person engaging in a drug-related felony offense, who intentionally kills or counsels, commands, or causes the intentional killing of an individual," but forbids the imposition of the death penalty against anyone who is mentally retarded who commits this particular crime.

DEATH PENALTY METHODS

The Eighth Amendment of the U.S. Bill of Rights, using the language of the English Bill of Rights of 1689,

TABLE 5.4

Method of execution, by state, 1999

Lethal injection		Electrocution	Lethal gas	Hanging	Firing squad
Arizona[a,b]	New Hampshire[a]	Alabama	Arizona[a,b]	Delaware[a,c]	Idaho[a]
Arkansas[a,d]	New Jersey	Arkansas[a,d]	California[a]	New Hampshire[a,e]	Oklahoma[f]
California[a]	New Mexico	Florida	Missouri[a]	Washington[a]	Utah[a]
Colorado	New York	Georgia	Wyoming[a,g]		
Connecticut	North Carolina	Kentucky[a,h]			
Delaware[a,c]	Ohio[a]	Nebraska			
Idaho[a]	Oklahoma[a]	Ohio[a]			
Illinois	Oregon	Oklahoma[f]			
Indiana	Pennsylvania	South Carolina[a]			
Kansas	South Carolina[a]	Tennessee[a,i]			
Kentucky[a,g]	South Dakota	Virginia[a]			
Louisiana	Tennessee[a,i]				
Maryland	Texas				
Mississippi	Utah[a]				
Missouri[a]	Virginia[a]				
Montana	Washington[a]				
Nevada	Wyoming[a]				

Note: The method of execution of Federal prisoners is lethal injection, pursuant to 28 CFR, Part 26. For offenses under the Violent Crime Control and Law Enforcement Act of 1994, the method is that of the State in which the conviction took place, pursuant to 18 U.S.C. 3596.

[a] Authorizes 2 methods of execution.
[b] Arizona authorizes lethal injection for persons whose capital sentence was received after 11/15/92; for those sentenced before that date, the condemned may select lethal injection or lethal gas.
[c] Delaware authorizes lethal injection for those whose capital offense occurred after 6/13/86; for those whose offense occurred before that date, the condemned may select lethal injection or hanging.
[d] Arkansas authorizes lethal injection for those whose capital offense occurred on or after 7/4/83; for those whose offense occurred before that date, the condemned may select lethal injection or electrocution.
[e] New Hampshire authorizes hanging only if lethal injection cannot be given.
[f] Oklahoma authorizes electrocution if lethal injection is ever held to be unconstitutional, and firing squad if both lethal injection and electrocution are held unconstitutional.
[g] Wyoming authorizes lethal gas if lethal injection is ever held to be unconstitutional.
[h] Kentucky authorizes lethal injection for persons whose capital sentence was received on or after 3/31/98; for those sentenced before that date, the condemned may select lethal injection or electrocution.
[i] Tennessee authorizes lethal injection for those whose capital offense occurred after 12/31/98; those whose offense occurred before that date may select lethal injection or electrocution.

SOURCE: Tracy L. Snell, "Table 3. Method of execution, by State, 1999," in *Capital Punishment 1999*, Bureau of Justice Statistics, Washington, DC, December 2000

prohibits the use of "cruel and unusual punishment" in carrying out an execution. Although one person was pressed to death (placed between two hard surfaces, eventually dying from the pressure) during the Salem witchcraft trials and some rebellious blacks were burned at the stake during the early 1700s, these were exceptional cases.

For the most part, neither the colonies nor the United States ever used excessive methods of execution, such as drawing and quartering, burying alive, boiling in oil, sawing in half, or crucifixion. Throughout most of the nineteenth century civilians sentenced to death were hanged, while the military usually shot spies, traitors, and deserters.

The federal government currently authorizes the method of execution under two different laws. Crimes prosecuted under 28 CFR, Part 26, call for execution by lethal injection, while offenses covered by the Violent Crime Control and Law Enforcement Act of 1994 (Public Law 103-322, also known as the Federal Death Penalty Act of 1994) are referred to the state where the conviction occurred. In 1999, 34 states used lethal injection as the primary method of execution. Sixteen states authorized more than one method of execution—lethal injection and

an alternative method—generally letting the condemned prisoner choose. Five of these sixteen states however, specified which method must be used, depending on the date of sentencing. (See Table 5.4.)

In 1999 only Delaware, New Hampshire, and Washington authorized the use of the gallows to hang the condemned. (See Table 5.4.) The condemned person, however, was given the alternative of death by lethal injection. Washington hanged two murderers in 1993 and 1994, while Delaware hanged a prisoner in January 1996. It was Delaware's first hanging in 50 years and the nation's third since 1965.

Idaho, Oklahoma, and Utah authorized the firing squad method if the condemned prisoner refused lethal injection. Oklahoma, however, concerned about legal challenges to its method of execution, could resort to electrocution if lethal injection was ruled unconstitutional and to the firing squad method if both lethal injection and electrocution were deemed unconstitutional. In January 1996 Utah executed its first prisoner by firing squad in two decades, almost 20 years after Gary Gilmore asked the state of Utah to carry out his execution using this method in 1977.

Electrocution

At the end of the nineteenth century, alternating current (AC) electricity became one of the dominant symbols of progress. Many people thought this modern convenience would provide a more humane method of execution. In 1888 New York built the first electric chair, and in 1890 executed William Kemmler with the crude mechanism. In 1999, 11 states authorized electrocution as the method of execution. (See Table 5.4.) In January 2000 the Florida legislature replaced electrocution with lethal injection as the state's primary execution method.

Lethal Gas

In 1921 Nevada became the first state to authorize the use of lethal gas for capital punishment. In 1924 Nevada executed Jon Gee using cyanide gas. This was the first time lethal gas was used for execution in the United States. The Nevada statute called for the condemned man to be executed in his cell, without warning, while asleep. Prison officials, unable to figure out a practical way to carry out the execution, ended up constructing a gas chamber. In 1994 a U.S. district judge in California ruled that lethal gas was an inhumane method of execution, a decision upheld by the U.S. Ninth Circuit Court of Appeals in 1995. The U.S. Supreme Court declined ruling on the case and remanded it back to the circuit court in 1996. In 1999 four states still authorized the use of lethal gas. (See Table 5.4.) The last execution using lethal gas was carried out in Arizona in 1999.

Lethal Injection

Over the past several years, most states have adopted lethal injection as a more humane alternative to other methods of execution. In 1977 Oklahoma became the first state to authorize lethal injection. It was not until 1982, however, that lethal injection was first used, when Texas executed Charlie Brooks. Following several legal challenges, the Supreme Court, in *Heckler v. Chaney* (470 U.S. 821, 1985), upheld the use of lethal injection as a method of execution. As of 1999, 34 states authorized lethal injection, either solely or as an alternative to another method. (See Table 5.4.)

PUBLIC AND PRIVATE EXECUTIONS

Early arguments for capital punishment centered around the issue of deterrence—that the thought of the death penalty might dissuade a person from committing a crime. Executions used to be held in public as a warning to others. Many executions were conducted in a circus atmosphere, leading to opposition to such a public display. In 1828 the state of New York passed a law allowing county sheriffs to hold executions in private. The law, however, was not mandatory, and no sheriff took advantage of it. In 1830 Connecticut became the first state to

pass a law prohibiting all public executions. The Pennsylvania legislature followed suit in 1834.

In 1835 the New York legislature, noting that county sheriffs continued to conduct public executions, probably due to fear of adverse public reactions, passed a law requiring that all public executions be held within the prison walls. The law further required that 12 respectable citizens be chosen to witness the hanging and report on the execution through the state newspaper.

The idea of private executions did not catch on quickly. Even when executions were confined to jail courtyards, it was often not difficult to find a perch from which to watch the hanging. By the end of the 1800s private executions had become the norm, although many public executions still took place. In 1936 an African American man was hanged before a crowd of about 20,000 in Owensboro, Kentucky. Many people found the holiday atmosphere, recorded on wire service photographs, so abhorrent that the Kentucky legislature banned public executions two years later. The last public hanging occurred on May 21, 1937, in Galena, Missouri, when Roscoe "Red" Jackson was executed before about 1,500 spectators. Historians disagree about which of the two should be considered the last public hanging. Although tickets to Jackson's hanging were sold to the public, some to people from out of state, the execution was conducted within a fenced-in area. The hanging in Owensboro could be viewed by anyone. In 1938 Missouri banned public hangings, and required executions to be conducted in a gas chamber by prison officials at a state penitentiary.

Today some opponents of capital punishment support the idea of public executions. They feel that private executions hide the acts from the public, making them more acceptable. Others have recommended televised executions. On the other hand, some proponents of the death penalty support public executions in the hope that they might act as deterrents to future murderers.

Sister Helen Prejean, director of the National Coalition to Abolish the Death Penalty and author of the book *Dead Man Walking* (Random House, New York, 1993), supported the worldwide televised broadcast of Timothy McVeigh's execution. She believes that American are so far removed from actual executions that we fail to see the consequences of our actions—that we are retaliating against evil deeds by performing evil deeds ourselves.

WITNESSES TO EXECUTIONS

Today most states limit the number of official witnesses present at an execution. Witnesses usually include prison officials, reporters, and the condemned person's family and friends. In celebrated cases, however, such as that of the Rosenbergs, the convicted spies (1953), the notorious California killer Caryl Chessman (1960), and convicted Oklahoma City bomber Timothy McVeigh (2001), the audience, including numerous reporters, grew substantially.

Robert Jay Lifton and Greg Mitchell, in *Who Owns Death? Capital Punishment, The American Conscience, and the End of Executions* (William Morrow, New York, 2000), reported that the number of witnesses allowed at an execution varies from state to state. For example, Pennsylvania and North Carolina allow six official witnesses, New Hampshire allows twelve, and other states have different required numbers. The authors observe, however, that as the numbers of executions rise, some prison authorities have resorted to going on the Internet to recruit witnesses. Others telephone the public to invite them to witness executions.

Victims' Families as Witnesses

The National Center for Victims of Crime (NCVC; Washington, D.C.) reported in *FYI: Rights of Survivors of Homicide* (1999) that, as of December 1998, the laws of 13 states—Alabama, Arkansas, California, Delaware, Kentucky, Louisiana, Mississippi, Nevada, Ohio, Oklahoma, South Carolina, Tennessee, and Washington—allowed victims' families to be present at executions.

According to the NCVC, the statutes of the different states vary in their procedural requirements, which victims' relatives have to follow in order to request notification and/or attendance. For example, the Nevada statute defines immediate family as those "who are related by blood, adoption or marriage, within the second degree of consanguinity (blood relationship) or affinity (relationship by marriage or adoption rather than by blood)." The victims' relatives may write the director of the prison department if they wish notification of the execution. Requests to view the execution also have to be submitted in writing.

The Oklahoma statute puts no limit on the number of immediate family members who may view the execution. Each family member has to be 18 years or older and may be "the spouse, a child by birth or adoption, a stepchild, a parent, a grandparent, or a sibling of the deceased victim." The family views the execution in an area separate from the other witnesses. If a separate room for direct viewing is not available, a closed-circuit television is provided. On the other hand, in Delaware and Louisiana, only a single family member or representative is allowed to attend the execution.

Seven other states—Florida, Illinois, Montana, North Carolina, Texas, Utah, and Virginia—allow victims' families to be present at executions by policy. Only one state, New Jersey, prohibits "any person who is related by either blood or marriage to the sentenced person or to the victim to be present at the execution."

Televising Executions

Timothy McVeigh was sentenced to die in 2001 for the 1995 Oklahoma City bombing. In April 2001 the Gallup Poll asked the American public if they thought the execution of Timothy McVeigh (initially set for May 16, 2001) should be televised. Of those polled, 43 percent indicated that they thought it should not be televised at all and 39 percent thought it should be televised only on closed-circuit television for the victims' families to watch. Very few people indicated that they thought the execution should be televised to the general public—only 17 percent.

The poll also asked if Americans would watch McVeigh's execution if it were nationally televised. Three-quarters (76 percent) of the respondents said they would not watch, while nearly one-quarter (23 percent) indicated they would watch. When asked, however, if they would watch if a family member had been a victim of the bombing, an additional 21 percent (for a total of 44 percent) said they would watch. Over half (52 percent) of the American people indicated they would not watch the televised execution under any circumstance. Of those polled, more men (52 percent) than women (37 percent) said they would watch the execution.

McVeigh's death sentence raised the question of how the prison facility would accommodate the hundreds of victims' relatives who would wish to witness the execution. Over 250 victims and family members requested to view the execution. On June 11, 2001, the day of the execution, 10 survivors of the bombing and members of victims' families chosen by lottery watched McVeigh die in Terre Haute, Indiana, behind tinted glass, unseen by the condemned. In addition, 10 journalists, 4 people selected by McVeigh, and several government officials witnessed the execution. Survivors and family members of the victims not chosen by lottery were allowed to witness the execution on closed-circuit television in a federal prison in Oklahoma City.

Does Witnessing an Execution Bring Closure?

Some family members of murder victims feel that witnessing the death of their loved ones' murderers has helped put closure to their tragedy. In August 1996 state senator Brooks Douglass (R-OK) witnessed the execution of Steven Hatch, one of the men who killed his parents, raped his sister, and shot him in the back in 1979. Douglass wrote the state law allowing family members of victims to be present at executions. After Hatch's execution, Senator Douglass stated, "It wasn't revenge; it wasn't retribution. But for the first time since I was 16, I felt some closure. I felt like I had finally put the past behind me. I know it was the right thing." The second person (Glen Ake) convicted for Douglass's parents' murder is serving a life sentence. The Supreme Court, in *Ake v. Oklahoma* (470 U.S. 68, 1985), overturned the man's conviction. He received two life sentences on retrial.

Witnessing the execution of the condemned, however, does not necessarily bring closure. The mother of Baylee

Almon, the dead one-year-old infant who, pictured in the arms of a firefighter, became a symbol of the Oklahoma City tragedy, admitted she did not believe McVeigh's execution would ever bring closure.

Media Witnesses

For the first time, on February 23, 1996, California used lethal injection as a method of execution. The use of the gas chamber had been ruled cruel and unusual punishment in 1994. In April 1996 the Society of Professional Journalists' Northern California Chapter and the California First Amendment Coalition filed a lawsuit, claiming that the new public witness procedure (Procedure 770) violated their First Amendment right by unlawfully limiting media access. At William Bonin's execution that February, officials of the San Quentin Prison admitted the witnesses to the observation room only after the condemned had been strapped to the gurney and the intravenous (IV) solution had been inserted and was running. After several minutes, they were told the inmate was dead. The journalists argued that since they were not allowed to see the entire execution, they could not inform the public of the whole process.

Up until 1936, when California used hanging as a method of execution, witnesses could watch the execution from the moment the inmate ascended the gallows to the time the trapdoor fell. When lethal gas replaced hanging in 1937, witnesses viewed the execution from the time the inmate was escorted into the gas chamber until death was pronounced.

San Quentin Prison officials maintained that with lethal injection executions it could take the execution team as long as 20 minutes to prepare the condemned, compared to about a one-minute preparation during lethal gas executions. They were concerned that the prolonged "exposure to witnesses will increase the likelihood of an identification of execution team members." This would in turn subject the staff and their families to possible repercussions that might affect their safety, their job performance, and prison security.

In February 1997 the U.S. District Court for the Northern District of California, in *California First Amendment Coalition v. Calderon* (956 F. Supp. 883 [N.D. Cal. 1997]) ruled that "the First Amendment requires prison officials to allow the public and the media to witness lethal injection from the time just before the prisoner is strapped down to a gurney until after death." The court found that a long history of access to executions has helped inform the public "on whether the state's 'awesome' power to commit executions was properly exercised."

In July 1998 prison officials appealed their case (*Northern California Chapter v. Calderon* (No. 97-15493). The U.S. Court of Appeals for the Ninth Circuit ruled that Procedure 770 does not violate the First Amendment rights of the press or the public by not allowing the viewing of executions in their entirety. The case was remanded to the district court so it could determine "whether the Coalition has presented 'substantial evidence' that Procedure 770 represents an exaggerated response to Calderon's security and safety concerns."

On July 26, 2000, in *California First Amendment Coalition v. Woodford* (No. C-96-1291-VRW), U.S. District Judge Vaughn Walker concluded that the prison officials' practice of restricting witness observation was "an exaggerated response to [their own] safety concerns." The judge ruled that media witnesses could view the execution procedure from the time the condemned is brought into the execution room to the time he or she is pronounced dead.

CHAPTER 6

EXECUTIONS—HISTORICAL STATISTICS

NUMBER OF EXECUTIONS

Until 1930 the U.S. government did not keep any record of the number of people executed under the death penalty. According to the Bureau of Justice Statistics (BJS) of the U.S. Department of Justice, from 1930 through 2000 a total of 4,542 executions were conducted under civil authority in the United States. (See Figure 6.1.) Military authorities carried out an additional 160 executions between 1930 and 1961, the date of the last military execution.

The number of executions generally declined between the 1930s and the 1960s. In 1930, 155 executions took place, reaching a high of 199 in 1935. By 1950 executions were down to 82, further dropping to 56 in 1960. (See Figure 6.1.) In 1967 a 10-year moratorium (temporary suspension) of the death penalty began as states waited for the U.S. Supreme Court to determine a constitutionally acceptable procedure for carrying out the death penalty. The moratorium ended in 1976, but no execution occurred that year. The first execution following the moratorium occurred in Utah in 1977. In 1999, 98 inmates were put to death, the most in one year since the death penalty was reinstated. In 2000 the number of executions (85) declined 13 percent from the previous year. Between 1976 and 2000, 683 persons had been put to death. (See Figure 6.2.)

LOCATIONS OF EXECUTIONS

The Death Penalty Information Center (DPIC), which provides up-to-date information on capital punishment, reported that, from 1976 to October 25, 2001, approximately 4 out of every 5 executions (593 of 731 civil executions) took place in the South. Thirty-one states executed prisoners, and the federal government executed 2 men. The largest single number (252) of executions occurred in Texas, followed by Virginia (82), Missouri (52), Florida (51), and Oklahoma (45). Together, these five states carried out nearly 66 percent of all executions during this 25-year period. (See Table 6.1.)

FIGURE 6.1

Executions, 1930–2000

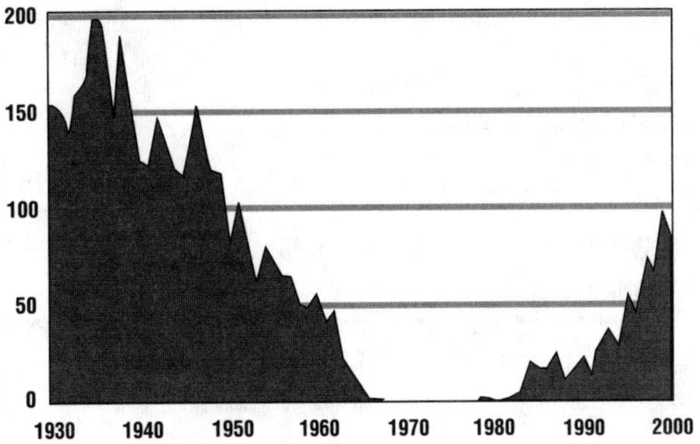

SOURCE: Tracy L. Snell, "Executions, 1930–2000," in *Capital Punishment 1999* [Online] http://www.ojp.usdoj.gov/bjs/glance/exe.htm [accessed October 9, 2001]

In 2000 Texas accounted for the largest number of executions (40), the most in a single year in any state in the nation's history, according to the DPIC. Texas was followed by Oklahoma (11), and Virginia (8). Florida executed 6 inmates, and Missouri executed 5. Alabama had 4 executions, Arizona had 3, and Arkansas had 2. Louisiana, South Carolina, North Carolina, Delaware, California, and Tennessee each put one prisoner to death. (See Table 6.1.) Tennessee executed its first inmate since 1960, while Arkansas put to death a female inmate, the first woman ever executed in that state.

GENDER

The NAACP Legal Defense & Educational Fund, Inc. (LDF), publishes the quarterly *Death Row USA,* which not only reports the number of death row inmates but also the number of inmates executed since January 1, 1976.

FIGURE 6.2

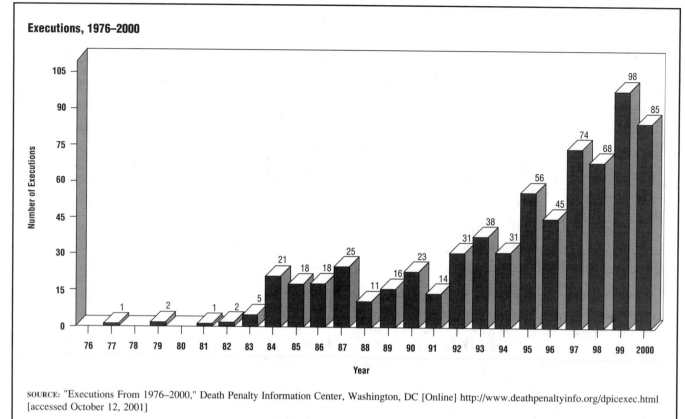

Executions, 1976–2000

SOURCE: "Executions From 1976–2000," Death Penalty Information Center, Washington, DC [Online] http://www.deathpenaltyinfo.org/dpicexec.html [accessed October 12, 2001]

TABLE 6.1

Number of executions by state, 1976–October 2001

(Last updated with execution in Georgia on October 25, 2001)

STATE	Total	2000	2001	STATE	Total	2000	2001
Texas	252	40	13	Indiana	9		2
Virginia	82	8	1	Utah	6		
Missouri	52	5	6	Mississippi	4		
Florida	51	6	1	Washington	4		1
Oklahoma	45	11	15	Maryland	3		
Louisiana	26	1		Nebraska	3		
S. Carolina	25	1		Pennsylvania	3		
Arkansas	24	2	1	Kentucky	2		
Alabama	23	4		Montana	2		
Georgia	23		1	Ohio	2		1
Arizona	22	3		Oregon	2		
N. Carolina	19	1	3	Colorado	1		
Delaware	13	1	2	Idaho	1		
Illinois	12			Tennessee	1	1	
California	9	1	1	Wyoming	1		
Nevada	9		1	*Federal*	2		2

SOURCE: "Number of Executions by State since 1976," Death Penalty Information Center, Washington, DC [Online] http://www.deathpenaltyinfo.org/dpicreg.html#region [accessed November 1, 2001]

The latest LDF report showed that, between 1976 and July 1, 2001, 715 men and 7 women had been executed. (See Table 6.2)

Professor Victor L. Streib of the Claude W. Pettit College of Law of the Ohio Northern University (Ada, Ohio) has been compiling information on female offenders and the death penalty since 1987. In *Death Penalty for Female Offenders: January 1, 1973, to December 31, 2000* (February 2001), Professor Streib reported that, as of December 31, 2000, 561 executions of women had been reported. Between 1900 and 2000 a total of 45 women were put to death. (See Table 6.3.)

In 1984 Margie Velma Barfield was executed in North Carolina for poisoning her boyfriend. Karla Faye Tucker of Texas was convicted of beating two people to death with a pickax, and in February 1998 Tucker was the first woman to be executed in Texas since the Civil War. (In 1863 Chipita Rodriguez, the last woman to be executed in Texas, was put to death by hanging.) In Florida, Judias Buenoano was convicted of poisoning her husband with arsenic. She was also convicted of drowning her paraplegic son and of trying to kill her boyfriend. In March 1998 Buenoano became the first woman to be executed in Florida since 1848, when a freed slave named Celia was hanged for killing her master.

In February 2000 Betty Lou Beets was executed in Texas for killing her fifth husband. Christina Marie Riggs, convicted of killing her two children, was executed in Arkansas in May 2000. The last woman put to death in Arkansas prior to Riggs—Lavinia Burnett—was hanged in 1845 for being an accessory to murder.

TABLE 6.2

Execution update (1976 to July 1, 2001)

Total number of executions since the 1976 reinstatement of capital punishment: 722

Year	76	77	78	79	80	81	82	83	84	85	86	87	88	89	90	91	92	93	94	95	96	97	98	99	00	01
Number of executions	0	1	0	2	0	1	2	5	21	18	18	25	11	16	23	14	31	38	31	56	45	74	68	98	85	39

Gender

Gender of defendants executed		Gender of victims	
total number 722		total number 928	
Female	7 (.97%)	Female	546 (48.58%)
Male	715 (99.03%)	Male	578 (51.42%)

Race

Race of defendants executed		Race of victims	
White	399 (55.26%)	White	908 (80.78%)
Black	258 (35.73%)	Black	155 (13.79%)
Latino/a	48 (6.65%)	Latino/a	38 (3.38%)
Native American	12 (1.66%)	Native American	2 (.18%)
Asian	5 (.69%)	Asian	21 (1.87%)

Defendant-victim racial combinations

	White Victim	Black Victim	Latino/a Victim	Asian Victim
White Defendant	373 (51.66%)	11 (1.52%)	4 (.55%)	3 (.42%)
Black Defendant	167 (23.13%)	73 (10.11%)	7 (.97%)	6 (.83%)
Latino/a Defendant	27 (3.74%)	2 (.28%)	16 (2.22%)	1 (.14%)
Asian Defendant	1 (.14%)	0 (0%)	0 (0%)	4 (.55%)
Native American Defendant	12 (1.66%)	0 (0%)	0 (0%)	0 (0%)
TOTAL:	569 (80.33%)	86 (11.91%)	27 (3.74%)	14 (1.94%)

Note: In addition, there were 15 defendants executed for the murders of multiple victims of different races. Of those, 8 defendants were white, 5 black and 2 Latino (2.08%).

SOURCE: "Execution Update (1976 to July 1, 2001)," in *Death Row USA, Summer 2001,* NAACP Legal Defense & Educational Fund, Inc., New York, NY, 2001

In January 2001 Wanda Jean Allen became the first woman to be executed in Oklahoma since 1903. She was convicted of killing her gay lover in 1988. In May 2001 Marilyn Kay Plantz, also of Oklahoma, was executed for the murder of her husband in 1988. Plantz hired two men to kill her husband. One of the men, William Bryson, was executed in June 2000 for the murder, and the other, Clinton McKimble, received a life sentence in exchange for his testimony against Plantz and Bryson.

RACE AND ETHNICITY

According to the BJS, more than half of those executed between 1930 and 1997 were black (52 percent), 47 percent were white, and 1 percent were categorized as "other" race. (See Table 6.4.) Data compiled by LDF show that, of the 722 prisoners executed from 1976 to July 1, 2001, over 55 percent were white (399), 35.7 percent were black (258), 6.6 percent were Hispanic (who may be of any race; 48), 1.7 percent were Native American (12), and less than 1 percent were Asian (5). (See Table 6.2.)

LDF maintains statistics not only on the race of the executed prisoners, but also on their victims. (See Table 6.2.) These types of statistics had been used in court cases to decide the constitutionality of the death penalty. The courts had to consider whether whites who murdered blacks got lighter sentences than blacks who murdered whites and whether those sentences violated the equal protection rights of the Constitution.

From 1976 through July 1, 2000, 51.7 percent of those executed were whites who had murdered other whites, while 1.5 percent were whites who had murdered black persons. About 23 percent of those executed were blacks who had murdered whites, and 10.1 percent were blacks who had murdered other blacks. (See Table 6.2.)

CRIMES WARRANTING THE DEATH PENALTY

The vast majority of executions from 1930 through 1997 were for murder (85.4 percent), followed by rape (10.6 percent). The remaining 1 percent of executions included 25 cases for armed robbery, 20 for kidnapping, 11 for burglary, 6 for sabotage, 6 for aggravated assault,

TABLE 6.3

Execution of female offenders by decade, 1900–2000

Decade	Executions: Women/Total	Jurisdictions
1900-09	3 / 1,200 (0.3%)	NY, OK, VT
1910-1919	1 / 1,050 (0.1%)	VA
1920-29	4 / 1,180 (0.3%)	LA, MS(2), NY
1930-39	11 / 1,700 (0.5%)	AL, IL, LA, MS, NY(3), OH, PA
1940-49	11 / 1,290 (0.9%)	CA(2), GA, LA, MS, NY, NC(2), PA(2), SC(2)
1950-59	8 / 716 (1.1%)	AL(2), CA, FED/MO, FED/NY, NY, OH(2)
1960-69	1 / 191 (0.5%)	CA (Elizabeth Duncan, 8-8-62)
1970-79	0 / 3 (0%)——	
1980-89	1 / 117 (0.9%)	NC (Velma Barfield, 11-2-84)
1990-99	2 / 478 (0.4%)	TX (Karla Faye Tucker, 2-3-98)
		FL (Judias Buenoano, 3-30-98)
2000[1]	2 / 85 (2.4%)	TX (Betty Lou Beets, 2-24-00)
		AR (Christina Marie Riggs, 5-2-00)
	45 / 8,010 (0.6%)	

[1] Information as of 12-31-00, omitting execution of Wanda Jean Allen in Oklahoma on 1-11-01

Victor L. Streib, "Table 1: Executions of Female Offenders by Decade, 1900–2000," in *Death Penalty for Female Offenders: January 1, 1973, to December 31, 2000* [Online] http://www.law.onu.edu/faculty/streib/femdeath.htm [accessed October 11, 2001]

and 2 for espionage. Since 1965 all those executed have been convicted on murder charges. (See Table 6.4.)

The last executions for rape occurred in 1964. Six executions for rape occurred in three states that year—Arkansas (1), Missouri (2), and Texas (3). In 1977 in *Coker v. Georgia* (433 U.S. 584), the Supreme Court ruled that rape did not warrant the death penalty. In December 1996, however, the Louisiana Supreme Court ruled that death is a just and constitutional punishment for the rape of a child under 12 years of age.

METHOD OF EXECUTION

Among the 598 prisoners executed between 1977 and 1999, most (438) received lethal injection, followed by electrocution (144). Eleven executions were carried out by lethal gas, 3 by hanging, and 2 by firing squad. Texas, the state with the largest number of prisoners executed, used lethal injection in all 199 cases. Virginia executed 48 inmates using lethal injection and 25 inmates using electrocution. Florida used electrocution to execute its 44 prisoners. (See Table 6.5.)

In 2000 lethal injection accounted for 4 of 5 (80 percent) executions. Of the 14 states that carried out executions, two states—Alabama (4) and Virginia (1)—used electrocution. (See Table 6.6.) While electrocution was the sole method of execution in Alabama, Virginia allowed the condemned prisoner to choose between lethal injection and the electric chair.

TABLE 6.4

Prisoners executed under civil authority, by race and offense, 1930–97

(- represents zero)

	Total				White				Black				Other			
	Total	Murder	Rape	Other offenses[a]	Total	Murder	Rape	Other offenses	Total	Murder	Rape	Other offenses	Total	Murder	Rape	Other offenses
1930-97	4,291	3,666	455	70	2,016	1,929	48	39	2,228	1,792	405	31	47	45	2	-
1997	74	74	-	-	45	45	-	-	27	27	-	-	2	2	-	-
1996	45	45	-	-	31	31	-	-	14	14	-	-	-	-	-	-
1995	56	56	-	-	33	33	-	-	22	22	-	-	1	1	-	-
1994	31	31	-	-	20	20	-	-	11	11	-	-	-	-	-	-
1993	38	38	-	-	23	23	-	-	14	14	-	-	1	1	-	-
1992	31	31	-	-	19	19	-	-	11	11	-	-	1	1	-	-
1991	14	14	-	-	7	7	-	-	7	7	-	-	-	-	-	-
1990	23	23	-	-	16	16	-	-	7	7	-	-	-	-	-	-
1989	16	16	-	-	8	8	-	-	8	8	-	-	-	-	-	-
1988	11	11	-	-	6	6	-	-	5	5	-	-	-	-	-	-
1987	25	25	-	-	13	13	-	-	12	12	-	-	-	-	-	-
1986	18	18	-	-	11	11	-	-	7	7	-	-	-	-	-	-
1985	18	18	-	-	11	11	-	-	7	7	-	-	-	-	-	-
1984	21	21	-	-	13	13	-	-	8	8	-	-	-	-	-	-
1983	5	5	-	-	4	4	-	-	1	1	-	-	-	-	-	-
1982	2	2	-	-	1	1	-	-	1	1	-	-	-	-	-	-
1981	1	1	-	-	1	1	-	-	-	-	-	-	-	-	-	-
1980	-	-	-	-	-	-	-	-	-	-	-	-	-	-	-	-
1979	2	2	-	-	2	2	-	-	-	-	-	-	-	-	-	-
1978	-	-	-	-	-	-	-	-	-	-	-	-	-	-	-	-
1977[b]	1	1	-	-	1	1	-	-	-	-	-	-	-	-	-	-
1967	2	2	-	-	1	1	-	-	1	1	-	-	-	-	-	-
1966	1	1	-	-	1	1	-	-	-	-	-	-	-	-	-	-
1965	7	7	-	-	6	6	-	-	1	1	-	-	-	-	-	-
1964	15	9	6	-	8	5	3	-	7	4	3	-	-	-	-	-
1963	21	18	2	1	13	12	-	1	8	6	2	-	-	-	-	-
1962	47	41	4	2	28	26	2	-	19	15	2	2	-	-	-	-
1961	42	33	8	1	20	18	1	1	22	15	7	-	-	-	-	-
1960	56	44	8	4	21	18	-	3	35	26	8	1	-	-	-	-
1959	49	41	8	-	16	15	1	-	33	26	7	-	-	-	-	-
1958	49	41	7	1	20	20	-	-	28	20	7	1	1	1	-	-
1957	65	54	10	1	34	32	2	-	31	22	8	1	-	-	-	-
1956	65	52	12	1	21	20	-	1	43	31	12	-	1	1	-	-
1955	76	65	7	4	44	41	1	2	32	24	6	2	-	-	-	-
1954	81	71	9	1	38	37	1	-	42	33	8	1	1	1	-	-
1953	62	51	7	4	30	25	1	4	31	25	6	-	1	1	-	-
1952	83	71	12	-	36	35	1	-	47	36	11	-	-	-	-	-
1951	105	87	17	1	57	55	2	-	47	31	15	1	1	1	-	-
1950	82	68	13	1	40	36	4	-	42	32	9	1	-	-	-	-
1949	119	107	10	2	50	49	-	1	67	56	10	1	2	2	-	-
1948	119	95	22	2	35	32	1	2	82	61	21	-	2	2	-	-
1947	153	129	23	1	42	40	2	-	111	89	21	1	-	-	-	-
1946	131	107	22	2	46	45	-	1	84	61	22	1	1	1	-	-
1945	117	90	26	1	41	37	4	-	75	52	22	1	1	1	-	-
1944	120	96	24	-	47	45	2	-	70	48	22	-	3	3	-	-
1943	131	118	13	-	54	54	-	-	74	63	11	-	3	1	2	-
1942	147	115	25	7	67	57	4	6	80	58	21	1	-	-	-	-
1941	123	102	20	1	59	55	4	-	63	46	16	1	1	1	-	-
1940	124	105	15	4	49	44	2	3	75	61	13	1	-	-	-	-
1939	160	145	12	3	80	79	-	1	77	63	12	2	3	3	-	-
1938	190	154	25	11	96	89	1	6	92	63	24	5	2	2	-	-
1937	147	133	13	1	69	67	2	-	74	62	11	1	4	4	-	-
1936	195	181	10	4	92	86	2	4	101	93	8	-	2	2	-	-
1935	199	184	13	2	119	115	2	2	77	66	11	-	3	3	-	-
1934	168	154	14	-	65	64	1	-	102	89	13	-	1	1	-	-
1933	160	151	7	2	77	75	1	1	81	74	6	1	2	2	-	-
1932	140	128	10	2	62	62	-	-	75	63	10	2	3	3	-	-
1931	153	137	15	1	77	76	1	-	72	57	14	1	4	4	-	-
1930	155	147	6	2	90	90	-	-	65	57	6	2	-	-	-	-

[a] Includes 25 executed for armed robbery, 20 for kidnaping, 11 for burglary, 6 for sabotage, 6 for aggravated assault, and 2 for espionage.
[b] There were no executions from 1968 through 1976.

SOURCE: Kathleen Maguire and Ann L. Pastore, eds., "Table 6.95: Prisoners executed under civil authority," in *Sourcebook of Criminal Justice Statistics 1999*, Bureau of Justice Statistics, Washington, DC, 2000

TABLE 6.5

Executions by state and method, 1977–99

State	Number executed	Lethal injection	Electro-cution	Lethal gas	Hanging	Firing squad
Total	598	438	144	11	3	2
Alabama	19	0	19	0	0	0
Arizona	19	17	0	2	0	0
Arkansas	21	20	1	0	0	0
California	7	5	0	2	0	0
Colorado	1	1	0	0	0	0
Delaware	10	9	0	0	1	0
Florida	44	0	44	0	0	0
Georgia	23	0	23	0	0	0
Idaho	1	1	0	0	0	0
Illinois	12	12	0	0	0	0
Indiana	7	4	3	0	0	0
Kentucky	2	1	1	0	0	0
Louisiana	25	5	20	0	0	0
Maryland	3	3	0	0	0	0
Mississippi	4	0	0	4	0	0
Missouri	41	41	0	0	0	0
Montana	2	2	0	0	0	0
Nebraska	3	0	3	0	0	0
Nevada	8	7	0	1	0	0
North Carolina	15	13	0	2	0	0
Ohio	1	1	0	0	0	0
Oklahoma	19	19	0	0	0	0
Oregon	2	2	0	0	0	0
Pennsylvania	3	3	0	0	0	0
South Carolina	24	19	5	0	0	0
Texas	199	199	0	0	0	0
Utah	6	4	0	0	0	2
Virginia	73	48	25	0	0	0
Washington	3	1	0	0	2	0
Wyoming	1	1	0	0	0	0

SOURCE: Tracy L. Snell, "Executions, by State and method, 1977–99," in *Capital Punishment 1999,* Bureau of Justice Statistics, Washington, DC, December 2000

TABLE 6.6

Advance count of executions, 2000

State	Number of executions	Method used
Texas	40	Lethal injection
Oklahoma	11	Lethal injection
Virginia	8	Lethal injection*
Florida	6	Lethal injection
Missouri	5	Lethal injection
Alabama	4	Electrocution
Arizona	3	Lethal injection
Arkansas	2	Lethal injection
Delaware	1	Lethal injection
Louisiana	1	Lethal injection
North Carolina	1	Lethal injection
South Carolina	1	Lethal injection
Tennessee	1	Lethal injection
California	1	Lethal injection
Total	85	

*Virginia executed 1 person by electrocution.

SOURCE: Tracy L. Snell, "Advance count of executions, : January 1, 2000–December 31, 2000," in *Capital Punishment 1999,* Bureau of Justice Statistics, Washington, DC, December 2000

CHAPTER 7

UNDER SENTENCE OF DEATH

AN EVER-INCREASING NUMBER

At year-end 1999 the Bureau of Justice Statistics (BJS) reported a total of 3,527 prisoners held under sentence of death in federal and state prisons—a nearly 2 percent increase over the previous year. The number of prisoners on death row has been increasing since 1976. (See Figure 7.1.)

The continually growing number of prisoners on death row reflects a rise in the number of death sentences being imposed. Moreover, just a small number of prisoners are removed from death row for reasons other than execution—resentencing, retrial, commutation (replacement of the death sentence with a lesser sentence), or death while awaiting execution (natural death, murder, or suicide).

From 1973 to 1999 a total of 6,707 persons received the death sentence. Of these, 598 were executed, 205 died while awaiting execution, 2,193 had their sentences or convictions overturned, and 154 had their sentences commuted. As of December 31, 1999, over half (52.6 percent, or 3,527 inmates) were still on death row awaiting execution. (See Table 7.1.)

Between January 1 and December 31, 1999, 32 states received 271 prisoners under sentence of death. The U.S. Bureau of Prisons received one inmate. All 272 prisoners had been convicted of murder. Eighty-eight prisoners from 21 states had their death sentences overturned or removed. Florida reported the most numbers (22) of vacated (annulled) capital sentences.

In summer 2001 the NAACP Legal Defense & Educational Fund, Inc. (LDF), reported 3,717 prisoners under sentence of death. (See Table 7.2.) The LDF statistics include persons who have been sentenced to death and are awaiting transfer to prison, while the BJS counts only those on death row awaiting execution.

GEOGRAPHIC DISTRIBUTION

As of July 1, 2001, more than half (53.9 percent) of the state prisoners awaiting execution were in the South

FIGURE 7.1

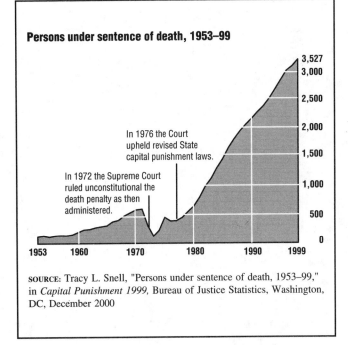

Persons under sentence of death, 1953–99

In 1976 the Court upheld revised State capital punishment laws.

In 1972 the Supreme Court ruled unconstitutional the death penalty as then administered.

SOURCE: Tracy L. Snell, "Persons under sentence of death, 1953–99," in *Capital Punishment 1999*, Bureau of Justice Statistics, Washington, DC, December 2000

(15 states). An additional 24.8 percent were in the 11 Western states, and 13.8 percent were in the 7 Midwestern states. The Northeastern states of Connecticut, New Jersey, New York, and Pennsylvania accounted for the remaining 7.5 percent. About 39 percent of the condemned were awaiting execution in three states—California (600), Texas (454), and Florida (383). Of the 38 jurisdictions with statutes authorizing the death penalty, only New Hampshire had no one under a capital sentence, while Montana, New York, New Mexico, South Dakota, Kansas, and Wyoming had six or fewer. (See Table 7.2.)

RACE

As of July 1, 2001, 46 percent of all death row inmates were white, and 43 percent were black. Hispanic

TABLE 7.1

Number sentenced to death and number of removals, by jurisdiction and reason for removal, 1973–99

State	Total sentenced to death, 1973-99	Number of removals, 1973-99					Under sentence of death, 12/31/99
		Executed	Died	Sentence or conviction overturned	Sentence commuted	Other removals	
U.S. total	6,707	598	205	2,193	154	30	3,527
Federal	22	0	0	2	0	0	20
Alabama	314	19	13	100	2	0	180
Arizona	223	19	9	73	5	1	116
Arkansas	94	21	1	30	2	0	40
California	722	7	31	116	15	0	553
Colorado	17	1	1	10	1	0	4
Connecticut	7	0	0	1	0	0	6
Delaware	40	10	0	13	0	0	17
Florida	821	44	29	363	18	2	365
Georgia	289	23	9	134	6	1	116
Idaho	37	1	1	12	2	0	21
Illinois	273	12	9	85	3	8	156
Indiana	92	7	1	37	2	2	43
Kansas	3	0	0	0	0	0	3
Kentucky	71	2	2	27	1	0	39
Louisiana	196	25	3	76	6	1	85
Maryland	48	3	1	24	3	0	17
Massachusetts	4	0	0	2	2	0	0
Mississippi	163	4	2	94	0	3	60
Missouri	158	41	7	25	2	0	83
Montana	15	2	0	6	1	0	6
Nebraska	24	3	2	8	2	0	9
Nevada	127	8	5	25	3	0	86
New Jersey	48	0	3	23	0	0	14
New Mexico	26	0	1	16	5	8	4
New York	8	0	0	3	0	0	5
North Carolina	468	15	9	237	5	0	202
Ohio	351	1	9	133	9	0	199
Oklahoma	294	19	7	128	1	0	139
Oregon	46	2	1	18	0	0	25
Pennsylvania	323	3	10	80	0	0	230
Rhode Island	2	0	0	2	0	0	0
South Carolina	163	24	4	67	3	0	65
South Dakota	3	0	0	0	0	0	3
Tennessee	192	0	9	81	0	2	100
Texas	829	199	21	103	45	1	460
Utah	26	6	0	9	1	0	10
Virginia	123	73	3	6	9	1	31
Washington	34	3	1	17	0	1	13
Wyoming	11	1	1	7	0	0	2
Percent	100%	8.9%	3.1%	32.7%	2.3%	0.4%	52.6%

Note: For those persons sentenced to death more than once, the numbers are based on the most recent death sentence.

SOURCE: Tracy L. Snell, "Number sentenced to death and number of removals, by jurisdiction and reason for removal, 1973–99," in *Capital Punishment 1999*, Bureau of Justice Statistics, Washington, DC, December 2000

prisoners (who may be of any race), whose ethnicity was known, accounted for 9 percent of those under a death sentence. Native Americans and Asians represented about 1 percent each of death row inmates. More than 8 in 10 (84 percent) of the Hispanics on death row were imprisoned in five states—California, Texas, Florida, Arizona, and Pennsylvania. (See Table 7.2.)

GENDER

As of July 1, 2001, nearly 99 percent (3,663) of all prisoners under sentence of death were males. Fifty-four females were awaiting execution.

In *Death Penalty for Female Offenders: January 1, 1973, to December 31, 2000* (February 2001), Professor Victor L. Streib of the Claude W. Pettit College of Law of the Ohio Northern University (Ada, OH) reported on female offenders on death row. Between 1973 and 2000, 137 females had been sentenced to death in the United States. Nearly two-thirds (65 percent) were white, and one-fourth (26 percent) were black. Eight women were Hispanic, and four were Native American. Of the 23 states with women on death row, North Carolina, Florida, California, Texas, and Ohio accounted for almost half (49 percent) of female inmates sentenced to death. (See Table 7.3.)

TABLE 7.2

Death row prisoners by state and ethnicity, July 1, 2001

State	Total	Black		White		Latino/a		Native American		Asian		Unknown	
Alabama	187	86	46%	99	53%	1	.5%	00	---	1	.5%	0	---
Arizona	127	16	13%	88	69%	19	15%	3	2%	1	.8%	0	---
Arkansas	39	23	59%	15	38%	1	3%	0	---	0	---	0	---
California	600	218	36%	240	40%	112	19%	14	2%	16	3%	0	---
Colorado	7	2	29%	2	29%	2	29%	0	---	1	14%	0	---
Connecticut	7	3	43%	3	43%	1	14%	0	---	0	---	0	---
Delaware	16	9	56%	7	44%	0	---	0	---	0	---	0	---
Florida	383	135	35%	210	55%	35	9%	1	.3%	2	.5%	0	---
Georgia	131	62	47%	66	50%	2	2%	0	---	1	.8%	0	---
Idaho	21	0	---	21	100%	0	---	0	---	0	---	0	---
Illinois	175	111	63%	54	31%	10	6%	0	---	0	---	0	---
Indiana	40	13	33%	27	68%	0	---	0	---	0	---	0	---
Kansas	4	0	---	4	100%	0	---	0	---	0	---	0	---
Kentucky	43	10	23%	32	74%	1	2%	0	---	0	---	0	---
Louisiana	92	62	67%	27	30%	2	2%	0	---	1	1%	0	---
Maryland	15	10	67%	5	33%	0	---	0	---	0	---	0	---
Mississippi	67	37	55%	30	45%	0	---	0	---	0	---	0	---
Missouri	75	32	43%	43	57%	0	---	0	---	0	---	0	---
Montana	6	0	---	6	100%	0	---	0	---	0	---	0	---
Nebraska	9	0	---	7	78%	1	11%	1	11%	0	---	0	---
Nevada	89	35	39%	43	48%	10	11%	0	---	1	1%	0	---
New Jersey	18	8	44%	10	56%	0	---	0	---	0	---	0	---
New Mexico	5	0	---	4	80%	1	20%	0	---	0	---	0	---
New York	6	2	33%	3	50%	1	17%	0	---	0	---	0	---
North Carolina	239	133	56%	89	37%	4	2%	12	5%	1	.4%	0	---
Ohio	202	100	50%	97	48%	2	1%	2	1%	1	.5%	0	---
Oklahoma	123	40	33%	68	55%	4	3%	9	7%	2	2%	0	---
Oregon	29	1	3%	24	83%	2	7%	1	3%	0	---	1	3%
Pennsylvania	246	155	63%	75	30%	14	6%	0	---	2	.8%	0	---
South Carolina	74	35	47%	39	53%	0	---	0	---	0	---	0	---
South Dakota	5	0	---	5	100%	0	---	0	---	0	---	0	---
Tennessee	102	37	36%	59	58%	2	2%	2	2%	2	2%	0	---
Texas	454	190	42%	157	35%	102	22%	0	---	5	1%	0	---
Utah	11	2	18%	6	55%	2	18%	1	9%	0	---	0	---
Virginia	29	12	41%	16	55%	1	3%	0	---	0	---	0	---
Washington	18	5	28%	12	67%	0	---	0	---	1	6%	0	---
Wyoming	2	0	---	2	100%	0	---	0	---	0	---	0	---
US Government	23	17	74%	3	13%	2	9%	0	---	1	4%	0	---
Military	7	5	71%	1	14%	0	---	0	---	1	14%	0	---
TOTAL	**3726**	**1606**	**43%**	**1699**	**46%**	**334**	**9%**	**46**	**1%**	**40**	**1%**	**1**	**.03%**

Note: 8 prisoners were sentenced to death in more than one state, 1 of them in 3 states. They are included in the chart above for each state in which they were sentenced to death, but the total number of prisoners under sentence of death is 3717.

SOURCE: "Summary of State Lists of Prisoners on Death Row (As of July 1, 2001)," in *Death Row USA, Summer 2001*, NAACP Legal Defense & Educational Fund, Inc., New York, NY, 2001

CHARACTERISTICS OF PRISONERS

The BJS collects additional information on death row inmates. In 1999 the median age of those under sentence of death was 37 years (this means that half of the inmates were younger than 37 and half were older than that age). About 7 in 10 (68.4 percent) were ages 25 to 44, and 4 of 10 (36.8 percent) were between 30 and 39 years old. Sixteen inmates were under age 20, and 80 inmates were over 60 years. The youngest inmate was 18 years old and was sentenced to death in November 1999. The oldest was 84, having been sentenced in June 1983 at the age of 68. Almost half (49.5 percent) of all inmates under sentence of death were ages 20 to 29 when they were arrested for their capital offense. (See Table 7.4.)

Among those for whom information about education was available as of December 31, 1999, more than half (51.6 percent) had not been graduated from high school, and only 1 in 10 had any college education. The median level of education was the eleventh grade. Most had never married (53 percent), and about one-fourth (24 percent) were separated, divorced, or widowed. (See Table 7.5.)

CRIMINAL HISTORY OF DEATH ROW INMATES

The BJS reported that, as of December 31, 1999, among prisoners on death row, nearly two-thirds (64.1 percent) had prior felony convictions. Almost 1 in 11 (8.4 percent) had been previously convicted of murder or manslaughter. About 2 of 5 (40.1 percent) had an active criminal justice record at the time of the murder for which they were condemned. Almost half of those with an active criminal record were out on parole when they committed their crime, and one-fourth were on probation. The others

TABLE 7.3

Death sentences for female offenders, 1973–2000

Rank	Sentencing State	White	Black	Latin	American Indian	Total Female Sentences
			Race of Offender			
1	North Carolina	10	4	0	2	16
2	Florida	11	3	1	0	15
3	California	7	3	4	0	14
4	Texas	10	3	0	0	13
5	Ohio	3	6	0	0	9
6	Alabama	6	2	0	0	8
7	Illinois	1	4	2	0	7
7	Mississippi	5	2	0	0	7
7	Oklahoma	6	1	0	0	7
10	Georgia	5	1	0	0	6
11	Missouri	4	0	1	0	5
11	Pennsylvania	2	3	0	0	5
13	Indiana	2	2	0	0	4
14	Kentucky	3	0	0	0	3
14	Maryland	1	0	0	2	3
16	Arizona	2	0	0	0	2
16	Arkansas	2	0	0	0	2
16	Idaho	2	0	0	0	2
16	Louisiana	1	1	0	0	2
16	Nevada	1	1	0	0	2
16	New Jersey	2	0	0	0	2
16	Tennessee	2	0	0	0	2
23	South Carolina	1	0	0	0	1
Totals		**89**	**36**	**8**	**4**	**137**

SOURCE: Victor L. Streib, "Table 3: State-by-State Breakdown of Death Sentences for Female Offenders, January 1, 1973, to December 31, 2000," in *Death Penalty for Female Offenders: January 1, 1973, to December 31, 2000* [Online] http://www.law.onu.edu/faculty/streib/femdeath.htm [accessed October 11, 2001]

TABLE 7.4

Age at time of arrest for capital offense and age of prisoners under death sentence, December 31, 1999

Age	At time of arrest		On December 31, 1999	
	Number*	Percent	Number	Percent
Total number under sentence of death on 12/31/99	3,232	100 %	3,527	100 %
17 or younger	80	2.5	0	
18-19	343	10.6	16	0.5
20-24	871	26.9	251	7.1
25-29	729	22.6	514	14.6
30-34	534	16.5	594	16.8
35-39	341	10.6	707	20.0
40-44	170	5.3	601	17.0
45-49	101	3.1	370	10.5
50-54	36	1.1	280	7.9
55-59	16	0.5	114	3.2
60 or older	11	0.3	80	2.3
Mean age	28 yrs		38 yrs	
Median age	27 yrs		37 yrs	

Note: The youngest person under sentence of death was a black male in Texas, born in December 1981 and sentenced to death in November 1999. The oldest person under sentence of death was a white male in Arizona, born in September 1915 and sentenced to death in June 1983.

* Excludes 295 inmates for whom the date of arrest for capital offense was not available.

SOURCE: Tracy L. Snell, "Table 8. Age at time of arrest for capital offense and age of prisoners under sentence of death at yearend 1999," in *Capital Punishment 1999,* Bureau of Justice Statistics, Washington, DC, December 2000

had charges pending, were in prison, had escaped from prison, or had some other criminal justice status. (See Table 7.6.)

Criminal history patterns varied slightly by race and Hispanic origin. Blacks (68.3 percent) had somewhat more prior felony convictions than whites (61.9 percent) and Hispanics (58.3 percent). Blacks (8.7 percent) and whites (8.3 percent) had a higher proportion of prior homicide convictions than Hispanics (6.9 percent). Hispanics (23.8 percent) and blacks (19.2 percent) were more likely than whites (15.5 percent) to be on parole when arrested for their capital crime. (See Table 7.6.)

Since 1988 the BJS has been collecting information on the number of death sentences imposed on the offenders entering the prison system. Among the 3,448 individuals admitted under sentence of death from 1988 to 1999, nearly 1 in 7 (15 percent) was admitted with two or more death sentences.

A LONG WAIT

It can be a long wait on death row. Between 1977 and 1999 a total of 6,365 offenders had been under a death sentence for varying periods. Of these, 598 (9.4 percent) were actually executed. Another 2,240 (35.2 percent)

were removed from under a death sentence because of appellate court decisions and reviews or commutations, or had died while awaiting execution.

For those executed from 1977 to 1999, the average time between the imposition of the most recent death sentence and the execution was about 9 years and 10 months. White prisoners had waited an average of 9.5 years, and black prisoners, 10.5 years, before their execution. In 1999 the 98 inmates executed were under sentence of death for an average of 11 years and 11 months. (See Table 7.7.)

Of the 3,527 persons under sentence of death on December 31, 1999, 58 (1.6 percent) were sentenced prior to 1980. Florida, Tennessee, Illinois, Indiana, and Idaho housed the inmates who had served the longest among all condemned inmates. On the other hand, South Dakota had no inmates sentenced to death prior to 1992; New Mexico, none prior to 1994; and Wyoming, New York, and Kansas, none prior to 1998. By year-end 1999 the average time spent under sentence of death by the condemned inmates still on death row was 7 years and 7 months, up 3 months from that of 1998. (See Table 7.8.)

GETTING OFF DEATH ROW

Prisoners can get off death row by different means. Table 7.9 breaks down the outcome of the sentences for the 6,707 inmates condemned to death for the period 1973 through 1999. During this period, 598 (8.9 percent) were executed. One-third (2,193 inmates) of those who left death row were sentenced in states where the death penalty was later overturned or had their sentences or convictions overturned by an appellate or higher court. Some (154) had their sentences commuted, while another 205 died while awaiting execution.

Using a single year as an example, of the 319 persons sentenced to death in 1995, 10 were executed, 7 died while in confinement, and 32 had their convictions or sentences overturned. (Conviction and sentencing are two separate trials under the two-part system required in death penalty cases.) Of these prisoners sentenced to death in 1995, 269 remained on death row as of December 31, 1999. (See Table 7.9.)

THE APPEALS PROCESS IN CAPITAL CASES

The appeals process in capital cases varies slightly from state to state but generally consists of similar procedures. The first step is the direct appeal in which the death sentence is automatically appealed from the trial court to the highest court of the state with criminal jurisdiction. The highest court of the state may be either the state supreme court or the highest court of criminal appeals. The state high court evaluates the trial court records for constitutional or legal errors. If the high court upholds the conviction and sentence, the defendant seeks *certiorari* in the U.S. Supreme Court. The *certiorari* is a petition to the Supreme Court to review the issues brought up in the direct appeal. If the Supreme Court denies *certiorari*, the trial court's ruling stands.

If the direct appeal is denied, the inmate may then seek state *habeas corpus* appeals, starting from the trial judge and going all the way to the state's highest court. This appeal differs from the direct appeal in that the condemned may raise issues that were not and could not have been raised during the direct appeal. These issues include the incompetence of the defense lawyer, jury bias, or the suppression of evidence by police or prosecution. If the state review is denied, the condemned can appeal to the U.S. Supreme Court.

A death row inmate who has exhausted all state appeals can file a petition for a federal *habeas corpus* review on grounds of violation of his or her constitutional rights. The right may involve a violation of the Eighth Amendment to the Constitution (the ban against cruel and unusual punishment), the Fourteenth Amendment (the right to due process), and the Sixth Amendment (the right to have the assistance of counsel for defense). The inmate files the appeal with the U.S. district court in the state in which he or she was convicted. If the district court denies the appeal, the inmate can proceed to the U.S. Circuit Court of Appeals. Finally, if the circuit court denies the

TABLE 7.5

Demographic characteristics of prisoners under death sentence, 1999

Characteristic	Prisoners under sentence of death, 1999		
	Yearend	Admissions	Removals
Total number under sentence of death	3,527	272	210
Gender			
Male	98.6%	98.9%	99.0%
Female	1.4	1.1	1.0
Race			
White	55.2%	57.7%	60.0%
Black	42.9	38.2	37.6
Other*	1.8	4.0	2.4
Hispanic origin			
Hispanic	10.2%	14.9%	11.6%
Non-Hispanic	89.8	85.1	88.4
Education			
8th grade or less	13.9%	14.2%	20.3%
9th-11th grade	37.7	38.6	38.5
High school graduate/GED	38.2	38.6	33.5
Any college	10.1	8.6	7.7
Median	11th	11th	11th
Marital status			
Married	22.9%	16.5%	31.7%
Divorced/separated	21.2	24.5	19.6
Widowed	2.8	3.8	2.6
Never married	53.0	55.3	46.0

Note: Calculations are based on those cases for which data were reported. Missing data by category were as follows:

	Yearend	Admissions	Removals
Hispanic origin	332	51	11
Education	499	39	28
Marital status	341	35	21

*At yearend 1998, "other" consisted of 27 American Indians, 20 Asians, and 12 self-identified Hispanics. During 1999, 4 American Indians, 6 Asians, and 1 self-identified Hispanic were admitted; 3 American Indians and 2 Asians were removed.

SOURCE: Tracy L. Snell, "Table 7. Demographic characteristics of prisoners under sentence of death, 1999," in *Capital Punishment 1999,* Bureau of Justice Statistics, Washington, DC, December 2000

appeal, the condemned can ask the U.S. Supreme Court for a *certiorari* review.

Automatic Review of Death Sentences

At year-end 1999, among the 38 states with capital punishment statutes, 36 states provided for automatic review of all death sentences regardless of the defendant's wishes. Of the remaining two states, South Carolina allowed the defendant to dispense with the sentence review if the court found him competent to decide for himself (*State v. Torrence,* 473 S.E.2d. 703 [S.C. 1996]). In Arkansas the state supreme court reviewed the trial court record for possible errors (*State v. Robbins,* 339 Ark. 379, 5 S.W.3d. 51 [1999]). The federal death penalty procedures, on the other hand, did not provide for automatic review after a death sentence was imposed.

Although most of the 36 states authorized an automatic review of both conviction and sentence, Idaho,

TABLE 7.6

Criminal history of prisoners under death sentence, 1999

	Prisoners under sentence of death							
	Number				Percent[a]			
	All[b]	White	Black	Hispanic	All[b]	White	Black	Hispanic
U.S. total	3,527	1,651	1,500	325	100%	100%	100%	100%
Prior felony convictions								
Yes	2,085	949	939	172	64.1%	61.9%	68.3%	58.3%
No	1,166	584	436	123	35.9	38.1	31.7	41.7
Not reported	276							
Prior homicide convictions								
Yes	290	134	128	22	8.4%	8.3%	8.7%	6.9%
No	3,166	1,487	1,337	297	91.6	91.7	91.3	93.1
Not reported	71							
Legal status at time of capital offense								
Charges pending	228	127	90	11	7.4%	8.6%	6.9%	4.0%
Probation	311	134	144	27	10.0	9.1	11.1	9.9
Parole	554	229	250	65	17.9	15.5	19.2	23.8
Prison escapee	39	25	10	3	1.3	1.7	0.8	1.1
Incarcerated	86	36	44	5	2.8	2.4	3.4	1.8
Other status	21	11	8	1	0.7	0.7	0.6	0.4
None	1,860	916	755	161	60.0	62.0	58.0	59.0
Not reported	428							

[a] Percentages are based on those offenders for whom data were reported.
Detail may not add to total because of rounding.
[b] Includes persons of other races.

SOURCE: Tracy L. Snell, "Table 9. Criminal history profile of prisoners under sentence of death, by race and Hispanic origin, 1999," in *Capital Punishment 1999*, Bureau of Justice Statistics, Washington, DC, December 2000

TABLE 7.7

Number of executions and average time under death sentence, 1977–99

Year of execution	Number executed			Average elapsed time from sentence to execution for:		
	All races*	White	Black	All races*	White	Black
Total	598	374	213	118 mo	114 mo	126 mo
1977-83	11	9	2	51 mo	49 mo	58 mo
1984	21	13	8	74	76	71
1985	18	11	7	71	65	80
1986	18	11	7	87	78	102
1987	25	13	12	86	78	96
1888	11	6	5	80	72	89
1989	16	8	8	95	78	112
1990	23	16	7	95	97	91
1991	14	7	7	116	124	107
1992	31	19	11	114	104	135
1993	38	23	14	113	112	121
1994	31	20	11	122	117	132
1995	56	33	22	134	128	144
1996	45	31	14	125	112	153
1997	74	45	27	133	126	147
1998	68	48	18	130	128	132
1999	98	61	33	143	143	141

Note: Average time was calculated from the most recent sentencing date.
*Includes American Indians and Asians.

SOURCE: Tracy L. Snell, "Table 12. Time under sentence of death and execution, by race, 1977–99," in *Capital Punishment 1999*, Bureau of Justice Statistics, Washington, DC, December 2000

Indiana, Kentucky, Oklahoma, and Tennessee required review of the sentence only. In Idaho inmates who wanted their convictions reviewed had to file an appeal or lose the right to do so. In Indiana and Kentucky, defendants were allowed to waive review of their convictions.

Generally, the state's highest court of appeals conducts the review whether or not the defendant requests it. If the appellate court vacates (annuls) the conviction or the sentence, the case could be returned to the trial court for additional proceedings or for retrial. Subsequent to the resentencing or retrial, the death sentence could be reinstated.

LEGAL RESOURCES

Right to Counsel

The Sixth Amendment to the U.S. Constitution guarantees the "assistance of counsel for defense" in federal criminal prosecution. In 1963 the U.S. Supreme Court extended the right to counsel to state criminal prosecution of indigent (poor) persons charged with felony (*Gideon v. Wainwright*, 372 U.S. 335). In 1972 the high court held that poor persons charged with any crime that carries a sentence of imprisonment have the right to counsel (*Argersinger v. Hamlin*, 407 U.S. 25).

TABLE 7.8

Prisoners under death sentence by state and year of sentencing as of December 31, 1999

State	Year of sentence for prisoners sentenced to and remaining on death row, 12/31/99												Under sentence of death, 12/31/99	Average number of years under sentence of death as of 12/31/99
	1974-79	1980-81	1982-83	1984-85	1986-87	1988-89	1990-91	1992-93	1994-95	1996-97	1998	1999		
Florida	22	10	17	31	31	37	48	44	47	31	27	20	365	9.2
California	8	17	44	37	46	64	54	72	59	78	31	43	553	8.5
Texas	8	11	9	17	31	42	41	63	83	67	40	48	460	6.9
Georgia	7	3	6	5	13	9	11	11	14	18	11	8	116	8.5
Tennessee	3	6	8	11	15	10	10	5	8	12	6	6	100	10.0
Nevada	2	3	7	10	4	10	11	1	15	16	2	5	86	8.8
Nebraska	2	2		1	1				1	2			9	*
Illinois	1	11	13	13	10	16	19	20	19	18	8	8	156	9.2
Alabama	1	3	9	9	16	17	11	14	33	31	24	12	180	7.0
North Carolina	1	2	3	4			13	45	48	42	20	24	202	4.9
Arizona	1	1	10	9	6	14	18	18	12	14	7	6	116	8.4
Kentucky	1	1	7	2	4	1	2	4	3	4	6	4	39	8.7
Arkansas	1				1	2	1	7	9	10	4	5	40	5.0
Indiana		2	4	4	6	3	5	5	5	4	3	2	43	9.3
Pennsylvania		1	14	14	28	33	16	27	41	25	16	15	230	8.0
Oklahoma		1	4	12	19	15	15	9	17	26	15	6	139	7.7
Mississippi		1	4		3	1	10	9	7	13	8	4	60	6.3
Maryland		1		3		2	1	1	1	5	2	1	17	7.6
Ohio			10	30	21	18	19	21	27	27	16	10	199	8.3
Louisiana			2	5	7	1	2	10	17	21	10	10	85	5.3
Missouri			2	5	6	5	8	11	17	16	6	7	83	6.4
Idaho			2	4	1	4	2	2	2	2	1	1	21	9.7
South Carolina			1	2	2	5	7	8	15	12	8	5	65	5.8
Utah			1	2		2	1	1		2		1	10	8.9
Montana			1		1			2		2			6	*
Delaware			1			1		7		4	2	2	17	5.4
New Jersey					1		2	1	4	4	1	1	14	5.2
Virginia					1		1	2	7	5	8	7	31	3.2
Colorado					1				1	1		1	4	*
Washington							2	2	2	4	3		13	4.5
Connecticut							2	1	1	1		1	6	*
Oregon							1	6	7	6	3	2	25	4.4
Federal system							1	4	2	7	5	1	20	3.5
South Dakota									1			1	3	*
New Mexico									2	2			4	*
Wyoming										1	1		2	*
Kansas											2	1	3	*
New York											1	4	5	*
Total	58	76	179	230	275	312	334	434	526	534	297	272	3,527	7.7

Note: For those persons sentenced to death more than once, the numbers are based on the most recent death sentence.
*Averages not calculated for fewer than 10 inmates.

SOURCE: Tracy L. Snell, "Appendix table 2. Prisoners under sentence of death on December 31, 1999, by State and year of sentencing," in *Capital Punishment 1999*, Bureau of Justice Statistics, Washington, DC, December 2000

Ineffective Counsel

The release near the end of the twentieth century of several inmates, who were found innocent after serving time on death row, called attention to the ineffective representation of defendants unable to afford private counsel. Death penalty experts claimed that some lawyers who defend capital cases are inexperienced and ill-trained. They cited the well-publicized cases of inmates exonerated as a result of college students finding evidence that defense lawyers had failed to uncover. In their November 1999 five-part series, "The Failure of the Death Penalty in Illinois" (*Chicago Tribune*, Chicago, IL), Ken Armstrong and Steve Mills examined all 285 death penalty cases since Illinois reinstated the death penalty in 1977. The

journalists reported that, at least 33 times, defendants sentenced to death in Illinois had lawyers who were later suspended or disbarred, "sanctions reserved for conduct so incompetent, unethical, or even criminal the lawyer's license [was] taken away."

Observers noted that, in an increasing number of death penalty cases, the nation's indigent defense system has not delivered effective counsel to the accused. States vary in fulfilling *Gideon*. Some states have undertaken the establishment and funding of an indigent defense system; others have passed the responsibility on to individual counties. In 2001 three states—Pennsylvania, South Dakota, and Utah—did not pay for indigent defense, leaving it to the counties to bear the costs. Across the United

TABLE 7.9

Prisoners under death sentence and the outcome sentence, by year of sentencing, 1973–99

				Number of prisoners removed from under sentence of death					
				Appeal or higher courts overturned					Under sentence of death, 12/31/99
Year of sentence	Number sentenced to death	Execution	Other death	Death penalty statute	Conviction	Sentence	Sentence commuted	Other or unknown reasons	
1973	42	2	0	14	9	8	9	0	0
1974	149	10	4	65	15	30	22	1	2
1975	298	6	4	171	24	67	21	2	3
1976	233	13	5	136	17	43	15	0	4
1977	137	19	3	40	26	32	7	0	10
1978	185	34	6	21	35	62	8	0	19
1979	152	26	12	2	28	58	5	1	20
1980	173	40	13	3	28	49	7	0	33
1981	227	48	13	0	43	75	4	1	43
1982	266	54	13	0	35	68	7	1	88
1983	253	53	14	1	25	60	7	2	91
1984	285	46	10	2	37	60	6	8	116
1985	269	31	5	1	43	68	4	3	114
1986	300	41	16	0	45	50	6	5	137
1987	290	34	14	4	36	56	2	6	138
1988	292	31	11	0	33	52	3	0	162
1989	259	19	9	0	29	49	3	0	150
1990	253	19	7	0	32	35	2	0	158
1991	264	13	9	0	30	33	3	0	176
1992	288	15	7	0	21	35	4	0	206
1993	290	13	9	0	15	20	5	0	228
1994	319	11	7	0	20	22	2	0	257
1995	319	10	7	0	13	19	1	0	269
1996	316	7	3	0	13	19	1	0	273
1997	276	1	3	0	5	6	0	0	261
1998	300	2	1	0	0	0	0	0	297
1999	272	0	0	0	0	0	0	0	272
Total, 1973-99	6,707	598	205	460	657	1,076	154	30	3,527

Note: For those persons sentenced to death more than once, the numbers are based on the most recent death sentence.

SOURCE: Tracy L. Snell, "Appendix table 1. Prisoners sentenced to death and the outcome sentence, by year of sentencing, 1973–99," in *Capital Punishment 1999*, Bureau of Justice Statistics, Washington, DC, December 2000

States, different jurisdictions use one or a combination of three systems to provide counsel to poor defendants. The first system used by some jurisdictions has public defenders who are usually government employees. Under the second system, the court-assigned counsel system, a judge appoints private lawyers to represent the poor. A third system involves contract lawyers who bid for the job of providing indigent defense.

Court-assigned lawyers belong to a list of private lawyers who accept clients on a case-by-case basis. In jurisdictions that employ these lawyers, judges appoint lawyers from a list of private bar members and determine their pay. In most cases the pay is very low. Beth A. Wilkinson, cochair of the Constitution Project's Death Penalty Initiative, testified before the U.S. Senate Judiciary Committee hearing (June 27, 2001) that many jurisdictions paid their court-appointed lawyers very low hourly rates for capital defense. For example, Alabama paid $20 to $40 an hour, with a limit of $2,000. This means that a lawyer spending 600 hours preparing for a capital case

earned a little over $30 dollars an hour. (According to the American Civil Liberties Union [ACLU], defending a capital case at the trial level takes about 700 to 1,000 hours.) Wilkinson added that while Tennessee paid $20 to $30 an hour, Mississippi had a $1,000 limit. Moreover, courts often refuse to authorize the needed funds for investigating the case and using expert testimony. In contrast, the prosecution usually has unlimited funds at its disposal.

Some states, such as Colorado and New York, not only have public defender offices, but capital defender offices that specialize in death penalty cases. When New York brought back capital punishment in 1995, the death penalty statute required the establishment of a capital defender office with a $15 million allotment to train trial lawyers and investigators. But other states, such as Alabama, Georgia, Mississippi, and Virginia, have no statewide public defender system. Until 2001, of Texas's 254 counties, only 3 had a public defender program. In June 2001, for the first time, legislation was passed requiring state funding for indigent defense.

Postconviction Review

While death row inmates have the right to seek review of their conviction and sentence, they do not have the right to counsel for postconviction proceedings. Since most of those awaiting execution are poor, they must find lawyers willing to handle appeals for free. In 1995 Congress discontinued federal funding of private organizations (called resource centers) that represent death row inmates in postconviction proceedings. As a result, private organizations and law firms, both proponents and opponents of the death penalty, concerned with the increasing problems in capital cases, volunteered their services. Some hold training seminars on the complex process of appellate review, while others provide research and investigation.

Some private organizations, however, cannot keep up with the large numbers of death row inmates, For example, the Equal Justice Initiative of Alabama, comprised of five lawyers and two fellows, has been representing a majority of the inmates seeking appeals. As of September 2001, Alabama had 187 death row inmates. Under state law, lawyers appointed to represent indigent inmates could not be paid more than $1,000 per case.

LIMITING FEDERAL APPEALS

Habeas corpus review, which affords state and federal prisoners the chance to challenge the constitutionality of their convictions or sentences, has long been considered an important safeguard in all criminal trials, especially those involving the death penalty. Some people fear that the limitations on federal *habeas corpus* petitions required by the Antiterrorism and Effective Death Penalty Act of 1996 (AEDPA; Public Law 104-132) may contribute to the execution of innocent persons.

The AEDPA requires death row inmates to file their *habeas corpus* petitions in the appropriate district courts within six months of the final state appeal. Prior to the enactment of this law, there was no filing deadline. Under the 1996 law, a defendant who fails to challenge his or her conviction or sentence within the time specified cannot file another petition unless approved by a three-judge appellate court. The AEDPA further dictates that federal judges will have to defer to the rulings of the state courts, unless the rulings violate the Constitution or the laws of the United States or contradict "the Supreme Court's recognition of a new federal right that is made retroactively applicable."

GOVERNMENT OFFICIALS ARE HAVING SECOND THOUGHTS

While the overwhelming majority of those sentenced to death are unquestionably guilty of murder, exonerations of wrongly convicted persons have caused some legislators, judges, and religious and international leaders to call for a suspension of executions. In December 1998 retiring Florida Supreme Court Justice Gerald Kogan told the *Washington Post*, "There are several cases where I had grave doubts as to the guilt of a particular person."

On July 8, 2001, federal judge Michael Ponsor of the U.S. District Court of Massachusetts wrote about his experience presiding over the case of Kristen Gilbert, the first death penalty case in Massachusetts in several decades ("Life, Death, and Uncertainty," *Boston Globe*). According to Judge Ponsor, having tried the case, he concluded that errors will eventually occur in the imposition of the death penalty because the legal system could not possibly carry out something that difficult perfectly in every instant.

The former attorney general of Virginia (1985–86), William G. Broaddus, under whose watch five inmates were executed, became a death penalty opponent. In 1996 he was co-counsel for Paraguayan Angel Francisco Breard, whose death sentence case caused an international uproar when the Republic of Paraguay sued Virginia state officials for failure to notify the Paraguayan consulate of Breard's arrest in compliance with the Vienna Convention. In addition, the case was appealed to the highest court of the United Nations, the International Court of Justice, which asked for a stay of execution. The U.S. Supreme Court denied the stay and Breard was executed in 1998. Two U.S. Supreme Court justices, Sandra Day O'Connor, a former supporter of the death penalty, and Ruth Bader Ginsburg, voiced their concern about the application of capital punishment.

In October 2001 New Mexico Governor Gary Johnson, in a letter sent to people who wrote him regarding the imminent execution of Terry Clark, indicated that, while he had no intention of declaring a moratorium (a temporary suspension) on executions, he believed that "eliminating the death penalty in the future may prove to be better public policy given the reality of the sentence today." He, therefore, was "open to a debate on this topic." On November 6, 2001, Clark was executed for the 1986 murder of a nine-year-old girl he had raped. He was the first inmate put to death in New Mexico in nearly 42 years.

INCREASING NUMBERS OF EXONERATION

From 1973 to December 31, 2000, 93 death row inmates in 22 states had been exonerated and released. Between 1973 and 1993 a total of 55 inmates were released, an average of 2.75 inmates each year. In 1996 that number had increased to 6 inmates freed from death row, rising to 8 inmates per year in both 1999 and 2000. (See Figure 7.2.)

Between 1973 and 2000 Florida accounted for the greatest number of exonerations (20), followed by Illinois (13), Oklahoma (7), and Texas (7). (See Figure 7.3.) By

FIGURE 7.2

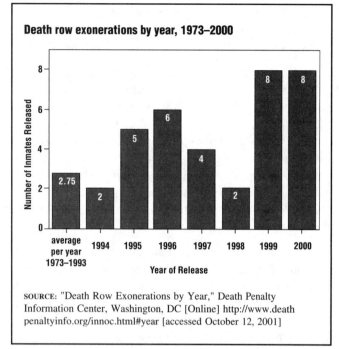

Death row exonerations by year, 1973–2000

SOURCE: "Death Row Exonerations by Year," Death Penalty Information Center, Washington, DC [Online] http://www.death penaltyinfo.org/innoc.html#year [accessed October 12, 2001]

October 15, 2001, the number of exonerations was up to 98, with Florida, Alabama, Massachusetts, Idaho, and Nebraska freeing 1 inmate each. Of the inmates released, 43 were black and 42 were white. Eleven were Hispanic, 1 was a Native American, and the last inmate was of "other" race. The inmates had spent an average of 8 years on death row.

A CALL FOR MORATORIUM

Anthony Porter of Illinois came within two days of being executed in September 1998. Questions regarding his mental competency (he had an IQ of 51) prompted the Illinois Supreme Court to stay his execution. Soon after, the collaborative efforts of private investigator Paul Ciolino and Professor David Protess and his investigative journalism students from Northwestern University (Evanston, IL) helped uncover evidence of Porter's innocence. In February 1999 another man confessed to the double murder. On March 11, 1999, Porter's conviction was reversed; he had been on death row for 17 years.

On January 31, 2000, Illinois became the first state to declare a moratorium. Governor George H. Ryan, a death penalty supporter, stopped all executions following the *Chicago Tribune* report showing that 13 inmates in his state had been released from death row since 1976. The governor stated,

> I now favor a moratorium, because I have grave concerns about our state's shameful record of convicting innocent people and putting them on death row. And, I believe, many Illinois residents now feel that same deep reservation. I cannot support a system, which, in its

administration, has proven to be so fraught with error and has come so close to the ultimate nightmare, the state's taking of innocent life. Thirteen people have been found to have been wrongfully convicted....

> Until I can be sure that everyone sentenced to death in Illinois is truly guilty, until I can be sure with moral certainty that no innocent man or woman is facing a lethal injection, no one will meet that fate. I am a strong proponent of tough criminal penalties, of supporting laws and programs to help police and prosecutors keep dangerous criminals off the streets. We must ensure the public safety of our citizens but, in doing so, we must ensure that the ends of justice are served.

Governor Ryan then appointed a commission composed of prosecutors, defense lawyers, judges, death penalty opponents, and nonlawyers to study the state's death penalty system. As of August 2001 at least 20 state legislatures had introduced bills calling for a moratorium on executions. Some states had authorized studies of the death penalty, including Connecticut, Illinois, Maryland, Missouri, Montana, North Carolina, and Pennsylvania.

DNA TESTING

The National Commission on the Future of DNA Evidence, in *Postconviction DNA Testing: Recommendations for Handling Requests* (National Institute of Justice, Washington, DC, September 1999), observed how, in *Herrera v. Collins* (506 U.S. 390, 1993), the Supreme Court noted that newly discovered evidence does not constitute grounds for a federal *habeas* relief if there is no evidence of a constitutional violation occurring during state criminal proceedings. Leonel Torres Herrera, 10 years after his initial trial, alleged that he was innocent of a double murder, presenting "actual evidence" that his brother, who had since died, had committed the crime. The commission, however, noted that today, with the availability of DNA testing, "the possibility of demonstrating actual innocence has moved from the realm of theory to the actual."

The science of deoxyribonucleic acid (DNA) testing is improving rapidly. When DNA testing was first used in criminal trials starting in the mid-1980s, not only were fresh DNA samples required, they also had to contain thousands of cells. As DNA technology has become more sophisticated, scientists are able to test a single cell for DNA patterns that could link suspects to hair or semen found on a victim. Today a crime laboratory can identify unique DNA patterns in a tiny sample of just 100 to 200 cells. DNA testing has played a substantial role in proving the innocence of a number of persons wrongly convicted. As of October 15, 2001, 11 of the 98 death row inmates released since 1973 were exonerated by DNA evidence.

When biological material has been left at the scene of the crime, DNA testing could, in some cases, establish

FIGURE 7.3

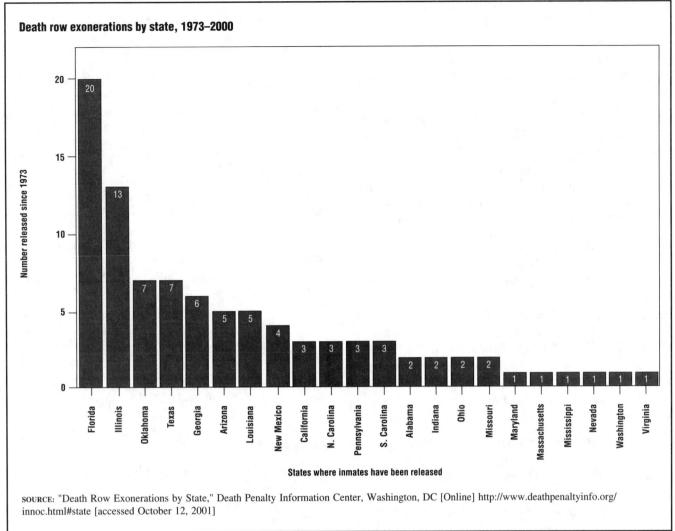

Death row exonerations by state, 1973–2000

SOURCE: "Death Row Exonerations by State," Death Penalty Information Center, Washington, DC [Online] http://www.deathpenaltyinfo.org/innoc.html#state [accessed October 12, 2001]

with near certainty a defendant's innocence or guilt. DNA, which stores the genetic code of the human body, is found in saliva, skin tissue, bones, blood, semen, and the root and shaft of hair. Biological samples that were difficult to test in the 1980s may yield more accurate information where previous results had proved inconclusive.

In 1996 Professor Protess and another group of students helped uncover new evidence that proved the innocence of four black men who were convicted for a 1978 gang rape and double murder. Two received life imprisonment while the other two were sentenced to death. DNA tests helped prove the men's innocence. In March 1999 the four men received a $36 million settlement from Cook County, Illinois, to resolve a lawsuit charging police misconduct. In 1986 Frank Lee Smith was sentenced to death in Florida for the rape and murder of an eight-year-old girl. DNA testing done in 2000 proved Smith's innocence; he had died of cancer the previous year while awaiting execution.

In December 2000 Congress authorized the U.S. Department of Justice to provide state crime laboratories

more than $30 million to analyze the backlog of DNA samples that had been collected but never tested. Under the DNA Analysis Backlog Reduction Act of 2000 (Public Law 106-546), states would receive funding to conduct tests on about a million samples collected from criminals and crime scenes that had never been analyzed. Each test costs about $2,000 to perform. Death row inmates whose cases involved biological evidence could receive funding.

In August 2001 the American Bar Association (ABA) called on Congress to pass legislation that would ensure every death row inmate the right to DNA testing. The ABA, while opposing the execution of mentally retarded persons and those who were minors when they committed their crimes, does not have a policy for or against the death penalty in other cases.

FAIRNESS AND THE DEATH PENALTY

Racial Questions

Death penalty cases raise a fairness issue. Opponents of the death penalty claim that minorities and poor defendants are more likely to be convicted and receive the death penalty than white and wealthy defendants. In 1987, on appeal, the lawyers for Warren McCleskey, a convicted murderer, brought before the Supreme Court the Baldus study (by Professors David C. Baldus, George Woodworth, and Charles Puianski), an analysis of 2,000 cases in Georgia in the 1970s.

This study showed that black defendants who were convicted of killing whites were more likely to receive death sentences than white murderers or blacks who killed blacks. The justices, in *McCleskey v. Kemp* (481 U.S. 279, 1987), rejected the study, declaring that "apparent disparities ... are an inevitable part of our criminal justice system" and that there were enough safeguards built into the legal system to protect every defendant.

In 1998 Dr. David Baldus and others, expanding on the Baldus study, found evidence of race-of-victim disparities in 26 out of 29 death penalty states ("Racial Discrimination and the Death Penalty in the Post-*Furman* Era: An Empirical and Legal Analysis with Recent Findings from Philadelphia," 83 *Cornell Law Review* 1661). The researchers found that the race of the victim was related to whether capital punishment was imposed. A defendant was more likely to receive the death penalty if the victim was white than if the victim was black.

These studies were consistent with a 1990 U.S. government study of capital punishment. The U.S. General Accounting Office (GAO), in *Death Penalty Sentencing: Research Indicates Pattern of Racial Disparities* (Washington, DC), reviewed 28 studies on race and the death penalty. The GAO reported that "in 82 percent of the studies, the race of the victim was found to influence the likelihood of being charged with capital murder or receiving the death penalty." The GAO found that when the victim was white, the defendant, whether white or black, was more likely to get the death sentence.

In the small number of horrendous murders, death sentences were more likely to be imposed, regardless of race. Nevertheless, when the offender killed a person while robbing him or when the murderer had a previous record, the race of the victim played a role. The studies also showed that for crimes of passion, the convicted person (regardless of race) rarely received the death penalty.

In September 1999, in his testimony before the Illinois House of Representatives' hearing on the state's system of capital punishment, Richard C. Dieter, executive director of the Death Penalty Information Center, noted,

> Ten out of 12 people who have been released from Illinois's death row are members of a minority. Most are African American. That doesn't prove bias, but it should raise concerns. Illinois's death row is made up of approximately 156 individuals, 97 of whom are Black—that's 62 percent in a state where the Black population is less

than 15 percent. Again, those figures do not prove any racial bias, but such a glaring disproportion is evidence that something is wrong at some level of society. If race is playing a role in who is sentenced to death, then it can also be playing a role in who is wrongly convicted.

Some persons claim that district attorneys, who alone decide which case to try as a death penalty case, may be motivated by politics or racial prejudice to impose the death penalty on a minority. Professor Jeffrey Pokorak of St. Mary's University School of Law, in "Probing the Capital Prosecutor's Perspective: Race of the Discretionary Actors" (83 *Cornell Law Review* 1811 [1998]), found that 97.5 percent (1,794 out of 1,838 prosecutors in the 38 states with capital punishment) were white. Only 1.2 percent each were black or Hispanic.

Racial Justice Legislation

In 1998 Kentucky became the first state to enact a racial justice law (Racial Justice Act, SB171), prohibiting the execution of a convicted person when evidence shows racial discrimination in prosecution or sentencing. Other states that have considered a similar legislation include Florida, Georgia, Indiana, Nebraska, New Mexico, North Carolina, Ohio, Oregon, and Texas. As of September 2001, however, no other state had passed similar legislation.

FIRST FEDERAL STUDY OF RACIAL AND ETHNIC BIAS

In July 2000 President Bill Clinton ordered the Department of Justice to review the administration of the federal death penalty system. This order came in the aftermath of the request for clemency by Raul Juan Garza, scheduled to be executed by the federal government on August 5, 2000. Garza's lawyer contended that it was unfair to execute his client because the federal death penalty discriminated against members of minorities.

On September 12, 2000, the Justice Department released *The Federal Death Penalty System: A Statistical Survey (1988–2000)*, providing information on the federal death penalty since the passage of the first federal capital punishment law in 1988 (the Anti-Drug Abuse Act). From 1988 to 1994 prosecutors in the 94 federal districts were required to submit to the U.S. attorney General for review and approval only those cases in which the U.S. attorney sought the death penalty. During this period the U.S. attorneys sought the death penalty in 52 cases and received authorization in 47 cases.

In 1995 the Justice Department adopted a new protocol, requiring the U.S. attorneys to submit for review all cases in which a defendant was charged with a crime subject to the death penalty, regardless of whether they intended to seek authorization to pursue the death penalty. These cases were first reviewed by the attorney general's Review Committee on Capital Cases, a committee of senior Justice Department lawyers.

TABLE 7.10

Distribution of defendants within each stage of the federal death penalty process, 1995–2000

STAGE	TOTAL		White		Black		Hispanic		Other	
	#	%	#	%	#	%	#	%	#	%
Submitted by U.S. attorneys	682	100.0%	134	19.6%	324	47.5%	195	28.6%	29	4.3%
No recommendation	5	100.0%	1	20.0%	1	20.0%	3	60.0%	0	0.0%
Recommendation not to seek death penalty (DP)	494	100.0%	85	17.2%	242	49.0%	153	31.0%	14	2.8%
Recommendation to seek DP	183	100.0%	48	26.2%	81	44.3%	39	21.3%	15	8.2%
Considered by review committee	618	100.0%	119	19.3%	301	48.7%	172	27.8%	26	4.2%
No recommendation	15	100.0%	4	26.7%	6	40.0%	4	26.7%	1	6.7%
Recommendation not to seek DP	420	100.0%	68	16.2%	215	51.2%	125	29.8%	12	2.9%
Recommendation to seek DP	183	100.0%	47	25.7%	80	43.7%	43	23.5%	13	7.1%
Considered by attorney general (AG)	588	100.0%	115	19.6%	287	48.8%	160	27.2%	26	4.4%
Decision deferred or pending	12	100.0%	3	25.0%	4	33.3%	4	33.3%	1	8.3%
Authorization not to seek DP	417	100.0%	68	16.3%	212	50.8%	124	29.7%	13	3.1%
Authorization to seek DP	159	100.0%	44	27.7%	71	44.7%	32	20.1%	12	7.5%
Authorized by AG to seek DP	159	100.0%	44	27.7%	71	44.7%	32	20.1%	12	7.5%
DP notice withdrawn – plea agreement	51	100.0%	21	41.2%	18	35.3%	9	17.6%	3	5.9%
DP notice withdrawn – subsequent AG decision	11	100.0%	1	9.1%	3	27.3%	5	45.5%	2	18.2%
DP notice dismissed or trial terminated	4	100.0%	0	0.0%	1	25.0%	3	75.0%	0	0.0%
Pending trial or completion of trial	51	100.0%	11	21.6%	23	45.1%	13	25.5%	4	7.8%
Not convicted of capital charge	1	100.0%	0	0.0%	1	100.0%	0	0.0%	0	0.0%
Convicted of capital charge	41	100.0%	11	26.8%	25	61.0%	2	4.9%	3	7.3%
Convicted of capital charge	41	100.0%	11	26.8%	25	61.0%	2	4.9%	3	7.3%
Jury verdict – DP not recommended	21	100.0%	7	33.3%	12	57.1%	0	0.0%	2	9.5%
Jury verdict – DP recommended	20	100.0%	4	20.0%	13	65.0%	2	10.0%	1	5.0%
Sentenced to death	20	100.0%	4	20.0%	13	65.0%	2	10.0%	1	5.0%
DP recommended by jury but not yet imposed	2	100.0%	0	0.0%	0	0.0%	2	100.0%	0	0.0%
DP vacated by court, further action pending	4	100.0%	1	25.0%	3	75.0%	0	0.0%	0	0.0%
Death sentence pending	14	100.0%	3	21.4%	10	71.4%	0	0.0%	1	7.1%

SOURCE: "Table 1A: Distribution of Defendants Within Each Stage of the Federal Death Penalty Process (1995–2000)," in *The Federal Death Penalty System: A Statistical Survey (1988–2000)*, U.S. Department of Justice, Washington, DC, September 12, 2000

The period 1995–2000, which provides a more extensive picture of the Justice Department's internal decision process as pertains to the federal death penalty, showed that between January 27, 1995, and July 20, 2000, at every phase of the federal process, minority defendants were overrepresented. Of the 682 defendants whose cases were submitted for review by federal prosecutors, 19.6 percent were white, 47.5 percent were black, and 28.6 percent were Hispanic. The prosecutors recommended seeking the death penalty for 183 of 682 cases submitted for review. Of these 183 cases, about two-thirds (44.3 percent blacks and 21.3 percent Hispanics) were members of minorities. The attorney general reviewed 588 of the cases and authorized the U.S. attorneys to seek the death penalty in 159 cases. Of the 159 defendants, 44.7 percent were black and 20.1 percent were Hispanic. Only about 28 percent were white. (See Table 7.10.)

Racial Disparity in Plea Bargaining

It should be noted that the attorney general's decision to seek the death penalty may be changed up until the jury has returned a sentencing verdict. This change may be sought by the defense lawyer, the U.S. attorney, the Review Committee, or by the attorney general. A plea agreement is one avenue that may result in the withdrawal of the death penalty. This means that the defendant entered into an agreement with the U.S. attorney resulting in a guilty plea, saving him or her from the death penalty. From 1995 to 2000, after the attorney general sought the death penalty for 159 defendants, 51 defendants entered into plea agreements. Almost twice as many white defendants (48 percent, or 21 out of 44) as blacks (25 percent, or 18 of 71) received a plea agreement. About 28 percent (9 of 32) of Hispanics entered into a plea agreement. (See Table 7.10.)

Government Defends Data

The National Institute of Justice observed that, "generally speaking, once submitted for review [to obtain a death penalty authorization], minorities proceeded to the next stages in the death penalty process at lower rates than whites." The institute claimed that the attorney general authorized the death penalty for a larger proportion of whites being considered (38 percent, or 44 of 115), compared to 25 percent (71 of 287) black defendants and 20 percent (32 of 160) Hispanic defendants. (See Table 7.10.)

SECOND FEDERAL STUDY OF RACIAL AND ETHNIC BIAS

On June 6, 2001, the Justice Department released a supplement to the September 2000 report—*The Federal Death*

Penalty System: Supplementary Data, Analysis and Revised Protocols for Capital Case Review. That same day Attorney General John Ashcroft told the Judiciary Committee of the U.S. House of Representatives that the report confirmed that the subsequent study of the administration of the federal death penalty showed no indication of racial or ethnic bias.

The follow-up study had been ordered by his predecessor, Attorney General Janet Reno. In addition to the 682 cases submitted by federal prosecutors for review in the first study of the federal death penalty, another 291 cases were analyzed, for a total of 973 cases. These included cases that should have been submitted for review for the first report but were not, those in which the defendant eventually entered into a plea agreement for a lesser sentence, and cases in which the death penalty could have been sought but was not. Among the 973 defendants, 17 percent (166) were white, 42 percent (408) were black, and 36 percent (350) were Hispanic.

According to the supplement, from 1995 and 2000, of the 973 defendants eligible for capital charges, federal prosecutors requested authorization to pursue the death penalty against 81 percent of whites, 29 percent of blacks, and 56 percent of Hispanics. The attorney general ultimately authorized seeking the death penalty for 27 percent of the white defendants, 17 percent of the black defendants, and 9 percent of the Hispanic defendants.

Critics of the supplementary report pointed out that the second federal review failed to address many issues. Following the release of the September 2000 survey, then Attorney General Reno ordered a study to find out how death penalty cases are taken into the federal system when there is a joint state and federal jurisdiction. The June report did not cover this issue. Instead, the report described a National Institute of Justice (NIJ) meeting on January 10, 2001, in which researchers and practitioners agreed that such a study "would entail a highly complex, multi-year research initiative" and that "even if such a study were carried out, it could not be expected to yield definitive answers concerning the reasons for disparities in federal death penalty."

Testifying before the Senate Judiciary Committee on June 11, 2001, Professor David C. Baldus (Joseph B. Tye Distinguished Professor of Law, College of Law, University of Iowa) reported that he was one of the researchers at the NIJ January 2001 meeting. Baldus claimed that, while it was true he and others at the meeting agreed that the study ordered by Attorney General Reno would likely take two years to complete, the consensus was that "such a study would provide the best possible evidence on the question." Baldus further pointed out that quite some time had elapsed since that meeting and the first report, and still the Justice Department had not taken any step to initiate such a study.

On July 20, 2001, the NIJ published a solicitation for research of the federal death penalty, including the deci-sion-making factors that determine whether a homicide case is prosecuted in the federal or state system, as well as issues of race/ethnicity and geography in the imposition of the death penalty.

The ACLU noted that, unlike the September 2000 report, the new Justice Department report did not include information on whether the supplemental 291 cases were from all or just some districts and, therefore, whether or not they represented all of the death penalty-eligible cases between 1995 and 2000. The ACLU also noted that, while the report found that federal prosecutors were less likely to submit cases of black and Hispanic defendants to the attorney general for death penalty authorizations and that the attorney general authorized capital punishment for more whites than blacks and Hispanics, there was no information about the decision-making process of prosecuting on the federal level and of offering plea agreements.

STUDIES OF THE U.S. DEATH PENALTY SYSTEM

Liebman Study

James S. Liebman, Jeffrey Fagan, and Valerie West conducted the first study of its kind—a statistical study of modern American capital appeals—for the U.S. Senate Judiciary Committee. The study, called *A Broken System: Error Rates in Capital Cases, 1973–1995* (June 12, 2000), examined all death penalty sentences (5,760) imposed in the United States over a twenty-year period.

On direct appeal, the state high courts reviewed 4,578 death sentences. It should be noted that the authors use "death sentences" and "capital judgments" interchangeably. The study found that 2 of every 3 death sentences (68 percent) reviewed by the courts all across the country were found to have serious errors. For every 100 death sentences, 41 were returned to the courts during state appeal because of serious errors. Of the 59 death sentences that reached the second state appeal, another six went back to court due to errors. At the third level of appeal—with the federal courts—21 more cases were remanded to the lower courts due to more errors found. All in all, of the original 100 death penalty sentences, 68 had serious errors that required retrial. Of the 68 persons who were retried, 82 percent (56 persons) were found not deserving of the death penalty. Another five inmates were found innocent of the capital crime for which they received the death sentence.

Latzer Study

Barry Latzer and James N. G. Cauthen noted that their reexamination of the Liebman study found that about one-fourth (27 percent)—and not two-thirds (68 percent)—of capital convictions were reversed between 1973 and 1995. In "Capital Appeals Revisited" (*Judicature*, Volume 84, Number 2, September–October 2000), the authors noted that the Liebman study did not differentiate between reversals of convictions and reversals of death sentences.

Latzer and Cauthen conducted their own investigation, based on the theory that many of the appeals resulted in reversed sentences but not reversed convictions. The study covered the period 1990–99, using reversal data in the same 26 states studied by Liebman and his colleagues. Latzer and Cauthen wanted more recent data of the death penalty system that would provide more complete reversal rate differences.

The authors found that, of the 837 death penalty reversals in state-level direct appeal or postconviction review, 61 percent were sentence reversals, and 39 percent were conviction reversals (reversals addressing the guilt or innocence of the defendant). Using Liebman's conclusion that 5 of 10 capital judgments were reversed at either the direct-appeal phase or postconviction review phase, Latzer and Cauthen applied this finding to their study and concluded that, of the 5 reversals, 3 were sentence reversals and 2 were conviction reversals.

The authors also investigated reversals at the federal level, using data from the Ninth Circuit Court of Appeals, the largest of the circuit courts. Of the 29 capital cases reversed by the court during the 10-year period, 21 (72.4 percent) were sentence reversals, and 8 (27.7 percent) were conviction reversals. This was consistent with the authors' findings regarding direct-appeal and postconviction sentence reversals. Using Liebman's finding that 68 of 100 capital judgments were reversed, Latzer and Cauthen concluded, "If 68 of 100 capital decisions are reversed after direct, post-conviction, and federal *habeas corpus* review, and 39 percent of these are conviction reversals, then convictions in 26.52 (39 percent of 68) of 100 capital decisions are reversed."

STATES' IMPOSITION OF THE DEATH PENALTY

Several states have commissioned studies of their death penalty system. These states include Arizona, Connecticut, Delaware, Illinois, Indiana, Maryland, Nebraska, Nevada, North Carolina, Texas, and Virginia. Results of studies conducted by three states are presented below.

Texas

In 1999 the Texas legislature passed a bill that would have required appointment of counsel for indigent representation; then Governor George W. Bush, however, vetoed the legislation. On June 14, 2001, Governor Rick Perry signed the Texas Fair Defense Act (Senate Bill 7), providing, for the first time, state funding for indigent defense services. The $12 million yearly appropriation will help establish public defender offices. Two lawyers will be provided in capital cases, unless the state indicates in writing that it will not seek the death penalty. The law also limits judges' powers by requiring appointments be made from a rotating list of qualified lawyers. Moreover, courts must pay reasonable fees, including necessary overhead reimbursements.

Under the new law, death penalty lawyers have to attend annual training on capital defense in order to remain on the rotating list. In addition, Senate Bill 7 establishes a Texas Task Force on Indigent Defense to be responsible for setting standards for lawyers for different cases. The task force will also monitor the operation of the public defender programs in the counties. The task force and the county capital appointment committee will review the list of lawyers who handle capital cases.

The Texas Fair Defense Act was passed as a result of findings by Texas Appleseed, a nonpartisan legal advocacy group. On December 12, 2000, Texas Appleseed reported that, unlike other active death penalty states, Texas had been "virtually alone" in not having a statewide program to assist indigent defendants with legal representation (*The Fair Defense Report: Analysis of Indigent Defense Practices in Texas*, Texas Appleseed Fair Defense Project, Austin, TX). As of November 20, 2000, among states that most actively imposed the death penalty, Texas was one of two states that did not fund indigent defense representation (Arizona was the other state). Texas was also the only state that had no statewide oversight commission, public defender agencies, and capital trial unit.

Texas Appleseed pointed out that Texas did not have an oversight commission that could have developed standards for appointment and compensation of lawyers in capital cases. In some states, a similar commission further monitors the performance of defense counsel and the judges' fee decisions.

Many death penalty states have a specialized statewide capital trial unit that assists court-appointed private defense lawyers. In addition, nine states—Colorado, Connecticut, Delaware, Maryland, Missouri, New Hampshire, New Jersey, New Mexico, and Wyoming—have a public defender program, most of which provide public defenders in every county statewide. Texas, on the other hand, used private lawyers appointed by judges on a case-by-case basis. These lawyers lacked the support of a public defender system that could have made available the expertise of other lawyers more experienced in capital cases, as well as the training programs that such a system provides.

North Carolina

On April 16, 2001, Isaac Unah and John Charles Boger released the most comprehensive study of North Carolina's death penalty system in the state's history (*Race and the Death Penalty in North Carolina, an Empirical Analysis: 1993–1997, Initial Findings*, University of North Carolina at Chapel Hill and the Common

Sense Foundation, NC). The researchers studied all 3,990 homicide cases between 1993 and 1997, including defendants who received death sentences, as well as those sentenced to life imprisonment.

On first analysis of all homicide cases, the researchers found that, overall, the death-sentencing rate where white victims were involved was almost twice as high (3.7 percent) as the rate where the victims were nonwhite (1.9 percent). In addition, the death-sentencing rate for nonwhite defendants/white victims (6.4 percent) was nearly 2.5 times higher than the rate for white defendants/white victims (2.6 percent).

When the researchers confined their investigation to death-eligible cases (those imposing the death penalty, such as a case involving the murder of a police officer), race determined whether the defendant received the death sentence. The death-sentencing rate in all death-eligible cases was so much higher in white-victim cases (8 percent) than in cases in which the victims were nonwhite (4.7 percent). As with all cases, nonwhite defendants in white-victim homicides received the death sentence at a higher rate (11.6 percent) than white defendants who murdered whites (6.1 percent).

After the initial analysis, Dr. Unah and Professor Boger performed a more comprehensive investigation involving 502 defendants, collecting 113 factors about each crime. These factors included the circumstances of the homicide, the evidence, the charges brought against the defendant, the character and background of the defendant and the victim, the presence or absence of aggravating or mitigating circumstances as specified under the law, as well as the presence or absence of aggravating or mitigating circumstances not specified under the law. The researchers also looked into other factors that might have influenced the imposition of the death penalty, such as the coming reelection of the district attorney prosecuting the crime. In the end, the researchers found that race—specifically the race of the victim—indeed played a role in the imposition of capital punishment in North Carolina from 1993 to 1997. On average, the odds of receiving the death penalty were increased by a factor of 3.5 times when the victim was white.

Nebraska

In May 1999 the Nebraska legislature became the first in the country to pass a bill proposing a two-year moratorium on executions. The bill also called for a study, during the moratorium, to determine the fairness of the administration of the death penalty. Governor Mike Johanns vetoed the bill. The governor also vetoed the proposed study, but the legislature overrode his veto.

On July 25, 2001, the Nebraska Commission on Law Enforcement and Criminal Justice released its findings of the state death penalty (David C. Baldus, George Wood-

worth, Gary L. Young, and Aaron M. Christ, *The Disposition of Nebraska Capital and Non- Capital Homicide Cases [1973–1999]: A Legal and Empirical Analysis*). The researchers reviewed over 700 homicide cases that resulted in a conviction. They then closely examined the decision-making process in 177 death-eligible cases, 27 of which received the death sentence. The study did not find racial bias in the use of the death penalty. White defendants (15 percent) were just as likely as nonwhite defendants (16 percent) to receive the death penalty. The study also concluded that there was no significant evidence of unfair treatment based on the victim's race—17 percent of defendants who murdered white victims and 11 percent of defendants who murdered minority victims were sentenced to death.

The study found, however, that death-eligible defendants who murdered victims of "high socioeconomic status" were nearly four times as likely to receive the death sentence than when the victims were poor, even when similar crimes had been committed. In addition, the study found geographic disparities in seeking the death penalty. Prosecutors in rural capital trials were more likely to seek the death penalty than their urban counterparts (31 percent versus 20 percent).

COSTS OF THE DEATH PENALTY

Most death penalty opponents advocate life imprisonment without the chance of parole as an alternative to the death sentence. Some people, however, believe that capital punishment costs the taxpayers less than a life sentence without parole. Several studies have found that the death penalty costs more than life imprisonment without parole. Hugo Adam Bedau, in *The Case against the Death Penalty* (American Civil Liberties Union, Washington, DC, 1997), found that a "murder trial normally takes longer when the death penalty is at issue than when it is not. Litigation costs—including the time of judges, prosecutors, public defenders, and court reporters, and the high costs of briefs—are mostly borne by the taxpayer."

In January 2000 the *Palm Beach Post* estimated that the death penalty cost Florida $51 million more than what it would cost to incarcerate all first-degree murderers sentenced to life without parole. According to the Department of Legislative Services of Maryland's General Assembly, it cost approximately $2.3 million to move a death row defendant through the system. In contrast, keeping the same inmate in prison cost about $19,200 annually, totaling about $768,000 for 40 years' confinement. Texas spent an estimated $2.3 million per death penalty case, about three times the cost of keeping a Texas inmate in prison for 40 years.

North Carolina

Phillip J. Cook and Donna B. Slawson, professors of public policy at Duke University, in *The Costs of Processing*

Murder Cases in North Carolina (1993), studied the total costs of every death penalty case in the state for over two years. They found that in North Carolina, the cost to try a noncapital murder case and imprison a convicted murderer for 20 years was $166,000. The cost to try a capital murder case, convict, and execute a prisoner after 10 years of imprisonment averaged $329,000. A noncapital murder case thus saved the state and local governments an estimated $163,000.

Only one-third (31 percent) of the capital murder trials, however, resulted in a sentence of death. Only about 10 percent of those condemned to death were actually executed. Many of those sentenced to death had retrials or new sentencing trials, which had different results than their original trials. Professors Cook and Slawson estimated that the extra cost for each case in which the defendant was sentenced to death was about $216,000. The extra cost per case in which the defendant was executed was more than $2.16 million.

Some of the costs incurred in a capital murder case—providing indigent defendants with two lawyers instead of one (which is their right), calling more expert witnesses, and filing more briefs—might not have been incurred in a noncapital murder trial in North Carolina. The appeals process had nine steps, some of which could be repeated.

New York

The state of New York established the Capital Defender Office upon the reinstatement of the death penalty in 1995. The state allocated about $15 million annually for capital defense expenses. As of December 1999, out of nearly 500 defendants charged with first-degree murder or the possibility of first-degree murder since 1995, New York prosecutors sought the death penalty in 37 cases. The nine death penalty cases tried so far resulted in five death sentences and four life imprisonments without parole.

No system is in place to track prosecution costs because district attorneys employ different methods to do so. Experts estimated that the prosecution costs probably equal, or exceed, that of defense expenses. Since death penalty cases often drag on for years, by the time the death row inmate is executed, the cost is tenfold. (In 1999, the 98 inmates executed nationwide were under sentence of death for an average of 11 years and 11 months; see Table 7.7.)

California

A study of the California system suggested a minimum cost of $500,000 per case (this included all capital cases, not just the ones that ended with a death sentence). In 1994 California set up the Office of Public Defender, which worked exclusively on appeals for poor defendants on death row at an annual cost of $8 million. Because the office cannot handle all the defendants, the state offered

private attorneys contracts for $75,000 to $200,000 to handle cases. Despite these efforts, about one-third of the prisoners on death row do not have lawyers to represent them in the appeals process. Many death penalty cases are on hold because lawyers cannot be found to handle the appeals.

Federal Death Penalty Costs

Since the passage of the Violent Crime Control and Law Enforcement Act (Public Law 103- 322; also known as the Federal Death Penalty Act of 1994), the number of federal prosecutions, including crimes punishable by death, has risen. The Subcommittee on Federal Death Penalty Cases of the Committee on Defender Services of the Judicial Conference of the United States, in *Federal Death Penalty Cases: Recommendations Concerning the Cost and Quality of Defense Representation* (Washington, DC, 1998), estimated that about 560 federal death penalty cases were filed between 1991 and 1997. The numbers increased each year. In 1991 there were 12 cases, rising nearly tenfold to 118 in 1995, and reaching 153 cases in 1997. (See Figure 7.4.)

Although the decision to charge a crime punishable by death is made by the local federal prosecutor, the U.S. attorney general alone authorizes the seeking of the death penalty. Between 1988 and December 1997, the U.S. attorney general authorized seeking capital punishment in 111 cases. The attorney general's decision to authorize seeking the death penalty makes a substantial difference in the cost of representing a defendant. From 1990 to 1997 the average total cost (for counsel and related services) per representation of a sample of cases in which the defendant was charged with an offense punishable by death and the attorney general authorized seeking the death penalty was $218,112. This included cases resolved by a guilty plea as well as cases resolved by a trial. In contrast, the average total cost per representation in which the defendant was charged with an offense punishable by death and the attorney general did not authorize seeking the death penalty was $55,772.

The decision whether to go to trial or to enter a guilty plea also affects the cost of representing the alleged offender. Between 1988 and 1997, of the 111 cases in which the attorney general sought the death sentence, 41 were tried for capital charges. Cases that ended in capital trials cost an average of $269,139, compared to $192,333 for cases resolved with a guilty plea.

Since a death penalty case differs from other cases in that a defendant's life is at stake, the defense generally devotes more time to the case. One time-consuming aspect of defense involves prolonged jury selection. While jury selection in noncapital cases may take a couple of days, in capital cases it may take several months. Table 7.11 shows the difference in the number of billable hours

FIGURE 7.4

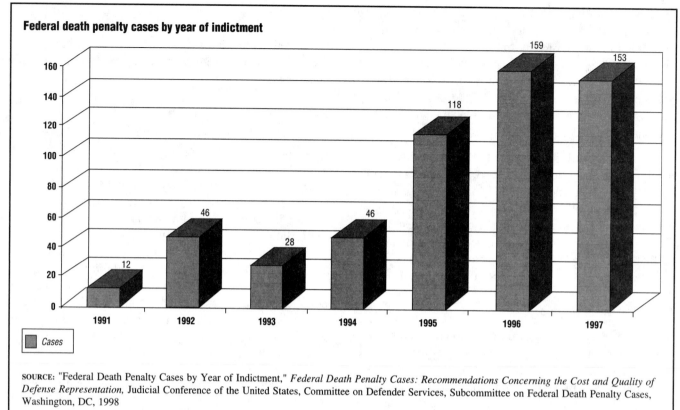

Federal death penalty cases by year of indictment

SOURCE: "Federal Death Penalty Cases by Year of Indictment," *Federal Death Penalty Cases: Recommendations Concerning the Cost and Quality of Defense Representation,* Judicial Conference of the United States, Committee on Defender Services, Subcommittee on Federal Death Penalty Cases, Washington, DC, 1998

TABLE 7.11

Average number of attorney hours billed in capital and non-capital homicide cases, 1992–97

	Case Type	In Court Hours	Out of Court Hours	Avg. Total Attorney Hours Per Representation
Non-Capital	Homicides	18	100	117
Capital	Auth. Denied	38	391	429
	Auth. Granted	231	1,233	1,464
	Capital Trial	409	1,480	1,889
	Plea	61	1,201	1,262
	Drug Cases	277	1,343	1,619

SOURCE: "Average Number of Attorney Hours Billed in Capital and Non-Capital Homicide Cases," *Federal Death Penalty Cases: Recommendations Concerning the Cost and Quality of Defense Representation,* Judicial Conference of the United States, Committee on Defender Services, Subcommittee on Federal Death Penalty Cases, Washington, DC, 1998

in capital and noncapital homicide cases as compiled by the Subcommittee on Federal Death Penalty Cases.

Those who support capital punishment, however, believe that the issue of justice should not be based upon cost. It might be more expensive to guarantee fairness to both the alleged perpetrator and the victim, but the cost is justified if the fair handling of the case is achieved.

CHAPTER 8

PUBLIC ATTITUDES TOWARD CAPITAL PUNISHMENT

Like all statistics, public opinion polls should be viewed cautiously. The way a question is phrased influences the respondents' answers. Many other factors may also influence a response in ways that are often difficult to determine. Respondents might never have thought of the issue until asked, or they might be giving the pollster the answer they think the pollster wants to hear. Organizations that survey opinions do not claim absolute accuracy. Their findings are approximate snapshots of the attitudes of the nation at a given time.

The surveys presented here have been selected from numerous polls taken on capital punishment. The Gallup Organization and Harris Interactive (formerly Louis Harris and Associates, Inc.), to name two such organizations, are well-respected in their fields, and their surveys are accepted as representative of public opinions. A typical, well-conducted survey claims accuracy to about plus or minus three points.

SUPPORT FOR THE DEATH PENALTY

Most Americans strongly favor capital punishment. In July 2001 the Harris Poll found that two-thirds (67 percent) of Americans believed in capital punishment. In 1965, two years before a death penalty moratorium (a temporary suspension) occurred, only two-fifths (38 percent) of the population believed in the imposition of the death penalty. By 1976, when the death penalty was reinstated, the proportion of Americans favoring the death penalty rose to 67 percent. The support for the death penalty peaked in 1997, with 3 out of 4 Americans (75 percent) favoring it and only 1 out of 5 (22 percent) opposing it. (See Table 8.1.)

In 1999 support for capital punishment dropped somewhat to 71 percent, and in 2000 it was down to 64 percent. The Harris Poll researchers believed that this might have been due to the well-publicized cases of wrongful convictions. In several cases DNA evidence has

TABLE 8.1

Support for capital punishment, 1965–2001

"Do you believe in capital punishment, that is the death penalty, or are you opposed to it?"

Base: All Respondents

	1965 %	1969 %	1970 %	1973 %	1976 %	1983 %	1997 %	1999 %	2000 %	July 2001 %
Believe in it	38	48	47	59	67	68	75	71	64	67
Opposed to it	47	38	42	31	25	27	22	21	25	26
Not sure/Refused	15	14	11	10	8	5	3	8	11	7

SOURCE: Humphrey Taylor, "Table 1: Believe in Capital Punishment," in *The Harris Poll #41,* August 17, 2001, Harris Interactive, Rochester, NY [Online] http://www.harrisinteractive.com/harris_poll/index.asp [accessed October 19, 2001]

helped exonerate innocent people who had been sentenced to death.

The July 2001 Harris Poll also found that men (74 percent) were more likely than women (62 percent) to support capital punishment. Whites (73 percent) tended to favor the death penalty more than Hispanics (who may be of any race; 63 percent) and blacks (46 percent). Republicans (85 percent) were more likely than independents (68 percent) and Democrats (54 percent) to believe in the death penalty. (See Table 8.2.)

The percentage of those believing in the death penalty varied with age and income. Those in the 18-24 and 30-39 age groups were more likely to favor the death penalty. More than 7 of 10 (73 percent) of persons earning $35,000 to $74,999 favored the death penalty. The support for the death penalty also varied with the degree of education, with those having a postgraduate degree favoring it least. In contrast to previous years, people living in the South were the least likely to favor the death penalty (63 percent). (See Table 8.2.) In 1999 three-quarters (74 percent) of those living in the South believed in the death penalty.

TABLE 8.2

Support for capital punishment by gender, race, age, and other characteristics, 2001

By demographic characteristics, United States, 2001[a]

Question: "Do you believe in capital punishment, that is, the death penalty, or are you opposed to it?"

	Believe in it	Opposed to it	Not sure/ refused
National	67%	26%	7%
Sex			
Male	74	22	4
Female	62	30	8
Race, ethnicity			
White	73	22	6
Black	46	43	10
Hispanic	63	33	4
Age			
18 to 24 years	72	23	5
25 to 29 years	66	23	11
30 to 39 years	71	24	5
40 to 49 years	63	33	4
50 to 64 years	66	28	6
65 years and older	67	22	11
Education			
College post graduate	53	40	7
College graduate	66	29	5
Some college	70	26	3
High school graduate or less	69	22	8
Income			
$75,000 and over	61	34	5
$50,000 to $74,999	73	25	2
$35,000 to $49,999	73	19	8
$25,000 to $34,999	65	27	8
$15,000 to $24,999	66	21	13
Less than $15,000	67	29	4
Region			
East	65	31	4
Midwest	74	20	6
South	63	28	9
West	70	23	8
Politics			
Republican	85	12	2
Democrat	54	36	10
Independent	68	25	6

[a] Percents may not add to 100 because of rounding.

SOURCE: Kathleen Maguire and Ann L. Pastore, eds., "Table 2.60: Attitudes toward the death penalty," in *Sourcebook of Criminal Justice Statistics,* Bureau of Justice Statistics, Washington, DC, 2000

ACCEPTABLE PENALTY FOR MURDER

In 1937, the first time the Gallup Organization polled Americans regarding their attitudes toward the death penalty for murder, 3 in 5 respondents (60 percent) favored the death penalty. For the next three decades support for capital punishment fluctuated, dropping to its lowest point in 1966 (42 percent). Starting in early 1972 support for capital punishment steadily increased, peaking at 80 percent in 1994. Since then support for capital punishment has mainly declined, dropping to 65 percent in May 2001, and rising slightly to 68 percent in October 2001.

The lowest proportion to support capital punishment for murder was 42 percent in 1966, a period of civil rights and anti-Vietnam War marches, "flower children," and the peace movement. It was also the only time in the 66 years (as of 2001) of Gallup polling that those who opposed capital punishment (47 percent) outnumbered those who favored it.

CRIMES DESERVING THE DEATH PENALTY

In June 2000 a *Newsweek* poll conducted by the Princeton Survey Research Associates found that, overall, nearly 2 of 5 Americans (38 percent) favored the death penalty for persons convicted of the most brutal murders, mass murders, and serial killings. More non-Hispanic whites (40 percent) than nonwhites (33 percent) supported the death penalty for such crimes. Another 23 percent preferred the death penalty for persons convicted of murder, other especially violent crimes, and major drug dealing. A larger proportion of non-Hispanic whites (24 percent) than nonwhites (15 percent) favored the death penalty for these crimes. About 12 percent of respondents thought any murderer should be sentenced to death. On the other hand, almost one-fifth (19 percent) of the American public opposed the death penalty in all cases.

EXECUTING MENTALLY RETARDED PERSONS WHO COMMIT MURDER

A Fox News/Opinion Dynamics Poll of June 6-7, 2001, found that more than two-thirds (67 percent) of Americans opposed the death penalty for persons convicted of premeditated murder if those persons have been found to be mentally retarded. About 19 percent supported the death penalty for convicted mentally retarded persons, and 14 percent were not sure.

DEATH PENALTY VERSUS LIFE IMPRISONMENT WITH NO PAROLE

Most people sentenced to life imprisonment are likely to get out on parole at some time in the future. Some people point to this as their reason for favoring the death penalty. In May 2001, when the Gallup Poll asked whether the penalty for murder should be execution or life imprisonment with no possibility of parole, support for the death penalty dropped to 52 percent, with 43 percent of respondents favoring a life sentence without parole. When this question was asked in 2000, the numbers were almost even, with 49 percent in favor of the death penalty and 47 percent preferring life imprisonment. Apparently, a substantial proportion of people who supported the death penalty would advocate life imprisonment if they could be guaranteed the killer would never get out of prison.

Gender Does Not Matter

In 1998 the Gallup Poll asked the same question, indicating the gender of the criminal offender. An almost equal proportion (54 percent for male offenders and 50 percent for females) of respondents thought capital punishment should be the penalty for murder. Similar percentages (36 percent for male offenders and 38 percent for females) of respondents chose life imprisonment with no possibility of parole.

REASONS FOR SUPPORTING THE DEATH PENALTY

In February 2001 the Gallup Poll asked capital punishment supporters why they favored the death penalty for people convicted of murder. Nearly half (48 percent) felt that the death penalty was the appropriate punishment for murder. Two in ten believed the death penalty saved taxpayers money. (Contrary to popular belief, studies show that the death penalty costs more than life imprisonment.) One in ten respondents thought that putting a murderer to death would set an example so that others would not commit the same crime.

SUPPORT FOR CAPITAL PUNISHMENT VARIES WITH SPECIFIC CASES

Although most Americans generally favor the death penalty, they tend to be more lenient when a survey mentions a specific offender. In August 1999, after Buford Furrow killed a postal carrier during a shooting spree in a Jewish community center in Los Angeles, a CNN/*USA Today*/Gallup Poll survey found that 55 percent of the American public favored the death penalty for Furrow if he were convicted. This figure is 16 percentage points lower than the 71 percent of general support for capital punishment that same year.

On June 20, 2001, Andrea Pia Yates of Houston, Texas, admitted to police that she killed her five children. Respondents to a June 28, 2001, Gallup Poll were split over whether or not Yates should be sentenced to death if convicted of killing her children (44 percent for and 43 percent against). Nearly two-thirds (63 percent) of the respondents believed that the defendant's postpartum depression at the time of murder should be taken into consideration during her trial.

In 1998 a *Dallas Morning News* survey found that although most (75 percent) Texans generally favored capital punishment, less than half (45 percent) supported the death penalty for Karla Faye Tucker, the second woman to be executed in the nation since the reinstatement of the death penalty in 1976.

Timothy McVeigh

Timothy McVeigh was initially scheduled to be executed on May 16, 2001, for the 1995 Oklahoma City bombing that killed 168 people. U.S. Attorney General John Ashcroft stayed McVeigh's execution when it was discovered that the FBI failed to turn over all documents to McVeigh's counsel. McVeigh was put to death on June 11, 2001. He was the first federal inmate executed since 1963, when Victor Harry Feguer was hanged in Iowa.

Prior to McVeigh's execution, a June 8–10, 2001, Gallup Poll found that about 3 of 5 (59 percent) respondents favored the death penalty and felt that McVeigh should be put to death. About 1 of 5 (19 percent) respondents opposed the death penalty but believed McVeigh should be executed. A slightly lower proportion (17 percent) indicated that they were against the death penalty and thought that McVeigh should not be executed.

Juan Raul Garza

Interestingly, in the same June 8-10, 2001, Gallup Poll, respondents who were asked similar questions regarding drug kingpin Juan Raul Garza gave slightly different responses. Garza was the second federal inmate set for execution on June 19, 2001, for murder. While nearly as many (50 percent) of the American public who supported the death penalty believed Garza should be executed, just 12 percent of those who opposed the death penalty stated that Garza should be put to death. Over one-fourth (27 percent) of those who opposed the death penalty believed he should not be executed, 10 percent more than those polled regarding McVeigh.

IS THE DEATH PENALTY IMPOSED TOO OFTEN?

Although the United States leads all Western countries in executions, just one-quarter (26 percent) of Americans surveyed by the Gallup Organization in February 2000 felt the death penalty is imposed too often. Three out of every five Americans (60 percent) thought it is not used often enough, while just 4 percent thought the level of death penalty imposition is about right.

The year before, in February 1999, the Gallup Poll found that nonwhites were more likely to oppose the death penalty than whites. Two in five (41 percent) nonwhites believed the death penalty is imposed too often, while one in five (22 percent) whites thought so. In contrast, two-thirds (66 percent) of whites indicated the death penalty is not used enough, while half (52 percent) of nonwhites said so.

Only One-Third of Americans Support an Increase in Executions

Since 1997 the proportion of Americans supporting an increase in execution of convicted criminals has continued to decline. In August 2001 the Harris Poll found that about one-third (35 percent) of Americans favored an increase in the number of executions, one-fourth (26 percent) favored a decrease, and 30 percent favored no change. In 1997 over half (53 percent) of the public favored an increase in the use of the death penalty, 14 percent favored a decrease, and 27 percent wanted no change.

TABLE 8.3

Opinion on percentage of people convicted of murder who are actually innocent, 2001

"For every one hundred people convicted of murder, how many would you guess are actually innocent?"

Base: Innocent people are sometimes convicted of murder (94%)

	Mean estimate		
	1999	2000	July 2001
All Adults	11%	13%	12%
Sex			
Men	8%	10%	9%
Women	13%	15%	14%
Race/Ethnicity			
White	10%	11%	10%
African-American	18%	22%	22%
Hispanic	11%	12%	15%
Education			
High school or less	13%	14%	14%
Some college	9%	12%	10%
College graduate	6%	9%	10%
Post graduate	7%	10%	8%
Party			
Republican	7%	10%	9%
Democrat	12%	13%	15%
Independent	8%	12%	11%

SOURCE: Humphrey Taylor, "Table 5: What Percent of People Convicted of Murder are Innocent?" in *The Harris Poll #41,* August 17, 2001, Harris Interactive, Rochester, NY [Online] http://www.harrisinteractive.com/harris_poll/index.asp [accessed October 19, 2001]

TABLE 8.4

Opinion on whether the death penalty is a deterrent, 1976–2001

"Do you feel that executing people who commit murder deters others from committing murder, or do you think such executions don't have much effect?"

Base: All Respondents

	1976 %	1983 %	1997 %	1999 %	2000 %	July 2001 %
Deters others	59	63	49	47	44	42
Not much effect	34	32	49	49	50	52
Not sure/Refused	7	5	2	4	7	7

SOURCE: Humphrey Taylor, "Table 2: Is Capital Punishment a Deterrent?" in *The Harris Poll #41,* Harris Interactive, Rochester, NY, August 17, 2001 [Online] http://www.harrisinteractive.com/harris_poll/index.asp [accessed October 19, 2001]

DEATH PENALTY FAVORED EVEN IF SOME ARE INNOCENT

The Death Penalty Information Center (Washington, D.C.), a nonprofit organization that opposes capital punishment, reported that between 1973 and 2000, 93 death row inmates were released from death row after proof of innocence. The center attributed the discovery of mistaken convictions to DNA tests, research by journalism students and reporters, and volunteer legal work "outside of the normal appeals process."

In August 2001 the Harris Poll found that virtually all Americans (94 percent) believed that, on average, for every 100 people convicted of murder, approximately 1 in 8 (12 percent) were innocent. Women guessed that this occurred more often (estimate of 14 percent) than men did (9 percent). Blacks estimated that 22 percent of people convicted of murder were innocent, compared to estimates by Hispanics (15 percent) and whites (10 percent). Democrats and those with a high school degree or less were more likely to believe that a higher proportion of innocent people (15 and 14 percent, respectively) were convicted of murder. (See Table 8.3.)

Though 94 percent of respondents indicated they believed that at least some of those charged with murder were innocent, the 12 percent error did not seem to qualify as "substantial." When asked if they would still support the death penalty if a "substantial" amount of innocent people were convicted of murder, only one-third (36 percent) said they would still support the death penalty. Over half (53 percent) would oppose it under those conditions. Nevertheless, the 36 percent who continued to support the death penalty was a smaller proportion compared to their counterparts in 2000 and 1999 (53 percent and 51 percent, respectively).

MORATORIUM

On January 31, 2000, Illinois governor George H. Ryan declared a moratorium on executions. In March 2001 over half (53 percent) of Gallup Poll respondents said they favored a moratorium on the death penalty in states with capital punishment. Such a moratorium was opposed by 40 percent.

In April 2001 an ABC News/*Washington Post* survey found that half (51 percent) of Americans believed there should be a moratorium on executions nationwide so that a commission could study whether or not the death penalty is administered fairly. A slightly smaller proportion (43 percent) of the American public believed enough safeguards are in place to prevent unfair or erroneous executions.

DETERRENT OR NOT?

A July 2001 Harris Poll found that about 4 of 10 Americans (42 percent) felt that capital punishment deters (discourages) people from committing murders. On the other hand, about 5 of 10 Americans (52 percent) believed capital punishment does not have much effect. In 1976, when the death penalty was reinstated, nearly 6 of 10 (59 percent) Americans thought capital punishment was a deterrent, compared to just over 3 in 10 (34 percent) who thought it was not a deterrent. (See Table 8.4.)

In May 2001, a month before Timothy McVeigh was put to death, the Gallup Poll asked the American people if they thought McVeigh's execution would serve as a deterrent to future acts of violence and murder. Two-thirds (66 percent) of respondents did not think so. Less than half that proportion (30 percent) believed the execution would act as a deterrent.

CHAPTER 9

CAPITAL PUNISHMENT AROUND THE WORLD

UNITED NATIONS RESOLUTIONS

Capital punishment is controversial not only in the United States but also in many other countries of the world. The ethical arguments that fuel the debate in the United States also characterize the discussion in other countries. The United Nations's position on capital punishment is a compromise among those countries that want it completely abolished, those that want it limited to very serious offenses, and those that want it left up to each country to decide. In 1957, after 11 years of debate, a statement on the death penalty was included in the International Covenant on Civil and Political Rights, which the General Assembly adopted in Resolution 2200 (XXI) of December 16, 1966. Article 6 of the Covenant states,

- Every human being has the inherent right to life. This right shall be protected by law. No one shall be arbitrarily deprived of his life.

- In countries that have not abolished the death penalty, sentence of death may be imposed only for the most serious crimes in accordance with the law in force at the time of the commission of the crime and not contrary to the provisions of the present Covenant and to the Convention on the Prevention and Punishment of the Crime of Genocide [systematic killing of a racial, political, or cultural group]. This penalty can only be carried out pursuant to a final judgment rendered by a competent court.

- When deprivation of life constitutes the crime of genocide, it is understood that nothing in this article shall authorize any State Party to the present Covenant to derogate [turn away] in any way from any obligation assumed under the provisions of the Convention on the Prevention and Punishment of the Crime of Genocide.

- Anyone sentenced to death shall have the right to seek pardon or commutation of the sentence [replacement of the death sentence with a lesser sentence]. Amnesty,

pardon, or commutation of the sentence of death may be granted in all cases.

- Sentence of death shall not be imposed for crimes committed by persons below eighteen years of age and shall not be carried out on pregnant women.

- Nothing in this article shall be invoked to delay or prevent the abolition of capital punishment by any State Party to the present Covenant.

The United Nations (UN) has dealt with the death penalty in several other documents and meetings. Among them is General Assembly Resolution 2393 (XXIII) of November 26, 1968, which specifies the following legal safeguards that should be offered to condemned prisoners by countries with capital punishment:

- A person condemned to death shall not be deprived of the right to appeal to a higher judicial authority or, as the case may be, to petition for pardon or reprieve [postponement or cancellation of punishment].

- A death sentence shall not be carried out until the procedures of appeal or, as the case may be, of petition for pardon or reprieve have been terminated.

- Special attention shall be given in the case of indigent [poor] persons by the provision of adequate legal assistance at all stages of the proceedings.

Since then the UN has come out more strongly for eliminating capital punishment. General Assembly Resolution 2857 (XXVI) of December 20, 1971, observed,

In order to guarantee fully the right to life, provided for in Article 3 of the Universal Declaration of Human Rights, the main objective to be pursued is that of progressively restricting the number of offenses for which capital punishment may be imposed, with a view to the desirability of abolishing this punishment in all countries.

The UN Economic and Social Council Resolution 1574 (L) of May 20, 1971, made a similar declaration. In 1984 the Economic and Social Council adopted the *Safeguards Guaranteeing Protection of the Rights of Those Facing the Death Penalty*, including persons younger than age 18 at the time the crime was committed. Subsequently, over the years, General Assembly and Economic and Social Council resolutions have called for the eventual abolition of the death penalty.

In 1989 the UN General Assembly adopted the Second Optional Protocol to the International Covenant on Civil and Political Rights, aimed at abolishing the death penalty. This international treaty allows countries to retain the death penalty in wartime as long as they reserve the right to do so at the time they become party to the treaty. As of 2001, 43 countries were parties to it, and seven more were signatories. By signing the treaty, a country indicates its intention to become a party at a later date.

Recent UN Initiatives

On April 28, 1999, the UN Commission on Human Rights voted 30-11, with 12 abstentions, in favor of a worldwide moratorium (a temporary suspension) on executions. The resolution was sponsored by the European Union. The United States and China, considered the most frequent users of the death penalty, voted against the moratorium. The other nine countries opposing the moratorium were Bangladesh, Botswana, Indonesia, Japan, Pakistan, Rwanda, South Korea, Sudan, and Qatar.

On August 24, 1999, the UN Sub-Commission on the Promotion and Protection of Human Rights called upon:

- All states which retain the death penalty and do not apply a moratorium on executions, in order to mark the millennium, to commute the sentences of those under sentence of death on 31 December 1999 at least to sentences of life imprisonment and to commit themselves to a moratorium on the imposition of the death penalty throughout the year 2000.

- [For the first time in a UN resolution] all states that retain the death penalty for refusal to undertake military services or for desertion not to apply the death penalty where the refusal to undertake military service or the desertion is the result of conscientious objection to such service.

On December 18, 2000, the secretary general of the United Nations, Kofi Annan, received a petition signed by over 3 million people from more than 130 countries, appealing for an end to executions. Subsequently, the secretary general called for a worldwide moratorium on the death penalty, noting that the taking of life as punishment for crime is "too absolute [and] too irreversible."

RETENTIONIST COUNTRIES

Amnesty International (AI), a human rights organization headquartered in London, United Kingdom, maintains information on capital punishment throughout the world. (AI vehemently opposes the death penalty, considering it the "ultimate form of cruel, inhuman, and degrading punishment.") The organization refers to countries that retain and use the death penalty as retentionist countries; those that no longer use the death penalty are known as abolitionist countries.

As of June 1, 2001, 86 countries and territories in the world retained and used the death penalty as a possible punishment for ordinary crimes. (See Table 9.1.) Ordinary crimes are crimes committed during peacetime. Ordinary crimes that could lead to the death penalty include murder, rape, and, in some countries, robbery or embezzlement of very large sums of money. Exceptional crimes, on the other hand, are military crimes committed during exceptional times, mainly wartime. Examples are treason, spying, or desertion (leaving the armed services without permission).

Although many of the retentionist countries had not executed anybody in many years, a small number of countries continue to carry out numerous executions. AI reported that the top 10 countries that continued executions were China, Iran, Saudi Arabia, the United States, Taiwan, Sierra Leone, Kazakstan, Nigeria, Belarus, and Kyrgyzstan.

AI reported that in 2000 at least 1,457 inmates were executed in 28 countries. Sixty-five countries sentenced over 3,000 people to death. AI believed that the actual numbers of those executed and sentenced to death were much higher than cases known to the organization.

In 2000 four countries accounted for 88 percent of all known executions worldwide—China (at least 1,000), Saudi Arabia (123), the United States (85), and Iran (75). Iraq reportedly put many people to death, but AI had not been able to determine the exact count.

United States

The United States remains the only Western country that practices capital punishment. (The federal government and 38 states have the death penalty.) In September 1997, for the first time, a UN monitor investigated the use of the death penalty in the United States. In his report to the UN Commission on Human Rights, the special investigator accused the United States of unfair, arbitrary, and racist use of capital punishment. He claimed that "allegations of racial discrimination in the imposition of death sentences are particularly serious in southern states, such as Alabama, Florida, Louisiana, Mississippi, Georgia and Texas, known as the 'death penalty belt.'"

FOREIGN NATIONALS. The Death Penalty Information Center (Washington, D.C.) reported that, as of September 27, 2001, 117 foreign nationals representing 34 nationalities were on death row in the United States. Capital punishment opponents claimed that the United States generally does not inform foreign nationals under arrest that they have the right to consult with the consulate of their home country as required by Article 36 of the Vienna Convention on Consular Relations. Article 36 requires local law enforcement to notify all detained foreigners "without delay" of their right to consular access. The United States had ratified (formally became a party to) this international agreement in 1969. In 1999 the United States executed five foreign nationals, and one each in 2000 and 2001.

THE UNITED STATES DEFIES THE UN'S HIGHEST COURT. Angel Francisco Breard, a Paraguayan national, was arrested on capital murder charges in 1992. In 1993 Breard was sentenced to death after his convictions for rape and capital murder. Following the denial of his appeals before the Virginia Supreme Court and the U.S. Supreme Court, Breard invoked the provision of the Vienna Convention on Consular Relations. The U.S. District Court, in *Breard v. Netherland* (945 F. Supp. 1255, 1266 [E.D. Va. 1996]), rejected Breard's claim because he had "procedurally defaulted" the claim when he failed to raise it in state court. In addition, the district court concluded that Breard could not show cause and prejudice for this default.

In the same year, 1996, the Republic of Paraguay brought suit against Virginia officials for violation of the Vienna Convention because they failed to notify the Paraguayan consulate of Breard's arrest. The district court dismissed the suit, which the appellate court affirmed. On April 3, 1998, the Republic of Paraguay brought the case before the International Court of Justice (ICJ; the UN's highest court), which ruled, on April 9, 1998, that the United States should stay Breard's execution pending the ICJ's final decision. Paraguay had also petitioned the U.S. Supreme Court.

On April 14, 1998, the day of execution, the U.S. Supreme Court, voting 6-3, refused to intervene in the case despite requests for a stay of execution from then-Secretary of State Madeleine Albright. In *Paraguay et al. v. Gilmore* (No. 97- 1390 [S-738]), the Court stated,

It is the rule in this country that assertions of error in criminal proceedings must first be raised in state court in order to form the basis for relief in *habeas*... Claims not so raised are considered defaulted. By not asserting his Vienna Convention claim in state court, Breard failed to exercise his rights under the Vienna Convention in conformity with the laws of the United States and the Commonwealth of Virginia. Having failed to do so, he cannot raise a claim of violation of those rights now on federal *habeas* review.

As for Paraguay's suits (both the original action and the case coming to us on petition for *certiorari* [a petition to the Supreme Court to review the issues brought up in

TABLE 9.1

Countries retaining the death penalty for ordinary crimes, 2001

Afghanistan	Liberia
Algeria	Libya
Antigua and Barbuda	Malawi
Armenia	Malaysia
Bahamas	Mauritania
Bahrain	Mongolia
Bangladesh	Morocco
Barbados	Myanmar
Belarus	Nigeria
Belize	North Korea
Benin	Oman
Botswana	Pakistan
Burundi	Palestinian Authority
Cameroon	Philippines
Chad	Qatar
China	Russian Federation
Comoros	Rwanda
Congo (Democratic Republic)	Saint Christopher & Nevis
Cuba	Saint Lucia
Dominica	Saint Vincent & Grenadines
Egypt	Saudi Arabia
Equatorial Guinea	Sierra Leone
Eritrea	Singapore
Ethiopia	Somalia
Gabon	South Korea
Ghana	Sudan
Guatemala	Swaziland
Guinea	Syria
Guyana	Taiwan
India	Tajikistan
Indonesia	Tanzania
Iran	Thailand
Iraq	Trinidad and Tobago
Jamaica	Tunisia
Japan	Uganda
Jordan	United Arab Emirates
Kazakstan	United States of America
Kenya	Uzbekistan
Kuwait	Vietnam
Kyrgyzstan	Yemen
Laos	Yugoslavia (Federal Republic)
Lebanon	Zambia
Lesotho	Zimbabwe

SOURCE: Adapted from "Abolitionist and Retentionist Countries," in *The Amnesty International Website against the Death Penalty,* Amnesty International, London, June 1, 2001 [Online] http://www.amnesty.org/ [accessed November 2, 2001]

the direct appeal]), neither the text nor the history of the Vienna Convention clearly provides a foreign nation a private right of action in United States courts to set aside a criminal conviction and sentence for violation of consular notification provisions... Though Paraguay claims that its suit is within an exemption dealing with continuing consequences of past violations of federal rights, we do not agree. The failure to notify the Paraguayan Consul occurred long ago and has no continuing effect.

In November 1998 the United States formally apologized to Paraguay for failing to inform Breard of his right to seek consular assistance. Paraguay withdrew its lawsuit following the apology.

GERMANY SUES THE UNITED STATES. In 1982 German brothers Karl and Walter LaGrand killed a bank employee during a robbery attempt in Tucson, Arizona. They were sentenced to death in 1984. In February 1999 Karl LaGrand was executed. The day before the execution of Walter LaGrand, Germany sued the United States before the ICJ. According to Germany, the United States violated Article 36 of the Vienna Convention by failing to inform the defendants without delay after their arrest of their right to contact the German consulate for help. Germany also claimed that Arizona prosecutors violated Article 36 because they knowingly failed to inform Germany of the arrests and convictions until 10 years after the murder. By that time it was too late, under "procedural default," for the brothers to raise the issue of the treaty violation.

The ICJ ordered the United States to stay Walter LaGrand's execution, but Arizona let the execution take place. Despite the execution, Germany proceeded with the lawsuit. During the November 2000 hearing before the ICJ, the United States argued that Article 36 does not confer personal rights to individual nationals. In other words, the United States conceded that, while it violated its treaty obligations to Germany, it did not violate its obligations to the brothers. The United States added that, although German authorities knew of the LaGrand case in 1992, they waited until 1999 to intervene for the brothers.

On June 27, 2001, the ICJ, in *Germany v. United States of America*, ruled 14-1 that the United States had violated its obligations to Germany and to the LaGrand brothers under the Vienna Convention on Consular Relations. The ICJ also ruled that domestic law must not prevent the review of the conviction and sentencing when a defendant's right to consular notification has been violated. In addition, the United States must provide review and remedies should a similar case arise.

China

Human rights groups have found that China executes more persons each year than all other nations combined. In October 1999 the Chinese government passed a law allowing the imposition of the death sentence on leaders of the Falun Gong movement charged with endangering national security and murder. The government claimed the "cult" movement has caused the death of over a thousand followers by dissuading them from seeking medical help.

In 2001 a massive rise in executions occurred as a result of a nationwide anticrime campaign called Strike Hard. Chinese officials had allegedly been very inconsistent in determining which crimes warranted the death penalty. Law enforcement, under pressure to achieve results, sped up the criminal process, reportedly subjecting defendants to torture to extract confessions. It is reported that the general public approves of the death penalty.

Persons convicted of nonviolent offenses, such as tax fraud, bribery, embezzlement, and counterfeiting, have been put to death. During the last Strike Hard campaign in

1996 AI reported over 4,400 inmates were shot to death. Between April and July 2001, nearly 3,000 death sentences had been handed down. About 1,780 were executed during those four months alone.

Japan

AI noted that "executions in Japan ... appear to be inflicted in an arbitrary fashion." The Japanese government does not announce any pending execution or notify families of death row inmates about the impending execution. Even the inmate scheduled to be put to death learns of his or her fate only about two hours before the execution.

Forum 90 is an abolitionist group that monitors capital punishment in Japan. In *The Hidden Death Penalty in Japan* (Sachiho Takahashi and Thomas Mariadason, eds., Tokyo, Japan, June 2001), Forum 90 reported that, in addition to the other secret elements of the death penalty in Japan, the public is not informed of the identities of those executed. Since Japan has no jury system, ordinary citizens find out about an execution only after the Ministry of Justice announces that it has occurred.

Death row inmates are forbidden from meeting with journalists and researchers collecting data on the death penalty. Any information gathered by these persons usually results from significant investigations of their own.

Japan is also known for its drawn-out process of appeals. A case that drew worldwide attention involved a prisoner who, in 1997, after having been on death row for 30 years, was executed in secrecy. The inmate had committed multiple murders at age 19 (a minor under Japanese law) but was convicted as an adult.

Between 1988 and 1992 the number of prisoners sentenced to death declined, from 12 in 1988 to 5 in 1992. No executions occurred between 1990 and March 1993. Since March 1993, when executions resumed, 7 prisoners have been put to death. As of December 2000, 53 persons were on death row. According to the U.S. Justice Department, polls indicate that the Japanese public generally approves of the death penalty.

ABOLITIONIST IN PRACTICE

Twenty countries are considered abolitionist in practice. (See Table 9.2.) They have death penalty laws but have not carried out any execution for the past 10 years or more. Some of these nations have not executed anyone for the past 30 years or more. Others have made an international commitment not to impose the death sentence.

ABOLITIONIST COUNTRIES

In 1863 Venezuela became the first nation to outlaw the death penalty. Since that time many countries have abolished capital punishment. Several countries, however,

TABLE 9.2

Countries that retain but do not impose the death penalty, 2001

Countries which retain the death penalty for ordinary crimes such as murder but can be considered abolitionist in practice in that they have not executed anyone during the past 10 years and are believed to have a policy or established practice of not carrying out executions. The list also includes countries which have made an international commitment not to use the death penalty

Bhutan	Nauru
Brunei Darussalam	Niger
Burkina Faso	Papua New Guinea
Central African Republic	Samoa
Congo (Republic)	Senegal
Gambia	Sri Lanka
Grenada	Suriname
Madagascar	Togo
Maldives	Tonga
Mali	Turkey

SOURCE: Adapted from "Abolitionist and Retentionist Countries," in *The Amnesty International Website against the Death Penalty,* Amnesty International, London, June 1, 2001 [Online] http://www.amnesty.org/ [accessed November 2, 2001]

TABLE 9.3

Countries whose laws do not provide for the death penalty for any crime, 2001

Andorra	Guineau-Bissau	Norway
Angola	Haiti	Palau
Australia	Honduras	Panama
Austria	Hungary	Paraguay
Azerbaijan	Iceland	Poland
Belgium	Ireland	Portugal
Bulgaria	Italy	Romania
Cambodia	Kiribati	San Marino
Canada	Liechtenstein	São Tomé and
Cape Verde	Lithuania	Príncipe
Colombia	Luxembourg	Seychelles
Costa Rica	Macedonia (former	Slovak Republic
Cote d'Ivoire	Yugoslav Republic)	Slovenia
Croatia	Malta	Solomon Islands
Czech Republic	Marshall Islands	South Africa
Denmark	Mauritius	Spain
Djibouti	Micronesia (Federated	Sweden
Dominican Republic	States)	Switzerland
East Timor	Moldova	Turkmenistan
Ecuador	Monaco	Tuvalu
Estonia	Mozambique	Ukraine
Finland	Namibia	United Kingdom
France	Nepal	Urugray
Georgia	Netherlands	Vanuatu
Germany	New Zealand	Vatican City State
Greece	Nicaragua	Venezuela

SOURCE: Adapted from "Abolitionist and Retentionist Countries," in *The Amnesty International Website against the Death Penalty,* Amnesty International, London, June 1, 2001 [Online] http://www.amnesty.org/ [accessed November 2, 2001]

including Argentina, Brazil, and Spain, restored it after previously rejecting it. Argentina revoked the death penalty in 1921 and then again in 1972, reinstating it in 1976 after a military takeover. Then, in 1984 it abolished capital punishment again. Brazil abolished the death penalty in 1882, restored it in 1969, and revoked it again in 1979.

Similarly, Spain repealed the death penalty in 1932, brought it back for certain crimes in 1934, totally restored it in 1938, and then abolished it again in 1978. The switching back and forth between the abolition and the reimposition of capital punishment often reflects these countries' shift between democracy and dictatorship.

As of June 1, 2001, 75 countries had abolished the death penalty for all crimes. (See Table 9.3.) Since 1976, when the United States reinstated the death penalty after a nine-year moratorium, many countries have stopped imposing capital punishment. In 1996 Belgium, the last of the Western European democracies to have the death sentence, abolished it for all crimes. In reality, Belgium has not executed any prisoner since 1950. Hong Kong went back under Chinese jurisdiction in July 1997. Having abolished capital punishment in 1993, the former British colony remains abolitionist. In 1999 East Timor, Turkmenistan, and the Ukraine became abolitionist nations for all crimes. In 2000 Cote D'Ivoire and Malta also abolished the death penalty for all crimes. (See Table 9.4 for a list of the countries that have abolished the death penalty since 1976.)

Abolitionist Countries for Ordinary Crimes Only

Fourteen countries do not impose the death penalty for ordinary crimes committed during peacetime, though they may impose it for exceptional crimes. (See Table 9.5.) Since 1997 five countries—Bolivia (1997), Bosnia-

Herzegovina (1997), Latvia (1999), Albania (2000), and Chile (2001)—have joined this group.

Capital Punishment Is Seldom Reintroduced

AI noted that once a country abolishes capital punishment, it seldom brings it back. Between 1985 and June 1, 2001, over 40 countries either enacted laws abolishing the death penalty or, having revoked it for ordinary crimes, eventually outlawed it for all crimes. During this period just four abolitionist countries reimposed the death penalty—Nepal, the Philippines, Gambia, and Papua New Guinea. Nepal, which reinstated the death penalty for murder, abolished it for all crimes in 1997. Gambia and Papua New Guinea remained abolitionist in practice. They retained the death penalty for ordinary crimes, but did not put any person to death during the 10 years from 1991 to 2001.

In late 1993 the Philippines reintroduced the death penalty. In February 1999 the first execution since 1976 took place, followed by six others. In March 2000 then-President Joseph Estrada suspended all executions in honor of the Christian Jubilee year. In October 2001 the new president, Gloria Macapagal Arroyo, announced the resumption of executions in light of the rising numbers of kidnapping cases. The president also planned to reverse the over 100 death sentences commuted by her predecessor. As

TABLE 9.4

Countries that have abolished the death penalty, 1976–2001

1976: **PORTUGAL** abolished the death penalty for all crimes.

1978: **DENMARK** abolished the death penalty for all crimes.

1979: **LUXEMBOURG, NICARAGUA** and **NORWAY** abolished the death penalty for all crimes. **BRAZIL, FIJI** and **PERU** abolished the death penalty for ordinary crimes.

1981: **FRANCE** and **CAPE VERDE** abolished the death penalty for all crimes.

1982: The **NETHERLANDS** abolished the death penalty for all crimes.

1983: **CYPRUS** and **EL SALVADOR** abolished the death penalty for ordinary crimes.

1984: **ARGENTINA** abolished the death penalty for ordinary crimes.

1985: **AUSTRALIA** abolished the death penalty for all crimes.

1987: **HAITI, LIECHTENSTEIN** and the **GERMAN DEMOCRATIC REPUBLIC** *(1)* abolished the death penalty for all crimes.

1989: **CAMBODIA, NEW ZEALAND, ROMANIA** and **SLOVENIA** *(2)* abolished the death penalty for all crimes.

1990: **ANDORRA, CROATIA** *(2)*, the **CZECH AND SLOVAK FEDERAL REPUBLIC** *(3)*, **HUNGARY, IRELAND, MOZAMBIQUE, NAMIBIA** and **SÃO TOMÉ AND PRÍNCIPE** abolished the death penalty for all crimes.

1992: **ANGOLA, PARAGUAY** and **SWITZERLAND** abolished the death penalty for all crimes.

1993: **GREECE, GUINEA-BISSAU, HONG KONG** *(4)* and **SEYCHELLES** abolished the death penalty for all crimes.

1994: **ITALY** abolished the death penalty for all crimes.

1995: **DJIBOUTI, MAURITIUS, MOLDOVA** and **SPAIN** abolished the death penalty for all crimes.

1996: **BELGIUM** abolished the death penalty for all crimes.

1997: **GEORGIA, NEPAL, POLAND** and **SOUTH AFRICA** abolished the death penalty for all crimes. **BOLIVIA** and **BOSNIA-HERZEGOVINA** abolished the death penalty for ordinary crimes.

1998: **AZERBAIJAN, BULGARIA, CANADA, ESTONIA, LITHUANIA** and the **UNITED KINGDOM** abolished the death penalty for all crimes.

1999: **EAST TIMOR, TURKMENISTAN** and **UKRAINE** abolished the death penalty for all crimes. **LATVIA** *(5)* abolished the death penalty for ordinary crimes.

2000 : **COTE D'IVOIRE** and **MALTA** abolished the death penalty for all crimes. **ALBANIA** *(6)* abolished the death penalty for ordinary crimes.

2001: **CHILE** abolished the death penalty for ordinary crimes.

Notes:
(1) In 1990 the German Democratic Republic became unified with the Federal Republic of Germany, where the death penalty had been abolished in 1949.
(2) Slovenia and Croatia abolished the death penalty while they were still republics of the Socialist Federal Republic of Yugoslavia. The two republics became independent in 1991.
(3) In 1993 the Czech and Slovak Federal Republic divided into two states, the Czech Republic and Slovakia.
(4) In 1997 Hong Kong was returned to Chinese rule as a special administrative region of China. Amnesty International understands that Hong Kong will remain abolitionist.
(5) In 1999 the Latvian parliament voted to ratify Protocol No. 6 to the European Convention on Human Rights, abolishing the death penalty for peacetime offences.
(6) In 2000 Albania ratified Protocol No. 6 to the European Convention on Human Rights, abolishing the death penalty for peacetime offences.

SOURCE: Adapted from "Abolitionist and Retentionist Countries," in *The Amnesty International Website against the Death Penalty,* Amnesty International, London, June 1, 2001 [Online] http://www.amnesty.org/ [accessed November 2, 2001]

TABLE 9.5

Countries that impose the death penalty only for exceptional crimes, 2001

Countries whose laws provide for the death penalty only for exceptional crimes such as crimes under military law or crimes committed in exceptional circumstances

Albania	Cyprus
Argentina	El Salvador
Bolivia	Fiji
Bosnia-Herzegovina	Israel
Brazil	Latvia
Chile	Mexico
Cook Islands	Peru

SOURCE: Adapted from "Abolitionist and Retentionist Countries," in *The Amnesty International Website against the Death Penalty,* Amnesty International, London, June 1, 2001 [Online] http://www.amnesty.org/ [accessed November 2, 2001]

of October 2001 over 1,500 persons were on death row, one of the largest per capita death row populations in the world.

DEATH PENALTY AGAINST MINORS

According to AI, since 1990 the execution of prisoners who were under the age of 18 when they committed their crime has continued in seven countries—the Democratic Republic of Congo, Iran, Nigeria, Pakistan, Saudi Arabia, the United States, and Yemen. Between 1997 and September 2001 the majority of executions of inmates who were under 18 during the commission of the crime—8 of 12 recorded executions—had occurred in the United States.

AI claimed that these countries were violating international human rights agreements. The International Covenant on Civil and Political Rights, the UN Convention on the Rights of the Child, and the American Convention on Human Rights all ban the imposition of the death sentence on persons who were less than 18 years old at the time of the crime. The UN Convention on the Rights of the Child further prohibits the sentence of life without the possibility of parole for those younger than 18 years old. Today virtually all countries in the world either have statutes prohibiting the execution of minors or are believed to be abiding by the provisions of one or another of the above treaties. In December 2000 Pakistan banned the juvenile death penalty.

CHAPTER 10

THE DEBATE—
CAPITAL PUNISHMENT SHOULD BE MAINTAINED

STATEMENT OF STEVEN D. STEWART, PROSECUTOR, CLARK COUNTY, INDIANA, NOVEMBER 7, 2001

Along with two-thirds of the public, I believe in capital punishment. I believe that there are some defendants who have earned the ultimate punishment our society has to offer by committing murder with aggravating circumstances present. I believe life is sacred. It cheapens the life of an innocent murder victim to say that society has no right to keep the murderer from ever killing again. In my view, society has not only the right, but the duty to act in self defense to protect the innocent.

Nevertheless, the value of the death penalty in our current system of justice is a limited one and should not be overstated. Because the death sentence is so rarely carried out, whatever deterrent value that exists is lessened in years of appeals and due process. Because of the unlimited power of judges, juries, and Prosecutors to show mercy, the difference between those who receive the death penalty and those who do not is minimal. Finally, because the system allows it, the financial costs to state and local governments can be staggering.

In spite of these shortcomings, it is my view that pursuing a death sentence in appropriate cases is the right thing to do. There is no adequate and acceptable alternative. Life Without Parole does not eliminate the risk that the prisoner will murder a guard, a visitor, or another inmate, and we should not be compelled to take that risk. It is also not unheard of for inmates to escape from prison. The prisoner will not be eligible for parole until the next legislative session, when the parole laws can be changed. Considering that a defendant sentenced to "life imprisonment" across the country actually serves on the average less than 8 years in prison, it is a good bet that "life without parole" will not have the meaning intended as years go by.

No system of justice can produce results which are 100 percent certain all the time. Mistakes will be made in

any system, which relies upon human testimony for proof. We should be vigilant to uncover and avoid such mistakes. Nevertheless, the risk of making a mistake with the extraordinary due process applied in death penalty cases is very small, and there is no credible evidence to show that any innocent persons have been executed at least since the death penalty was reactivated in 1976. The estimated 50–85 inmates "exonerated" and released from death row, as trumpeted by antideath penalty activists, should be considered in context of over 7,000 death sentences handed down since 1973. The inevitability of a mistake should not serve as grounds to eliminate the death penalty any more than the risk of having a wreck should make automobiles illegal. At the same time, we should never ignore the risks of allowing the inmate to kill again. Our "system" was created by legislators and judges. In order for the death penalty to remain a meaningful and effective punishment, those same legislators and judges need to make necessary changes to reflect the will of the people in a democratic society.

STATEMENT OF SENATOR ORRIN G. HATCH (R-UT) BEFORE THE SUBCOMMITTEE ON CONSTITUTION, FEDERALISM AND PROPERTY RIGHTS OF THE SENATE JUDICIARY COMMITTEE, JUNE 13, 2001

The death penalty is a subject on the minds of many Americans in light of the execution this week of Timothy McVeigh for the murder of 168 innocent people in the worst incident of domestic terrorism in our nation's history. The death penalty is the ultimate punishment society can impose, and it is appropriate that we scrutinize its use in our federal criminal justice system.

While we may disagree about whether capital punishment should be permitted in our country, we all agree that it must be meted out fairly. In my view, the studies released by former Attorney General Reno and Attorney

General Ashcroft show that there is no invidious racial discrimination in the application of the federal death penalty. Indeed, if anything these studies show that the federal government has sought the death penalty for proportionately fewer minorities than white....

Nevertheless, we all must share Attorney General Ashcroft's concern that nearly 80 percent of defendants in federal capital cases are minorities. We also must commit ourselves to identifying and solving the socioeconomic factors that underlie these statistics. Doing something about this, however, requires that we first have the courage to acknowledge a painful but undeniable fact: the offenses that may lead to homicides and capital charges in the federal system are not evenly distributed across all population groups. Moreover, while many complain about the racial disparity among death penalty defendants, there is hardly a mention of the disparity among murder victims. As former Deputy Attorney General Eric Holder pointed out last year, "although young African-American men are only 1 percent of our nation's population, they are fully 18 percent of our nation's homicide victims.... Although black people make up 12 to 15 percent of the nation's population, they are about 50 percent of the nation's homicide victims."....

... Predictably, some death penalty opponents still insist there should be a moratorium on all pending executions until completion of these additional research projects. I respectfully submit that such an action is simply not warranted on the facts before us. That was the conclusion of the prior administration, as made clear by the public statements of President Clinton, Attorney General Reno, and Deputy Attorney General Eric Holder. It is not surprising, therefore, that the current administration takes the same position.

As stated last year by Attorney General Reno, there simply is no question of the guilt of the current defendants on death row. While we can—and will—continue to seek to better understand and improve the current system, there is no justifiable reason to fail to carry out the sentences properly imposed in these cases.

The case of Juan Garza, who is scheduled to be executed next week, illustrates why the call for a moratorium is misguided. No one seriously questions that he is guilty of murdering three members of his drug-trafficking organization. The evidence also shows that he was responsible for five additional murders, and that while in custody pending trial, Garza threatened prosecutors and jurors....

Like all of the defendants on federal death row, Mr. Garza faces execution not because of his race, ethnicity, or place of residence, but because he is guilty of committing heinous crimes. Attorney General Ashcroft, like Attorney General Reno before him, is right to reject calls for a moratorium.

STATEMENT OF PRESIDENT GEORGE W. BUSH ABOUT THE EXECUTION OF TIMOTHY MCVEIGH, JUNE 11, 2001

This morning, the United States of America carried out the severest sentence for the gravest of crimes. The victims of the Oklahoma City bombing have been given not vengeance, but justice. And one young man met the fate he chose for himself six years ago. For the survivors of the crime and for the families of the dead, the pain goes on. The final punishment of the guilty cannot alone bring peace to the innocent. It cannot recover the loss or balance the scales, and it is not meant to do so.

Today, every living person who was hurt by the evil done in Oklahoma City can rest in the knowledge that there has been a reckoning. At every point from the morning of April 19, 1995, to this hour, we have seen the good that overcomes evil. We saw it in the rescuers who saved and suffered with the victims. We have seen it in a community that has grieved and held close the memory of the lost. We have seen it in the work of detectives, marshals, and police. And we have seen it in the courts. Due process ruled. The case was proved. The verdict was calmly reached. And the rights of the accused were protected and observed to the full, and to the end. Under the laws of our country, the matter is concluded. Life and history bring tragedies, and often they cannot be explained. But they can be redeemed. They are redeemed by dispensing justice, though eternal justice is not ours to deliver.

By remembering those who grieve, including Timothy McVeigh's mother, father, and sisters, and by trusting in purposes greater than our own, may God in his mercy grant peace to all, to the lives that were taken six years ago, to the lives that go on, and to the life that ended today.

LETTER WRITTEN BY STATE SENATOR RON KLEIN (D-FL) TO GOVERNOR JEB BUSH TO CONSIDER LETHAL INJECTION AS THE METHOD OF EXECUTION, JULY 12, 1999

For those of us who are strong proponents of capital punishment, once due process has been met, a quick and efficient means of execution is an absolute requirement in order to sufficiently create the deterrent which is intended. Every time the constitutionality of the electric chair is challenged, we jeopardize the swift implementation of justice, undermine the impact and deterrence value of a death sentence, and prolong the pain and suffering of victims' families. We should, once and for all, adopt lethal injection as the means of execution in Florida for all future death warrants.

Each time we execute an inmate in Florida by electrocution, we risk the potential of another mishap that will be the catalyst for additional stays and delays. The method of execution should not take priority over the most efficient, constitutional means of carrying out a death sentence. I have said many times before that "dead is dead."

Lethal injection is being successfully administered as the sole method of execution in 16 states and as a choice in 16 others. In Texas, for example, 128 inmates (more than any other state in the nation) were executed by lethal injection without incident between 1977 and 1997. Over 77 percent of executions nationwide are now carried out by lethal injection because it has met constitutional muster over and over again.

It is time for Florida to take the issue of the electric chair, which is forcing delays, appeals and stays, out of the equation. By providing timely and efficient justice, we can begin to send a strong message to criminals and accomplish the goal with which the public has charged us.

I look forward to your support and leadership on this issue during the upcoming legislative session.

STATEMENT OF REPRESENTATIVE HENRY J. HYDE (R-IL), CHAIRMAN, HOUSE OF REPRESENTATIVES JUDICIARY COMMITTEE, DECEMBER 10, 1997

With regard to the issue of capital punishment, it is my view that the death penalty, if imposed fairly and without undue delay, can serve a deterrent purpose in our criminal justice system. There are some cases of murder that are so heinous and brutal that society must impose its ultimate penalty. These cases would include terrorism, treason, hijacking resulting in the death of a hostage, or the killing of a police [officer] or prison guard acting in the line of duty. If, under careful deliberation, it is determined that such a crime has occurred and the defendant in the crime has been proven guilty beyond a reasonable doubt, then I would support the imposition of capital punishment.

Society has a right to impose whatever punishment it collectively determines befits the violation of its laws. Denying society the ability to impose the death penalty on those convicted of murder devalues the lives of its citizens.

STATEMENT OF SENATOR DON NICKLES (R-OK) AFTER THE OKLAHOMA CITY BOMBER, TIMOTHY MCVEIGH, WAS SENTENCED TO DEATH, JUNE 13, 1997

Oklahomans everywhere breathed a deep sigh of relief when Denver jurors found Timothy McVeigh guilty of the Oklahoma City bombing recently.

It is no longer speculation that McVeigh is guilty of the most horrific case of domestic terrorism in our nation's history. His murderous and carefully plotted attack against America killed 169 people, including 19 children. We will always remember their faces, treasure their lives, and honor their dreams and hopes. And we will

help bear the physical and emotional burdens of more than 460 others who were scarred and injured in the blast.

Now, Oklahoma turns its attention toward making sure McVeigh's sentence is carried out fully and taking another step toward putting the tragedy behind us....

I am ... pleased by the legislative changes passed by Congress in the wake of the Oklahoma City bombing. The Oklahoma congressional delegation was unified in our work to provide trial coverage on closed-circuit television; give survivors and victims' family members the ability to both view a trial and testify during the sentencing phase; and strengthen penalties for the use of explosive devices and killing federal law officers. Importantly, Congress also curbed the nearly limitless stream of appeals by death row inmates.

STATEMENT OF REPRESENTATIVE ROBERT K. DORNAN (R-CA), DECEMBER 4, 1995

As a U.S. congressman, one of my primary concerns is the rule of law. Over the last 30 years, our nation has experienced a crippling decline in effective law enforcement resulting from the erosion of the concept of swift and sure punishment for law breakers. This has resulted from multiple causes, including a politicized judiciary, which all too often has been more sympathetic to the criminal than the victim, and as well, to a general judicial philosophy which has become more concerned with questions of procedure than the search for truth....

As a conservative, I believe there are certain crimes for which the death penalty is justified. Some individuals commit crimes so reprehensible that they forfeit their right to live in society. And some commit crimes so heinous that they do not deserve to be supported for life by the society they injured. These are the people who should be sentenced to death. The death penalty should remain our most severe punishment and should be used only in extraordinary cases. But as has always been the standard in our justice system, the punishment should fit the crime.

STATEMENT OF REPRESENTATIVE SAM JOHNSON (R-TX), NOVEMBER 8, 1995

Regarding capital punishment, I continue to believe that the best way to prevent crime is to target repeat offenders. Criminals must understand the consequences of their actions. We should make prisoners serve out their entire sentences and enforce stiffer penalties, such as capital punishment against felons convicted of heinous crimes, such as rape, murder, and drug-related deaths. I am aware of the need for individual responsibility in determining the death penalty's applicability, and we must always be diligent not to punish the innocent. However, in spite of these risks, I believe that capital punishment is a morally justifiable, necessary, and effective punishment.

Thirty-six states currently administer capital punishment. Texas alone has executed 99 criminals in the past seven years. The people of Texas have made it known that violent crime will not be tolerated.

STATEMENT OF SENATOR JESSE HELMS (R-NC), NOVEMBER 6, 1995

Although I wish that the death penalty was never necessary, I do believe that it should be available to our courts to punish those responsible for especially violent crimes. I believe that the death penalty protects society from further harm by the offender. I also think that it is useful in deterring others from committing similar crimes.

American society will be increasingly plagued by violent crime without the use of the death penalty. In order to combat crime, we must give our police officers and judges the support and encouragement necessary to get tough with criminals. The death penalty is one step in the *right* direction.

EXCERPTS FROM JUSTICE ANTONIN SCALIA'S CONCURRING OPINION IN THE SUPREME COURT DECISION *CALLINS V. COLLINS* (510 U.S. 1141, 1994), DENYING REVIEW OF THE DEATH PENALTY CASE (IN RESPONSE TO JUSTICE HARRY A. BLACKMUN'S DISSENT)

The Fifth Amendment provides that "no person shall be held to answer for a capital crime, unless on a presentment or indictment of a Grand Jury ... nor be deprived of life ... without due process of law." This clearly permits the death penalty to be imposed and establishes beyond doubt that the death penalty is not one of the "cruel and unusual punishments" prohibited by the Eighth Amendment.

Convictions in opposition to the death penalty are often passionate and deeply held. That would be no excuse for reading them into a Constitution that does not contain them, even if they represented the convictions of a majority of Americans. Much less is there any excuse for using that course to thrust a minority's views upon the people. Justice Blackmun ... describ[es] with poignancy the death of a convicted murderer by lethal injection. He chooses ... one of the less brutal of the murders—the murder of a man ripped by a bullet suddenly and unexpectedly, with no opportunity to prepare himself and his affairs, and left to bleed to death on the floor of a tavern. The death-by-injection, which Justice Blackmun describes, looks pretty desirable next to that. It looks even better next to some of the other cases currently before us, which Justice Blackmun did not select as the vehicle for his announcement that the death penalty is always unconstitutional—for example, the case of the 11-year-old girl raped by four men and then killed.... How enviable a quiet death by lethal injection compared with that! If the people conclude ... that ... brutal deaths may be deterred by capital punishment, indeed, if they merely conclude that justice requires such brutal deaths to be avenged by capital punishment, the creation of false, untextual, and unhistorical contradictions within the "Court's Eighth Amendment jurisprudence" should not prevent them.

STATEMENT OF PAUL G. CASSELL, ASSOCIATE PROFESSOR OF LAW, UNIVERSITY OF UTAH, SALT LAKE CITY, BEFORE THE SENATE JUDICIARY COMMITTEE, APRIL 1, 1993

The paucity [smallness of number] of examples of innocent defendants who have been executed provides compelling evidence that the risk of mistaken execution is virtually non-existent. If opponents of the death penalty are able to produce no better examples of mistaken executions [in the testimony], then the overwhelming majority of Americans who support capital punishment can rest assured that the criminal justice system is doing an admirable, if not indeed perfect, job of preventing the execution of innocent defendants....

Capital sentences, when carried out, save innocent lives by permanently incapacitating murderers. Some persons who commit capital homicide will slay other innocent persons if given the opportunity to do so. The death penalty is the most effective means of preventing such killers from repeating their crimes. The next most serious penalty, life imprisonment without possibility of parole, prevents murderers from committing some crimes but does not prevent them from murdering in prison.

At least five federal prison officers have been killed since December 1982, and the inmates in at least three of the incidents were already serving life sentences for murder....

While the innocent lives saved through the incapacitative effect of capital punishment are important, the penalty also saves far more innocent lives through its general deterrent effect....

Logic supports the conclusion that the death penalty is the most effective deterrent for some kinds of murders—those that require reflection and forethought by persons of reasonable intelligence and unimpaired mental facilities. Many capital offenses are quintessential [the most typical] contemplative offenses. Murder for hire, treason, and terrorist bombings all require extensive planning. It stands to reason that capital punishment deters such persons more than the next most serious penalty, life imprisonment without parole.

Anecdotal evidence in support of the deterrent value of capital sentences comes from examples of persons who have been deterred from murdering, or risking a murder, because of the death penalty. For instance, Justice McComb of the California Supreme Court collected from the files of the Los Angeles Police Department 14 examples within a four-year period of defendants who, in explaining their refusal to take a life or carry a weapon, pointed to the presence of the death penalty....

Statistical studies support the proposition that capital sentences, like other criminal sanctions, have a deterrent effect. To be sure, some statistical surveys, often conducted by opponents of the death penalty, have found no such effect....

One of the most recent substantial econometric studies [applying statistical methods to economics to study problems] was performed by Professor Stephen K. Layson of the University of North Carolina at Greensboro, who analyzed data for the United States from 1936 to 1977. Layson concluded that increases in the probability of execution reduced the homicide rate. Specifically, Layson found that, on average, each execution deterred approximately 18 murders....

Through the imposition of just punishment, civilized society expresses its outrage and sense of revulsion toward those who, by contravening [violating] its laws, have not only inflicted injury upon discrete [separate and distinct] individuals, but also weakened the bonds that hold communities together. Certain crimes constitute such outrageous violation of human and moral values that they demand retribution. It was to control the natural human impulse to seek revenge and, more broadly, to give expression to deeply held views that some conduct deserves punishment, that criminal laws, administered by the state, were established. The rule of law does not eliminate feelings of outrage but does provide controlled channels for expressing such feelings. People can rely on society to sanction criminal conduct and to carry out deserved punishments....

The death penalty's retributive function thus vindicates the fundamental moral principle that a criminal should receive his or her just desserts. Through the provision of just punishment, capital punishment affirms the sanctity of human life and thereby protects it.

... The system imposes a vast array of due process protections to assure that no innocent person is convicted of a crime.

STATEMENT OF MIRIAM SHEHANE, STATE PRESIDENT, VICTIMS OF CRIME AND LENIENCY, MONTGOMERY, ALABAMA, BEFORE THE SENATE JUDICIARY COMMITTEE, APRIL 1, 1993

My daughter, Quenette, was brutally murdered in 1976....

Time will not permit nor will I burden you with the gory details of how one of the defendants described her hours of torture and final death, but the memory is imprinted in my mind permanently. The three men who killed her were arrested and brought to trial—literally

seven trials over a period of six years.... The frustrations the families go through when they think justice will soon prevail, only to receive jolt after jolt as they learn the case is going back for trial due to technicalities, [are] enough to cause fatal health problems.

... As you know, 36 states have determined that the death penalty is the most appropriate punishment for certain brutal and vicious murders. As the parent of a murder victim, I feel this punishment is not only fair, it is essential. What is not fair is when this punishment is prolonged by extensive appeals, stays, and postponements. We victims need a closure to our grief. I did not rejoice when Wallace Norrell was executed July 13, 1990, for murdering Quenette, but I certainly felt relief. I could not have a sense of completion and finally put my dear Quenette to rest if I didn't [sic] have to worry about two others being released at some point....

I can assure you that the system, as it now operates, gives far more consideration to death row inmates than it affords the victims and their families. What are the safeguards for the victim when a murderer is tried, acquitted by a jury, but can never be retried no matter how much evidence is produced in the future? Are the scales of justice earnestly balanced when a convicted murderer is not executed for 13.5 years? Lest we forget, in addition to the extensive appeals of the courts, every state with a capital punishment statute has a procedure for executive clemency.

STATEMENT OF BRUCE FEIN, PRIVATE ATTORNEY SPECIALIZING IN CONSTITUTIONAL AND COMMUNICATIONS LAWS, BEFORE THE HOUSE JUDICIARY COMMITTEE, MAY 23, 1990

Although the death penalty certainly is not the answer to the worrisome ... levels of crime today, it is an important tool, I think, in creating a right kind of moral climate that suggests there are certain standards of behavior that must be accepted in order to avoid degeneration of society, anarchy, and a level of bestiality....

We must recognize that death laws have tongues. They speak to a moral universe that places some kind of conduct simply beyond the level of decent mankind....

It seems to me as well that certainly when you speak of the need for a death penalty for [killing] prison wardens, that would not threaten somebody who is already in prison under a life term with no possibility of parole, and who has very little incentive to do anything to control his conduct, to try to escape, to kill to escape because there isn't any further punishment that is available if death is not an option.

I think we owe a certain decency toward our prison wardens who undertake very dangerous positions to have that death penalty option there.

STATEMENT OF JOHN C. SCULLY, COUNSEL, WASHINGTON LEGAL FOUNDATION, WASHINGTON, D.C., BEFORE THE HOUSE JUDICIARY COMMITTEE, MAY 3, 1990

The overwhelming majority of Americans, black and white, support the death penalty. The Supreme Court has consistently upheld the constitutionality of the death penalty. The drug-war killings and the other murders that occur daily in our country demonstrate the need for the death penalty. The death penalty is a deterrent to future murders. Finally, some murders are so shocking that it is evident that there is no other punishment that fits the crime.

Yet, the will of the majority of the people is regularly frustrated by the opponents of the death penalty who repeatedly devise new and often bizarre forms of lethal attacks upon the death penalty. The rejection by the U.S. Supreme Court of the statistical disparity-death-by-racial-quota theory has led the anti-death penalty advocates to seek a legislative vehicle to attack the death penalty....

WLF [Washington Legal Foundation] strongly opposes racial discrimination in the justice system. Individuals sentenced to death should and do have the right and opportunity to challenge any act of racial discrimination in the justice system.

... The BJS [Bureau of Justice Statistics] report showed that for every 1,000 whites arrested on homicide charges, approximately 16 were given a death sentence, while fewer than 12 blacks were sent to death row for every 1,000 blacks arrested for homicide. This means that white murderers are 36 percent more likely to be sentenced to death than their black counterparts.

Does that mean that white murderers are the victims of racial discrimination? Of course not. There are numerous individual circumstances that comprise each murder case; those circumstances make it impossible to use statistics to prove discrimination in a manner similar to that utilized in employment discrimination cases.

... Studies, unable to show racial discrimination against blacks by examining the race of the defendant, also examined the race of the victim. The Baldus study concluded that for some types of murders, if the victim of the crime was white, then the murderer was more likely to receive a death sentence than if the victim was black.

The race-of-the-victim theory, if accepted, means that even a white murderer can level charges of racism at a jury that sent him to death row for killing a white person....

The Katz study showed that the black defendant/white victim cases are the most aggravated of the four defendant-victim racial combinations. The interracial nature of this kind of homicide minimized the possibility that the killing arose due to a family dispute or fight between friends, neighbors, or relatives.

The black defendant/black victim homicides occurred most frequently and were characterized by poor defendants who kill family members, friends, or other acquaintances during a fight or argument. Those types of murders generally have the most mitigating circumstances.

The white defendant/white victim homicides reflected a mix between killings precipitated by a dispute similar to those precipitating black-on-black homicides, but with a substantial percent (about one-third) of the killings comparable to the black-on-white homicides.

Only 27 of the 1,082 cases were characterized as white defendant/black victim homicides. The relatively small number of such homicides made them difficult for Katz to classify.

STATEMENT OF JAMES C. ANDERS, SOLICITOR, FIFTH JUDICIAL CIRCUIT OF SOUTH CAROLINA, BEFORE THE SENATE JUDICIARY COMMITTEE, SEPTEMBER 19, 1989

I believe that in certain cases, the death penalty can be shown to be the only rational and realistic punishment for an unspeakable crime.... Obviously, the most basic right a citizen has is the right to be secure in his person, the right to be safe from physical or economic harm from another. Laws to protect citizens and advance the harmony of society are founded upon these principles. To enforce these laws, created in the best interest of society as a whole, there has to be a deterrent for a breach of the law. Therefore, deterrence is the first aim of a system of punishment.

Deterrence is only one side of the punishment coin, however. An equally fundamental reason to punish lies in society's compelling desire to see justice done. Punishment expresses the emotions of the society wronged, the anger and outrage felt, and it solidifies and reinforces the goals, values, and norms of acceptable behavior in the society....

The deterrent effect of the death penalty is the favorite criticism of the opponents of capital punishment. The social scientists' studies have been mixed at best, and there is no authoritative consensus on whether or not the death penalty deters anyone from committing a crime. Threats of punishment cannot and are not meant to deter everybody all of the time. They are meant to deter most people most of the time. Therefore, the death penalty can only be a deterrent if it is meted out with a reasonable degree of consistency. The deterrence effect lies in the knowledge of the citizenry that it will more likely than not be carried out if the named crime is committed.

Even if one is not fully convinced of the deterrent effect of the death penalty, he or she would surely choose the certainty of the convicted criminal's death by execution over the possibility of the deaths of new victims.

Death penalty opponents argue that if life is sacred, then the murderer's life, too, is sacred ... and for the state to punish him by execution is barbaric and causes the state to bend to the murderer's level. The only similarity between the unjustified taking of an innocent life and the carrying out of a convicted murderer's execution is the end result—death. The death penalty is a legal sentence, enacted by the legislatures of various states, which presumably reflect their constituents' desires. It is a penalty that can finally be carried out only after a trial where the defendant is afforded all of his constitutional rights....

Death penalty opponents are also troubled by the studies that purport to show that the death penalty is applied capriciously [unpredictably] that it discriminates racially and economically.... Assuming that premise for the sake of argument, is that a rational reason to abolish the death penalty? Is the fact that some guilty persons escape punishment sufficient to let all guilty persons escape it?

... If the death penalty can deter one murder of an innocent life or if it can make a statement to the community about what will and will not be tolerated, then it is justified.

Opponents of the death penalty advocate the life sentence in prison as a viable alternative to execution.... Early release programs, furloughs, and escape combine to place a shockingly high number of convicted murderers back on the streets in record time.

The life without parole sentence is no solution either. First, the possibility of escape cannot be completely eliminated, even in the most secure of institutions.... Second, the life without parole sentence places a tremendous burden on prison administrators. Faced with controlling inmates who have already received the worst punishment society can mete out, they can only throw their hands up in frustration. Lastly, the true lifer is not only capable of continuing to murder, but may actually be more likely to do so. Every prison in the country has its own stories of the lifer who killed another inmate over a cigarette or a piece of chicken.

STATEMENT OF ROBERT B. KLIESMET, PRESIDENT, INTERNATIONAL UNION OF POLICE ASSOCIATIONS, BEFORE THE SENATE JUDICIARY COMMITTEE, SEPTEMBER 19, 1989

Street cops, in their pragmatic view, believe, as does 86 percent of the public, that the death penalty is a viable deterrent for persons convicted of certain crimes. A search of the literature shows there are a number of studies and articles that show a direct deterrent effect by imposing and carrying out the death penalty. One study goes as far as to point out that for each execution for a homicide, up to 15 lives can be saved through the deterrent effect. The

safety of society, which is the real goal of the criminal justice system, is being compromised by saving the life of a convicted offender. This compromise is a needless sacrifice of a blameless victim's life.

STATEMENT OF REPRESENTATIVE NEWT GINGRICH (R-GA), JANUARY 31, 1988

[The state] should use the death penalty for such serious crimes as murder and treason. Criminals might think twice before committing such acts if they knew that the consequences of their actions could result in the death penalty. People must be held accountable for the crimes they commit. I don't believe we can just slap someone on the hand and hope [he or she] never misbehave[s] again.

Right now, there are over a thousand prisoners on death row. Many of them have been there since the early 1970s because our current criminal justice system encourages them to seek endless appeals in order to delay their sentence of death.

I believe this is wrong. That's why I'm working on legislation to establish a unified appeals process that would place a two-year time limit on appeals to federal courts. This would prevent persons convicted of crimes from deliberately dragging out their appeals simply to delay the death sentence.

STATEMENT OF SENATOR JOHN P. EAST (R-NC), JANUARY 16, 1986

With the tougher attitude towards crime that we have taken in the past five years, the murder rate has gone down, but day after day we still read newspaper accounts of murders, many of which are carried out with chilling cruelty and detachment. The American people deserve continued protection from this wave of killing, protection often denied them by a system that often still gives lenient penalties to the most vicious criminals.

Death is the only suitable penalty for reprehensible crimes, such as premeditated murder. Murder does not simply differ in magnitude from extortion or theft. It differs in kind as well, and its punishment also should differ in kind. Murderers have not simply injured their victims, but they have weakened the most important bond that holds communities together—respect for life. By imposing the supreme penalty in cases of murder, society expresses its moral outrage at such a crime; it sends a signal that innocent human life is precious; and it declares that such life cannot be violated without a like consequence to the killer. By imposing the death penalty, it also deters other would-be murderers, and it prevents the murderer from killing again.

I am convinced that there needs to be a federal death penalty statute. In particular, we need to be able to impose the death penalty for the assassination of high government officials. We also need to provide for capital punishment in cases where convicted killers, already confined in a federal prison and serving life sentences, commit murder again. At present, such people have no incentive not to kill because they are already suffering the severest penalty that federal law has to offer. As a result, the number of gruesome murders at federal correctional institutions is on the rise.

TESTIMONY OF ERNEST VAN DEN HAAG, ADJUNCT PROFESSOR OF SOCIAL PHILOSOPHY, NEW YORK UNIVERSITY, BEFORE THE SUBCOMMITTEE ON CRIMINAL LAW AND PROCEDURES OF THE SENATE JUDICIARY COMMITTEE, MARCH 15, 1972

It is suggested that the death penalty discriminates against the poor and the black.... If true, ... the suggestion would be nonetheless wholly irrelevant. It concerns the unfair way in which the penalty is distributed, not the fairness or unfairness of the penalty.

Any penalty ... could be unfairly or unjustly applied. The vice is not in the penalty, but in the process by which it is inflicted. It is unfair to inflict unequal penalties on equally guilty parties, or on any innocent parties, regardless of what the penalty is.... You should try to correct the judicial processes by which, it is alleged, the penalties are unfairly inflicted....

All penalties—including fines, prison sentences, and the death penalty—are deterrent roughly in proportion to their severity.... Were that not the case, we would certainly not have varied penalties, but might impose a uniform penalty of $5 for any crime whatsoever. We impose penalties roughly differentiated because we feel that crimes of different gravity deserve different punishment.

On the basis of the statistics available, no logical conclusion one way or the other can be reached. It cannot be proven that the death penalty is additionally deterrent; it cannot be proven either that it is not.

No penalty can deter the irrational, perhaps. But penalties do influence those who are rational enough to be influenced. In this respect the data suggest the death penalty has been very effective, precisely because very few murders are committed by rational persons.

CHAPTER 11

THE DEBATE— CAPITAL PUNISHMENT SHOULD BE ABOLISHED

STATEMENT OF SENATOR RUSSELL D. FEINGOLD (D-WI), ON INTRODUCING THE FEDERAL DEATH PENALTY ABOLITION ACT OF 2001 (S. 191) BEFORE THE SENATE, JANUARY 25, 2001

I rise today to introduce the Federal Death Penalty Abolition Act of 2001. This bill will abolish the death penalty at the federal level. It will put an immediate halt to executions and forbid the imposition of the death penalty as a sentence for violations of federal law.

... We've heard about violence in our schools and neighborhoods. Some say it's because of the availability of guns to minors. Some say Hollywood has contributed to a culture of violence. Others argue that the roots of the problem are far deeper and more complex. Whatever the causes, a culture of violence has certainly infected our nation. As schoolhouse killings have shown, our children are now reached by that culture of violence, not merely as casual observers, but as participants and victims.

But, I'm not so sure that we in government don't contribute to this casual attitude we sometimes see toward killing and death. With each new death penalty statute enacted and each execution carried out, our executive, judicial, and legislative branches, at both the state and federal level, add to a culture of violence and killing. With each person executed, we're teaching our children that the way to settle scores is through violence, even to the point of taking a human life. Sadly, total executions in the last two years—98 in 1999 and 85 in 2000—mark the highest number of total annual executions since the death penalty was reinstated in 1976.

... In the wake of recent controversies involving DNA technology and the discovery of condemned innocents, we are once again having a national debate on this important issue of justice. Those who favor the death penalty should be pressed to explain why fallible human beings should presume to use the power of the state to extinguished the life of a fellow human being on our collective behalf ...

Our nation is a great nation. We have the strongest democracy in the world. We have expended blood and treasure to protect so many fundamental human rights at home and abroad and not always for only our own interests. But we can do better. We should do better ... Across the globe, with every American who is executed, the entire world watches and asks how can the Americans, the champions of human rights, compromise their own professed beliefs in this way ...

What is even more troubling in the international context is that the United States is now one of only six countries that imposes the death penalty for crimes committed by children ... These are countries that are often criticized for human rights abuses. When will we rectify this clear human rights violation—the execution of people who were not even adults when they committed the crimes for which they were sentenced to die?

... Is the death penalty a deterrent for our children's conduct, as well as that of adult Americans? The numbers prove that those who believe that capital punishment is an effective deterrent are sadly, sadly mistaken. The federal government and most States in the U.S. have a death penalty, while our European counterparts do not. Following the logic of death penalty supporters who believe it is a deterrent, you would think that our European allies, who don't use the death penalty, would have a higher murder rate than the United States. Yet, they don't and it's not even close. In fact, the murder rate in the U.S. is six times higher than the murder rate in Britain, seven times higher than in France, and five times higher than in Sweden.

But we don't even need to look across the Atlantic to see that capital punishment has no deterrent effect on crime ... Let's compare Wisconsin and Texas ... Wisconsin has been death penalty-free for nearly 150 years. In contrast, Texas is the most prodigious user of the death penalty, having executed 241 people since 1976 ... During the period 1995 to 1998, Texas has had a murder rate that is nearly double the murder rate in Wisconsin. The same trend can also be detected on a regional scale. The Southern region of the United States has a higher murder rate than any other region. Yet, executions taking place in that region constituted almost 90 percent of executions in the nation as a whole. These and countless other data continue to call into question the argument that the death penalty is a deterrent to murder.

The fact that our society relies on killing as punishment is disturbing enough. Even more disturbing, however, is the fact that the states' and federal use of the death penalty is often not consistent with principles of due process, fairness, and justice. These principles are the foundation of our criminal justice system and, in a broader sense, the stability of our nation. It is clearer than ever before that we have put innocent people on death row. In addition, statistics show that those States that have the death penalty are more likely to put people to death for killing white victims than for killing black victims ...

... Some argue that the discovery of the innocence of a death row inmate proves that the system works. This is absurd. How can you say the criminal justice system works when a group of students—not lawyers or investigators but students with no special powers, who were very much outside the system—discover that a man about to be executed was, in fact, innocent? ...

A primary reason why our justice system has sometimes been less than just is a series of U.S. Supreme Court decisions that seem to fail to grasp the significance and responsibility of their task when a human life is at stake. The Supreme Court has been narrowly focused on procedural technicalities, ignoring the fact that the death penalty is a unique punishment that cannot be undone to correct mistakes. In *Jones v. United States,* which involved an inmate on death row in Texas and the interpretation of the 1994 Federal Death Penalty Act, the judge refused to tell the jury that if they deadlocked on the sentence, the law required the judge to impose a sentence of life without possibility of parole. As a result, some jurors were under the grave misunderstanding that lack of unanimity would mean the judge could give a sentence where the defendant might one day go free. The jurors therefore returned a sentence of death. The Supreme Court upheld the lower court's imposition of the death penalty. And one more person will lose a life, when a simple correction of a misunderstanding could have resulted in a severe, yet morally correct, sentence of life without parole.

... Another reason we need to abolish the death penalty is the continuing evidence of racial bias in our criminal justice system.... In some cases, racism can be found at every stage of a capital trial—in the selection of jurors, during the presentation of evidence, when the prosecutor contrasts the race of the victim and defendant to appeal to the prejudice of the jury, and sometimes during jury deliberations.

... At the federal level, 20 people currently sit on death row. Another seven men sit on the military's death row. Of those 20 defendants on the federal government's death row, 14 are black and only four are white. One defendant is Hispanic and another Asian. That means 16 of the 20 people on federal death row are members of a racial or ethnic minority. That's 80 percent. And the numbers are worse on the military's death row. Six of the seven, or 86 percent, on military death row are minorities.

... One thing is clear: no matter how hard we try, we cannot overcome the inevitable fallibility of being human. That fallibility means that we will be unable to apply the death penalty in a fair and just manner. The risk that we will condemn innocent people to death will always lurk ...

... At the beginning of 2001, at the end of a remarkable century and millennium of progress and at the beginning of a new century and millennium with hopes for even greater progress, I cannot help but believe that our progress has been tarnished by our nation's not only continuing, but increasing use of the death penalty ... We are a nation that prides itself on the fundamental principles of justice, liberty, equality, and due process. We are a nation that scrutinizes the human rights records of other nations. We are one of the first nations to speak out against torture and killings by foreign governments. It is time for us to look in the mirror.

... At the beginning of 2001, as we enter a new millennium, our society is still far from fully just. The continued use of the death penalty demeans us. The penalty is at odds with our best traditions. It is wrong and it is immoral. The adage "two wrongs do not make a right" could not be more appropriate here. Our nation has long ago done away with other barbaric punishments like whipping and cutting off the ears of suspected criminals. Just as our nation did away with these punishments as contrary to our humanity and ideals, it is time to abolish the death penalty as we enter the next century. And it's not just a matter of morality. The continued viability of our justice system as a truly just system requires that we do so. And in the world's eyes, the ability of our nation to say truthfully that we are the leader and defender of freedom, liberty and equality demands that we do so.

A JOINT STATEMENT, *TO END THE DEATH PENALTY,* BY THE NATIONAL JEWISH/CATHOLIC CONSULTATION (COSPONSORED BY THE NATIONAL COUNCIL OF SYNAGOGUES AND THE BISHOPS' COMMITTEE FOR ECUMENICAL AND INTERRELIGIOUS AFFAIRS OF THE NATIONAL CONFERENCE OF CATHOLIC BISHOPS), DECEMBER 3, 1999

"A Sanhedrin [Jewish court of law] that puts one person to death once in seven years is called destructive.

Rabbi Eliezer ben Azariah says: Or even once in seventy years. Rabbi Tarfon and Rabbi Akiba say: Had we been the Sanhedrin, none would ever have been put to death." *Mishnah Makkot, 1:10 (2nd Century, C.E.)*

"A sign of hope is the increasing recognition that the dignity of human life must never be taken away, even in the case of someone who has done great evil. Modern society has the means of protecting itself, without definitively denying criminals the chance to reform. I renew the appeal for a consensus to end the death penalty, which is both cruel and unnecessary." *Pope John Paul II, January 27, 1999, St. Louis, Missouri*

Almost two millennia separate these two statements, which together embody the collective wisdom and moral insights of our two ancient religious traditions, Rabbinic Judaism and Roman Catholicism, on a burning issue of our time, capital punishment. At our meeting of March 23, 1999, we religious leaders, Catholic and Jewish, probed and shared our own traditions with each other. [The National Jewish/Catholic Consultation has been meeting twice a year since 1987.] The result was a remarkable confluence of witness on how best in our time to interpret the eternal word of God.

Both traditions begin with an affirmation of the sanctity of human life. Both, as the above statements imply, acknowledge the theoretical possibility of a justifiable death penalty, since the Scriptures mandate it for certain offenses. Yet both have, over the centuries, narrowed those grounds until, today, we would say together that it is time to cease the practice altogether. To achieve this consensus [majority opinion], we analyzed the statements of our respective bodies going back to the late 1970s and we agree that in them we found a growing conviction that the arguments offered in defense of the death penalty are less than persuasive in the face of the overwhelming mandate in both Jewish and Catholic traditions to respect the sanctity of human life.

Some would argue that the death penalty is needed as a means of retributive justice [exacting punishment for offense done] to balance out the crime with the punishment. This reflects a natural concern of society, and especially of victims and their families. Yet we believe that we are called to seek a higher road even while punishing the guilty, for example through long and in some cases life-long incarceration, so that the healing of all can ultimately take place.

Some would argue that the death penalty is needed as a deterrent to crime. Yet the studies that lie behind our statements over the years have yet to reveal any objective evidence to justify this conclusion. Criminals tend to believe they will escape any consequences for their behavior, or simply do not think of consequences at all, so an escalation of consequences is usually irrelevant to their state of mind at the time of the crime.

Some would argue that the death penalty will teach society at large the seriousness of crime. Yet we say that teaching people to respond to violence with violence will, again, only breed more violence.

Some would argue that our system of justice, trial by jury, can ensure that capital punishment will be meted out equitably [fairly] to various groups in society and that the innocent will never be convicted. This is the least persuasive argument of all. Statistics, however weighted, indicate that errors are made in judgment and convictions. Recent scientific advances, such as DNA testing, may reveal that persons on death row, despite seemingly "overwhelming" circumstantial evidence, may in fact be innocent of the charges against them. Likewise, suspiciously high percentages of those on death row are poor or people of color. Our legal system is a very good one, but it is a human institution. Even a small percentage of irreversible errors is increasingly seen as intolerable. God alone is the author of life.

The strongest argument of all is the deep pain and grief of the families of victims and their quite natural desire to see punishment meted out to those who have plunged them into such agony. Yet it is the clear teaching of our traditions that this pain and suffering cannot be healed simply through the retribution of capital punishment or by vengeance. It is a difficult and long process of healing, which comes about through personal growth and God's grace. We agree that much more must be done by the religious community and by society at large to solace and care for the grieving families of the victims of violent crime.

... We affirm that we came to these conclusions because of our shared understanding of the sanctity of human life. We have committed ourselves to work together, and each within our own communities, toward ending the death penalty.

STATEMENT OF SAMUEL JORDAN, DIRECTOR, PROGRAM TO ABOLISH THE DEATH PENALTY, AMNESTY INTERNATIONAL U.S.A., MARCH 4, 1998

The death penalty as imposed in the United States has the power to mislead even the most attentive social observer. Despite its fatal brutality, the death penalty is permitted by the Constitution, honored by custom, and upheld by the courts—as was slavery. Beneath the veneer, the practice of executions is accompanied by a resolute defiance of internationally accepted standards of human rights and fairness.

Repeatedly, studies have shown that capital punishment is imposed arbitrarily with disproportionate weight given to race—of the victim. Although African-Americans account for 50 percent of the homicide victims in the nation, 82 percent of death row offenders have been convicted for the murder of whites. Poverty as well as race often determines the allocation of the death sentence. Inadequate, inexperienced representation for indigent [poor] defendants characterizes most capital litigation. In addition, imposition of the death penalty often costs as much as three times the expense of lifetime incarceration. The system of executions has also sought to lower the age of offenders against whom it may be applied, thus ensnaring juveniles. And sadly, there are no reliable statistics on the numbers of mentally deficient victims of the executioner.

Many organizations have begun to support the call for a moratorium on the death penalty. They argue that the same conditions persist today, which led the U.S. Supreme Court to order a moratorium on executions in 1972 in the landmark case, *Furman v. Georgia*. The resumption of executions after *Gregg v. Georgia* in 1976 has not been marked by the abatement of racial disparities, arbitrariness, and substandard representation in the judicial process leading to the death sentence.

While the moratorium effort draws attention to the shortcomings of the judicial process, we must not rely upon the courts alone to settle matters of public morality and human rights. The role of the abolitionist in the struggle to rid our nation of the death penalty is not unlike the task that confronted abolitionists in the era of chattel slavery [slaves were treated as personal property] in the United States. The answer will not be found in the law. Laws which permit executions must be changed. They must reflect instead an attempt by our society to respect and enhance the dignity of human life without regard to race, wealth, and prestige.

The first challenge for the modern abolitionist is to topple the death penalty from its pedestal of broad, popular acceptance and to expose it for what it is, a brutal and dehumanizing rationale for legal murder. Next, we must demand that all sectors of the society, especially religious organizations, take command of the moral and humanitarian dimensions of this issue. In the end, to be successful, we must drive a wedge between those who promote capital punishment for selfish reasons, including vote totals and public image, and those who might honestly believe that there is a connection between the death penalty and fairness.

Meeting these challenges will release enormous social energies which can be employed to change the laws. Only then will we join the 101 of the 194 nations of the world which have abandoned the practice of state-sanctioned killing. We deserve a criminal justice system free of the ritual of human sacrifice.

STATEMENT OF RICHARD C. DIETER, EXECUTIVE DIRECTOR, DEATH PENALTY INFORMATION CENTER, WASHINGTON, D.C., DECEMBER 31, 1997

As the number of executions reached a record high, the discriminatory nature of the death penalty became more apparent. Of the 74 executions this year, only 10 percent were punishment for the murder of a black person, yet blacks are victims in about 50 percent of the murders committed in the U.S. Their deaths rarely merit the attention and the expenditures associated with the death penalty. Since the death penalty was reinstated, six white defendants have been executed for murdering a black person, while 112 black people have been executed for the murder of a white person.

Lack of competent representation continued to contribute to the arbitrariness of the death penalty. Exzavious Gibson, a poor black man in Georgia, went before the Georgia courts to appeal his death sentence without a lawyer to plead his case. He lost the appeal. In Mississippi, a federal civil rights suit was filed on behalf of death row inmates against the state, which provides no money and no attorneys for the post-conviction appeals process. The suit cited the results of psychological testing given to the inmates, which showed that one-third suffered from mental retardation. The inmates also were given the Law School Admission Test to test the assumption that they could act as their own lawyers (none of the inmates scored above the 1 percent level) ...

... In the past, representation in Georgia and Mississippi might have been provided by the death penalty resource centers, which were established to help with appeals. But federal funding for these centers in 20 states around the country was cut off in 1996, leaving many inmates unrepresented.

The increasing frequency of executions in the U.S. has done little to settle the issue in the eyes of the public. Opposition has moved from candlelight vigils outside of penitentiaries to national and international critiques of the continuing arbitrariness and inequity in the implementation of the death penalty. Public disillusionment with the political promises made for capital punishment is evidenced in the high support for alternatives to executions. While the trend toward more executions will likely continue because of the vast number of people on death row and the shorter appeals process, there are signs that the public may be shifting its focus away from the death penalty as a solution to crime.

STATEMENT OF REPRESENTATIVE HENRY B. GONZALEZ (D-TX) IN THE HOUSE OF REPRESENTATIVES, JUNE 30, 1995

I believe that the death penalty is an act of vengeance veiled as an instrument of justice. Not only do I believe that there are independently sufficient moral objections to the principle of capital punishment to warrant its abolition, but I also know that the death penalty is meted out to the poor, to a disproportionate number of minorities, and does not either deter crime or advance justice.

Violent crimes have unfortunately become a constant in our society ... The sight of any brutal homicide excites a passion within us that demands retributive [exacting punishment for offense done] justice ... We cannot allow ourselves to punish an irrational action with an equally irrational retaliation—murder is wrong, whether it is committed by an individual or by the state.

... The United Nations Universal Declaration of Human Rights states, "No one shall be subjected to torture or to cruel, inhuman, or degrading treatment or punishment." The death penalty is torture, and numerous examples exist, emphasizing the cruelty of the execution ...

... Studies fail to establish that the death penalty either has a unique value as a deterrent or is a more effective deterrent than life imprisonment. We assume that perpetrators will give greater consideration to the consequences of their actions if the penalty is death, but the problem is that we are not always dealing with rational actions. Those who commit violent crimes often do so in moments of passion, rage, and fear—times when irrationality reigns.

... Proponents advocate that some crimes simply deserve death. This argument is ludicrous. If a murderer deserves death, I ask why then do we not burn the arsonist or rape the rapist? Our justice system does not provide for such punishments because society comprehends that it must be founded on principles different from those it condemns. How can we condemn killing while condoning execution?

... In practice, capital punishment has become a kind of grotesque lottery. It is more likely to be carried out in some states than in others ... The death penalty is far more likely to be imposed against blacks than whites ... It is most likely to be imposed upon the poor and uneducated—60 percent of death row inmates never finished high school ...

... There are moves in Congress to speed up the execution process by limiting and streamlining the appeals process. But when the statistics show how arbitrarily the death penalty is applied, how can we make any changes without first assuring fairness? ... There are no do-overs in this business when mistakes are made.

EXCERPTS FROM JUSTICE HARRY A. BLACKMUN'S DISSENTING OPINION IN THE SUPREME COURT DECISION *CALLINS V. COLLINS* (510 U.S. 1141, 1994), DENYING REVIEW OF THE DEATH PENALTY CASE (SEE JUSTICE ANTONIN SCALIA'S CONCURRING OPINION IN CHAPTER 10)

Twenty years have passed since this Court declared that the death penalty must be imposed fairly, and with reasonable consistency, or not at all, and, ... despite the effort of the states and courts to devise legal formulas and procedural rules to meet this daunting challenge, the death penalty remains fraught with arbitrariness, discrimination, caprice, and mistake ... Experience has taught us that the constitutional goal of eliminating arbitrariness and discrimination from the administration of death ... can never be achieved without compromising an equally essential component of fundamental fairness—individualized sentencing ...

From this day forward, I no longer shall tinker with the machinery of death. For more than 20 years, I have endeavored—indeed, I have struggled—along with a majority of this Court, to develop procedural and substantive rules that would lend more than the mere appearance of fairness to the death penalty endeavor. Rather than continue to coddle the Court's delusions that the desired level of fairness has been achieved and the need for regulation eviscerated [removed], I feel morally and intellectually obligated simply to concede that the death penalty experiment has failed. It is virtually self-evident to me now that no combination of procedural rules or substantive regulations ever can save the death penalty from its inherent constitutional deficiencies ... The problem is that the inevitability of factual, legal, and moral error gives us a system that we know must wrongly kill some defendants, a system that fails to deliver the fair, consistent, and reliable sentence of death required by the Constitution ...

There is little doubt now that *Furman's* essential holding was correct. Although most of the public seems to desire, and the Constitution appears to permit, the penalty of death, it surely is beyond dispute that, if the death penalty cannot be administered consistently and rationally, it may not be administered at all.

Delivering on the *Furman* promise, however, has proved to be another matter. *Furman* aspired to eliminate the vestiges of racism and the effects of poverty in capital sentencing; it deplored the "wanton" and "random" infliction of death by a government with constitutionally limited power. *Furman* demanded that the sentencer's discretion be directed and limited by procedural rules and objective standards in order to minimize the risk of arbitrary and capricious sentences of death.

... It soon became apparent that discretion could not be eliminated from capital sentencing without threatening the fundamental fairness due a defendant when life is at stake. Just as contemporary society was no longer tolerant of the random or discriminatory infliction of the penalty of death, ... evolving standards of decency required due consideration of the uniqueness of each individual defendant when imposing society's ultimate penalty ...

... While one might hope that providing the sentencer with as much relevant mitigating [lessening the gravity of crime] evidence as possible will lead to more rational and consistent sentences, experience has taught otherwise. It seems that the decision whether a human being should live or die is so inherently subjective—rife with all of life's understandings, experiences, prejudices, and passions—that it inevitably defies the rationality and consistency required by the Constitution ...

STATEMENT OF SENATOR CAROL MOSELEY-BRAUN (D-IL) BEFORE THE SENATE JUDICIARY COMMITTEE, APRIL 1, 1993

The Supreme Court's recent holding in the *Herrera* case, that a death row inmate's claim of actual innocence does not entitle him to *habeas* relief (a prisoner's petition to be heard in federal court), is deeply troubling in an era when Congress and state legislatures are rushing to make more and more crimes punishable by death yet simultaneously curtailing the right to appeal at both the state and federal levels ...

When human judgment becomes infallible, our system will be infallible. Until then, those who would strip the system of vital safeguards lead us ever closer to the day when, in the name of the state, we will execute an innocent man. And that, in the word of Justice Brennan's dissent in the *Herrera* case, "comes perilously close to simple murder."

STATEMENT OF WALTER MCMILLIAN, MONROEVILLE, ALABAMA, BEFORE THE SENATE JUDICIARY COMMITTEE, APRIL 1, 1993

My name is Walter McMillian. I was sentenced to die in the electric chair and spent nearly six years on death row in Alabama awaiting execution for a murder that I did not commit, a murder that I knew nothing about, a murder that I had nothing to do with. Today, the state of Alabama has acknowledged that I am an innocent man and that I was wrongfully convicted. What happened to me could have happened to you, or to anyone else. I was convicted and sentenced to death on the false testimony of one man. I am here today to urge you to do all that is in your power to prevent what happened to me from happening to anyone else.

TESTIMONY OF JULIUS L. CHAMBERS, DIRECTOR-COUNSEL, NAACP LEGAL DEFENSE & EDUCATIONAL FUND, INC., BEFORE THE HOUSE JUDICIARY COMMITTEE, MARCH 14, 1990

Passage of the proposed death penalty bills would not advance—but would instead retard—resolution of the vexing problems associated with urban crime. While holding up the mirage of fighting and deterring crime, these death penalty bills would surely result in furthering the historical and well-documented racial disparities in the imposition of capital punishment in the United States.

Our concern is squarely grounded in the stark reality, which black people have traditionally faced. For more than three centuries, the weight of the death penalty in this country has been borne far more heavily by blacks than by whites ...

... There is no question that the financial cost of sentencing a single person to death is astronomical ... For example, the GAO [General Accounting Office] noted that one study done on "death penalty costs in New York estimated it would cost at least $1.8 million to defend and prosecute a capital case." By contrast, the cost of feeding and housing the defendant convicted in that same case for a period of 40 years would only be $602,000. The proposed statutes are absolutely silent as to where the millions of dollars would come from to "foot the bill ..."

Perhaps the true purpose of the bills is to divert the public's attention away from considering measures which could truly serve to fight crime. One commentator correctly observed that ... "the death penalty debate enables public officials and legislators to falsely assert that they are being tough on crime because they favor the death penalty." More emphasis should be placed on the less glamorous side of fighting crime. Most major cities in the country, for example, cannot afford to offer adequate treatment to young offenders who have become ensnared with the drug world.

TESTIMONY OF HENRY SCHWARZSCHILD, DIRECTOR, AMERICAN CIVIL LIBERTIES UNION CAPITAL PUNISHMENT PROJECT, BEFORE THE HOUSE JUDICIARY COMMITTEE, MARCH 14, 1990

The American Civil Liberties Union ... hold[s] capital punishment to be inherently cruel and unusual punishment, barred by the Eighth Amendment of the Constitution. We conclude, furthermore, that in its application, the death penalty violates the due-process-of-law clause of the Fifth Amendment and the equal-protection-of-the-law clause of the Fourteenth. These judgments are grounded in the evidence that the retention of the death penalty in no way contributes to a lessening of the incidence of violent crime, that executions are a barbaric spectacle inflicted upon isolated individual criminal offenders in circumstances redolent with arbitrariness, racial and sex discrimination, as well as status bigotry, that entirely innocent persons are unavoidably executed on occasion, and that the death penalty is not only staggeringly expensive to administer but radically distorts the entire scheme of criminal sentencing.

No one—I want to emphasize—opposes the death penalty because we think that violent crime is not so terrible or that punishment for it should not be proportionately severe. It is the *limits* of severity that is in controversy, not deep anguish about violent crime; that latter, we all, of course, share. When 200 years ago Western countries, including ours, abolished medieval forms of criminal punishment—drawing and quartering, boiling in oil, burning at the stake, gibbeting [hanging], and their like—we did so not because crimes were no longer thought to be so bad or because criminals had become nicer people: Those brutal forms of execution were abolished because we had come to think of *ourselves* as too civilized to do that sort of thing to another human being, no matter who he or she was or what [he or she] had done. *That,* and not the baseless claim that execution makes for less crime, is the issue.

THE REVEREND GUILLERMO CHAVEZ, CHAIRMAN, NATIONAL INTERRELIGIOUS TASK FORCE ON CRIMINAL JUSTICE, BEFORE THE HOUSE JUDICIARY COMMITTEE, NOVEMBER 7, 1985

I question the notion of "standards of decency" as an accepted rationale upon which to base public policy. We need to remember that, about 200 years ago, slaveholding was not considered offensive to the then-current "standards of decency."

... As people of religious and ethical conscience, we seek the restoration and the renewal of wrongdoers, not their deaths. Capital punishment makes it possible for human error or prejudice to send innocent persons to their death. It eliminates forever the healing possibilities of human love and respect. Penal history provides us with prominent examples of innocent persons falsely condemned. Our Judeo-Christian heritage affirms that for the state to assume the power of absolute judgment is to assume a power that belongs only to God.

Another issue that concerns us is that the value of life, when confronted with the death penalty, is cheapened. In this regard, we are especially concerned with what the death penalty does to a society that inflicts it.

As the United Presbyterian Church has declared, "The use of the death penalty tends to brutalize the society that condones it." In denying the humanity of those we put to death, even those guilty of the most terrible crimes, including espionage or treason, we deny our own humanity, and life is further cheapened. Nothing is achieved by taking one more life or adding one more victim.

REMARKS OF SUPREME COURT JUSTICE THURGOOD MARSHALL AT A JUDICIAL CONFERENCE OF THE SECOND CIRCUIT IN HERSHEY, PENNSYLVANIA, SEPTEMBER 6, 1985

Capital defendants frequently suffer the consequences of having trial counsel who are ill-equipped to handle capital cases. Death penalty litigation has become a specialized field of practice, and even the most well-intentioned attorneys often are unable to recognize, preserve, and defend their client's rights. Often trial counsel simply are unfamiliar with the special rules that apply in capital cases. Counsel—whether appointed or retained—often are handling their first criminal cases, or their first murder cases, when confronted with the prospect of a death penalty. Though acting in good faith, they inevitably make very serious mistakes ... The federal reports are filled with stories of counsel who presented *no* evidence in mitigation [lessening of the gravity of the crime] of their client's sentences because they did not know what to offer or how to offer it, or had not read the state's sentencing statute.

... The Court has not yet recognized that the right of effective assistance must encompass a right to counsel familiar with death penalty jurisprudence at the trial stage. Instead, in all but the most egregious [outstanding for undesirable qualities] case, a court cannot or will not make a finding of ineffective assistance of counsel, because counsel has met what the Supreme Court has defined as a minimal standard of competence for criminal lawyers. As a consequence, many capital defendants find that errors by their lawyers preclude presentation of substantial constitutional claims, but that such errors—with the resulting forfeitures of rights—are not sufficient in themselves to constitute ineffective assistance.

Contrary to popular perceptions, all capital defendants have *not* spent years filing frivolous claims in federal courts. Many of these defendants have not yet filed *any* federal claims when their execution dates are set. We simply cannot allow this inaccurate view to blind us to reality or to accept the hasty review process on the ground that defendants already have had the benefits of an untruncated [lengthy] review process. Until an execution date is set and the situation becomes urgent, capital defendants simply have been unable to secure counsel.

Once the execution date is set, the race is on. Prisoners who have not yet sought state or federal *habeas corpus* relief have roughly one month to do so.... But the new attorney often has no knowledge of the record, has not met the client, and has only a few days to read hundreds of pages of transcripts and prepare a petition. This petition, hastily prepared, must include all claims that the defendant might raise, because subsequent petitions will likely be declared abusive of the process if they entertain collateral attacks.

IMPORTANT NAMES AND ADDRESSES

American Bar Association
Criminal Justice Section
740 15th St. NW
10th Floor
Washington, DC 20005-1009
(202) 662-1500
(202) 662-1501
URL: http://www.abanet.org/crimjust/home.
html

American Civil Liberties Union
Capital Punishment Project
122 Maryland Ave. NE
Washington, DC 20002
(202) 675-2319
(202) 546-0738
E-mail: capitalpunishment@dcaclu.org
URL: http://www.aclu.org/death-penalty

Amnesty International U.S.A.
National Office
322 Eighth Ave.
New York, NY 10001
(212) 807-8400
FAX: (212) 627-1451

Amnesty International U.S.A.
The Program to Abolish
the Death Penalty
600 Pennsylvania Ave. SE
5th Floor
Washington, DC 20003
(202) 544-0200
FAX: (202) 546-7142
E-mail: padp@aiusa.org
URL: http://www.aiusa.org/abolish

Bureau of Justice Statistics
U.S. Department of Justice
810 Seventh St. NW
Washington, DC 20531
(202) 307-0765
FAX: (202) 307-5846
(800) 732-3277
E-mail: askbjs@ojp.usdoj.gov
URL: http://www.ojp.usdoj.gov/bjs

Death Penalty Information Center
1320 18th St. NW
5th Floor
Washington, DC 20036
(202) 293-6970
FAX: (202) 822-4787
E-mail: dpic@essential.org
URL: http://www.deathpenaltyinfo.org

Federal Bureau of Investigation
J. Edgar Hoover Building
935 Pennsylvania Ave. NW
Washington, DC 20535-0001
(202) 324-3000
FAX: (202) 323-2083
URL: http://www.fbi.gov

Federal Bureau of Prisons
Office of Public Affairs
320 First St. NW
Washington, DC 20534
(202) 307-3198
E-mail: webmaster@bop.gov
URL: http://www.bop.gov

Innocence Project
Benjamin N. Cardozo School of Law
55 Fifth Ave., 11th floor
New York, NY 10003-4391
(212) 790-0200
E-mail: info@innocenceproject.org
URL: http://www.innocenceproject.org

International Association of
Chiefs of Police
515 N. Washington St.
Alexandria, VA 22314
(703) 836-6767
FAX: (703) 836-4543
(800) THE-IACP (843-4227)
E-mail: information@theiacp.org
URL: http://www.theiacp.org

Justice Research and
Statistics Association
777 N. Capitol St. NE
Suite 801
Washington, DC 20002
(202) 842-9330
FAX: (202) 842-9329
E-mail: cjinfo@jrsa.org
URL: http://www.jrsa.org

Murder Victims' Families
for Reconciliation
2161 Massachusetts Ave.
Cambridge, MA 02140
(617) 868-0007
FAX: (617) 354-2832
URL: http://www.mvfr.org

NAACP Legal Defense &
Educational Fund, Inc.
99 Hudson St.
Suite 1600
New York, NY 10013
(212) 965-2200
FAX: (212) 226-7592
E-mail: dfins@naacpldf.org
URL: http://www.naacpldf.org

National Association of
Criminal Defense Lawyers
1025 Connecticut Ave. NW
Suite 901
Washington, DC 20036
(202) 872-8600
FAX: (202) 872-8690
E-mail: assist@nacdl.com
URL: http://www.nacdl.org

National Center for Victims of Crime
2000 M St. NW
Suite 480
Washington, DC 20036
(202) 467-8700
FAX: (202) 467-8701
(800) 394-2255
E-mail: webmaster@ncvc.org
URL: http://www.ncvc.org

National Criminal Justice Reference Service
P.O. Box 6000
Rockville, MD 20849-6000
(301) 519-5500
FAX: (301) 519-5212
(800) 851-3420
E-mail: askncjrs@ncjrs.org
URL: http://www.ncjrs.org

National District Attorneys Association
99 Canal Center Plaza
Suite 510
Alexandria, VA 22314
(703) 549-9222
FAX: (703) 836-3195
E-mail: webmaster@ndaa-apri.org
URL: http://www.ndaa.org

The Sentencing Project
514 10th St. NW
Suite 1000
Washington, DC 20004
(202) 628-0871
FAX: (202) 628-1091
E-mail: staff@sentencingproject.org
http://www.sentencingproject.org

U.S. Commission on Civil Rights
Public Affairs Office
624 9th St. NW
Washington, DC 20425
(202) 376-8312
(202) 376-8513
(800) 552-6843
URL: http://www.usccr.gov

U.S. Department of Justice
950 Pennsylvania Ave. NW
Washington, DC 20530-0001
(202) 514-2007
FAX: (202) 514-5331
E-mail: askdoj@usdoj.gov
URL: http://www.usdoj.gov

U.S. House Committee on the Judiciary
2138 Rayburn House Office Bldg.
Washington, DC 20515
(202) 225-3951
E-mail: judiciary@mail.house.gov
URL: http://www.house.gov/judiciary

U.S. Senate Committee on the Judiciary
224 Dirksen Bldg.
Washington, DC 20510
(202) 224-7703
FAX: (202) 224-9516
URL: http://www.senate.gov/~judiciary

U.S. Sentencing Commission
Office of Publishing and Public Affairs
1 Columbus Circle NE
Suite 2-500
Washington, DC 20002-8002
(202) 502-4590
FAX: (202) 502-4699
E-mail: pubaffairs@ussc.gov
URL: http://www.ussc.gov

U.S. Supreme Court
1 First St. NE
Washington, DC 20543
(202) 479-3211
URL: http://www.supremecourtus.gov

RESOURCES

The U.S. Department of Justice collects statistics on death row inmates as part of its National Prisoner Statistics (NPS) program. Based on voluntary reporting, the NPS program collects and interprets data on state and federal prisoners. Begun by the U.S. Bureau of the Census in 1926, the program was transferred to the Federal Bureau of Prisons in 1950, to the now-defunct Law Enforcement Assistance Administration (LEAA), and then to the Bureau of Justice Statistics (BJS) in 1979.

Since 1972 the Bureau of the Census, as the collecting agent for the LEAA and the BJS, has been responsible for compiling the relevant data. The BJS annually prepares a bulletin titled *Capital Punishment*, which provides an overview of capital punishment in the United States. The BJS *Sourcebook of Criminal Justice Statistics*, prepared by the Hindelang Criminal Justice Research Center of the State University at Albany, New York, is the most complete compilation of criminal justice statistics.

The Department of Justice has released two reports on the federal death penalty. They are *The Federal Death Penalty System: A Statistical Survey (1988-2000)* (2000) and *The Federal Death Penalty System: Supplementary Data, Analysis and Revised Protocols for Capital Case Review* (2001). *Postconviction DNA Testing: Recommendations for Handling Requests*, a report by the National Commission on the Future of DNA Evidence of the National Institute of Justice (1999), was helpful in the preparation of this book. *Federal Death Penalty Cases: Recommendations Concerning the Cost and Quality of Defense Representation*, prepared by the Subcommittee on Death Penalty Cases of the Committee on Defender Services of the Judicial Conference of the United States (1998), provides information on the cost of federal death penalty cases.

The NAACP Legal Defense & Educational Fund, Inc. (LDF; New York, NY), is a private institution that maintains statistics on capital punishment. LDF is strongly opposed to the death penalty. Despite its name, LDF is not part of the National Association for the Advancement of Colored People (NAACP), although it was founded by that organization. For over 30 years, the New York-based LDF has had a separate board of directors, program, staff, office, and budget. LDF publishes *Death Row U.S.A.*, a periodic compilation of capital punishment statistics and information, including the names of all those currently on death row. Data from this quarterly release were helpful in preparing this book.

The Death Penalty Information Center (DPIC; Washington, DC), a nonprofit organization, provides the media and general public with information and analysis regarding capital punishment. The DPIC, which is against the death penalty, serves as a resource to those working on this issue and its reports and charts on capital punishment were used for this book.

Amnesty International is the Nobel Prize–winning human rights organization headquartered in London, United Kingdom. It strongly opposes the death penalty. Amnesty International maintains information on the death penalty and torture throughout the world and periodically publishes its findings.

Charts and data from the *Death Penalty for Female Offenders: January 1, 1973, to December 31, 2000* (2001) and *The Juvenile Death Penalty Today: Death Sentences and Executions for Juvenile Crimes: January 1, 1973-December 31, 2000* (2001) by Professor Victor L. Streib of the Claude W. Pettit College of Law of the Ohio Northern University (Ada, OH) were also used in the preparation of this book.

Other studies used in this book include *A Broken System: Error Rates in Capital Cases, 1973-1995* (2000) by James S. Liebman, Jeffrey Fagan, and Valerie West; "Capital Appeals Revisited," *Judicature*, Volume 84, Number

2, September-October 2000, by Barry Latzer and James N. G. Cauthen; *The Fair Defense Report: Analysis of Indigent Defense Practices in Texas* (2000) by the Texas Appleseed Fair Defense Project (Austin, TX); *Race and the Death Penalty in North Carolina, an Empirical Analysis: 1993-1997, Initial Findings* (2001) by Isaac Unah and John Charles Boger (University of North Carolina at Chapel Hill and the Common Sense Foundation, NC); and *The Disposition of Nebraska Capital and Non-Capital Homicide Cases (1973-1999): A Legal and Empirical Analysis* (2001) by David C. Baldus, George Woodworth, Gary L. Young, and Aaron M. Christ.

Forum 90, an abolitionist group that monitors capital punishment in Japan, provided information on the imposition of the death penalty in Japan in *The Hidden Death Penalty in Japan* (Sachiho Takahashi and Thomas Mariadason, eds., Tokyo, Japan, 2001).

In *FYI: Rights of Survivors of Homicide* (1999) the National Center for Victims of Crimes (Washington, DC), a nonprofit organization that supports victims' rights and promotes victim assistance, describes some state statutes and policies that allow victims' families to witness executions. Other information about victims' families as execution witnesses comes from *Who Owns Death? Capital Punishment, the American Conscience, and the End of Executions* (William Morrow, New York, NY, 2000) by Robert Jay Lifton and Greg Mitchell.

Polls taken by the Gallup Organization (Princeton, NJ) and Harris Interactive (New York, NY) were also used in this book.

INDEX

Godfrey v. Georgia, 17
Godinez v. Moran, 31
Gomez, Fierro v., 35
Gonzalez, Henry B., 94–95
Gregg v. Georgia, 8–9
Guidelines, sentencing, 9–10
Guilty pleas, 40, 65

H

Habeas corpus review, 19, 36–37, 57, 61
Hanging, 34–35, 43
Harris, Pulley v., 17–18
Harris poll, 71, 74
Harris v. Alabama, 13
Hatch, Orrin G., 83–84
Heckler v. Chaney, 34
Helms, Jessie, 86
Herrera v. Collins, 22–23
Hitchcock v. Dugger, 15
Hyde, Henry J., 85
Hynes v. Tomei, 40

I

Idaho, Lankford v., 21–22
Illinois, Witherspoon v., 10
Illinois moratorium on executions, 62
Income, public opinion on the death penalty by, 72t
Increase in executions, support of, 73
Indigent defendants
　due process, 28–29
　ineffective counsel, 59–60
　right to counsel, 18–19, 58, 61
　Texas, 67
Ineffective counsel, 59–60
Innocence of convicted people, opinion poll on, 74
Insanity, 28–29, 29–30
Intent, 16
International Court of Justice, 79–80
International Covenant on Civil and Political Rights, 41–42, 77
International trends
　abolitionism, 5, 80–82, 82(t9.4)
　extradition, 5–6
　International Covenant on Civil and Political Rights, 41–42
　minors, 82
　retentionist countries, 79t
　United Nations resolutions, 77–78, 82
　See also Individual countries

J

Japan, 80
Johnson, Gary, 61
Johnson, Penry v., 31
Johnson, Sam, 85–86
Johnson v. Texas, 27
Jordan, Samuel, 93–94
Judges and sentencing, 9–10, 12–13
Jurek v. Texas, 9
Juries
　advisory, 13
　consideration of parole, 12
　exclusion of jurors, 10
　flexible guidelines, 9–10

lesser charge consideration, 11
　racial composition of, 33–34
　racial prejudice, 3, 31–33
　sense of responsibility, 11–12
Juvenile offenders, 25–27, 41–42, 82

K

Kennedy, Anthony M., 27
Kennedy, Stanford v., 26
Kentucky's Racial Justice Act, 64
Kidnapping, 15
Klein, Ron, 84–85
Kliesmet, Robert B., 89
Kyles v. Whitley, 23

L

LaGrand, Karl and Walter, 79–80
Lankford v. Idaho, 21–22
Latzer Study, 66–67
Legislation and international treaties
　Anti-Drug Abuse Act, 3, 42
　Antiterrorism Act of 2001 (New York), 5
　Antiterrorism and Effective Death Penalty Act, 3, 4, 36–37, 61
　DNA Analysis Backlog Reduction Act of 2000, 63
　General Assembly Resolutions 2393 and 2857, 77
　International Covenant on Civil and Political Rights, 41–42, 77
　Racial Justice Act (Kentucky), 64
　Safeguards Guaranteeing Protection of the Rights of Those Facing the Death Penalty, 78
　Second Optional Protocol to the International Covenant on Civil and Political Rights, 78
　Texas Fair Defense Act, 67
　Violent Crime Control and Law Enforcement Act, 3
　See also Federal law; Statutes
Lesser charge consideration, 11
Lethal gas, 35, 44
Lethal injection, 34, 44, 84–85
Liebman Study, 66
Life imprisonment without parole, 72, 73
Lockett v. Ohio, 15
Lockhart v. McCree, 10–11
Louisiana, 40
Louisiana, Roberts v., 10
Louisiana v. Wilson, 40
Lynaugh, Penry v., 30–31

M

Malice, 20–21
Marital status of death row inmates, 57t
Marshall, Thurgood, 8, 11, 12, 18, 29–30, 97
Maryland, Booth v., 23–24
Maryland moratorium on executions, 4
McCree, Lockhart v., 10–11
McFarland v. Scott, 19
McMillian, Walter, 96
McVeigh, Timothy, 3, 45, 73–75, 84, 85
Media witnesses to executions, 46
Mentally retarded persons
　Anti-Drug Abuse Act, 42

mitigating circumstances, 30–31
　public opinion on execution of, 72
　statutes regarding execution of, 42
Methods of execution, 34–36, 42–44, 43t, 50, 52(t6.6), 84–85
Military law, 3
Minorities. See Discrimination
Minors. See Juvenile offenders
Miscarriage of justice claims, 23
Mississippi, Caldwell v., 11–12
Missouri, Wilkins v., 26
Mitigating circumstances, 15, 25–27, 30–31
Moore, Provenzano v., 35–36
Moran, Godinez v., 31
Moratorium on executions
　Illinois, 62
　Maryland, 4
　public opinion on, 74
　United Nations call for, 78
Moseley-Braun, Carol, 96
Murder
　classifications of, 39
　consideration of circumstances, 15–17
Murray, Turner v., 31–32
Murray v. Giarratano, 18

N

National Jewish/Catholic Consultation, 92–93
Native Americans. See American Indians
Nebraska, 68
Netherlands, Breard v., 79
New Hampshire abolition bills, 4–5
New York
　capital defense expenses, 69
　expansion of death penalty law, 5
　plea-bargaining provisions, 40
　private execution statutes, 44
Newsweek poll, 72
Nickles, Don, 85
North Carolina
　costs of capital murder cases, 68–69
　Race and the Death Penalty in North Carolina, an Empirical Analysis: 1993-1997, Initial Findings, 67–68
North Carolina, Woodson v., 9–10
Northern California Chapter v. Calderon, 46

O

O'Connor, Sandra Day, 5, 16, 17, 26, 27, 30
Ohio, Lockett v., 15
Oklahoma, Eddings v., 25
Oklahoma, Thompson v., 25–26
"Outrageously and wantonly vile" murder, 17

P

Paraguay et al. v. Gilmore, 79
Parole, jurors' consideration of, 12
Payne v. Tennessee, 23–24
Penry v. Johnson, 31
Penry v. Lynaugh, 30–31
Philippines, 81–82
Plea bargaining, 40, 65
Political affiliation and public opinion, 72t, 74(t8.3)
Ponsor, Michael, 61